MINORITY RELIGIONS IN AMERICA

Minority
Religions
In America

William J. Whalen

Associate Professor of Communication
Purdue University

alba house
A DIVISION OF THE SOCIETY OF ST. PAUL
STATEN ISLAND, NEW YORK 10314

Library of Congress Cataloging in Publication Data

Whalen, William Joseph.
  Minority religions in America.

  Includes bibliographies.

  1. Sects — U.S.   I. Title.

BR516.5.W438   291'.0973   79-38979

ISBN: 0-8189-0239-6

Nihil Obstat:
  Daniel V. Flynn, J.C.D.
  Censor Librorum

Imprimatur:
  James P. Mahoney
  Vicar General, Archdiocese of New York
  November 27, 1971

The Nihil Obstat and Imprimatur are official declarations that a book or pamphlet is free of doctrinal or moral error. No implication is contained therein that those who granted the Nihil Obstat and Imprimatur agree with the contents, opinions or statements expressed.

Designed, printed and bound in the U.S.A. by the Pauline Fathers and Brothers of the Society of St. Paul, 2187 Victory Blvd., Staten Island, N. Y. 10314 as part of their communications apostolate.

ALTHOUGH MOST CHURCH members in America identify themselves as Catholics, Jews, Eastern Orthodox or adherents of mainline Protestant denominations, millions of others belong to minority religions. The major religious denominations shape the direction of organized religion but we cannot understand the total religious scene unless we know something about the minority religions as well.

A minority religion publishes one of the nation's most respected daily newspapers (*The Christian Science Monitor*); another minority group operates the largest church-related university (Brigham Young University); a third edits the religious magazine with the largest circulation in the world (*The Watchtower*). These and other smaller sects often outstrip the traditional churches in missionary efforts and therefore in membership growth.

Minority religions differ among themselves in many respects. Some claim only a few thousand followers while others report worldwide memberships in the millions. Some carry on their work in rented halls and storefront churches and others erect imposing temples. Some go back to the 18th century and others date their beginnings as recently as the 1930's.

The United States has provided a fertile soil for religious movements: Spiritualism, Mormonism, Adventism, Christian Science, the Unity School of Christianity, I AM, Jehovah's Witnesses, the Nation of Islam. Although all of these were founded in this country, several now count far more members in foreign countries than they do in the United States.

We have tried to treat all religious bodies with the respect they deserve. Sometimes an observer of a particular religious movement may be forced to conclude that the founder was deluded or dishonest but he also knows that every faith enrolls people of goodwill and basic sincerity.

In studying and writing about minority religions for more than 20 years I have been helped by dozens of people. Only two or three groups have ever refused cooperation. I cannot thank everyone by name but I would like to express my appreciation to Peter Anson, James A. Decker, Noel Duerden, Fr. Edward Finn, S.J., Bishop Leon Grochowski, David J. Johnston, Brigadier Andrew S. Miller, Robert W. Nixon, Richard L. Pierce, Bishop William H. Pitkin, David E. Sleeper, Dr. Dorothy T. Spoerl, and J. C. Wenger. They should not be held accountable for any errors I may have made nor should it be assumed that they endorse everything I have written about their own religious traditions.

Several of these accounts originally appeared in somewhat different form in *U. S. Catholic* magazine; I am indebted to the magazine, Claretian Publications, and managing editor Robert E. Burns for permission to use this material. Finally I would like to thank Mrs. Leslie Jones and Mrs. Chris Mettes who typed most of the manuscript.

W. J. W.
August 1971
Lafayette, Indiana

CONTENTS

MINORITY RELIGIONS
IN AMERICA

The Adventists

ONE HUNDRED YEARS AGO all the Seventh-day Adventists in the world could have met in a high school gymnasium. The 4,000 Adventists in 1868 lived in the United States and Canada.

Since then the Adventists have quietly extended their network of churches, schools, missions, hospitals, and publishing houses throughout a world that they confidently believe to be entering its final days. Today this American-born Church operates in 190 countries and reports more than 1,700,000 adult members. It has been growing at the rate of 5 percent a year.

Unlike most Christian denominations the Seventh-day Adventist Church has barely been touched by the current ecumenical movement. Mainline Protestant Churches have no more contacts with the Adventists than do Catholics, Eastern Orthodox, or Jews. Some theologians lump the Adventists with the Mormons, Christian Scientists, and Jehovah's Witnesses as cultists while others, even including some influential fundamentalists, have recently urged their fellow Protestants to take a second look at Adventism and perhaps reverse this judgment.

Roman Catholicism has always fared rather poorly in Adventist preaching and periodicals. Some SDA authors carry on an old fashioned vendetta against the Church of Rome whose popes were responsible for changing the observance of the Sabbath from Saturday to Sunday and thereby heading Christendom down the road to apostasy.

Like Catholics the Seventh-day Adventists are deeply involved in parochial education. In fact, the Adventists maintain the largest worldwide private school system next to that maintained by the Roman Catholic Church. Their educational system includes 6,200 schools with 400,000 pupils from kindergarten to graduate and medical schools.

An Adventist congregation will try to open a grade school if as few as 20 pupils are ready to enroll. In the United States only the Catholic Church and the Lutheran Church-Missouri Synod conduct more parochial schools. Yet the Adventists no doubt enroll a higher percentage of their young people in church schools than any other church. Right now the Adventists educate six out of ten of their school-age members in their own institutions from first grade through college.

This relatively small Church which reports 407,766 adult members in the United States supports two universities and nine colleges. Its highly regarded medical center at Loma Linda University in California trains physicians, dentists, and medical technologists. The SDA Church runs more colleges and universities than the Protestant Episcopal Church which is ten times its size or the Christian Churches (Disciples of Christ) which is seven times as large as the Adventist Church. A recent survey indicates that there are three times as many Adventists who are college graduates than you would find in the general American population.

The Adventist educational network does not run on pennies. The Adventists consistently rank near the top of all church members according to per capita contributions to their church. Most Adventists fall into the middle and lower middle classes; they are rarely found in the upper echelons of corporations or on Wall Street. But in

1968 the Adventists contributed an average of $304.38 to their church in tithes and offerings. This figure is per member not per family; we might multiply these figures by three to obtain the average family contributions: about $1,000.

A Seventh-day Adventist is expected to contribute 10 percent of his gross income before taxes. Besides this basic tithe many Adventists contribute another 10 percent to support their church's missionary, welfare, educational, medical, and publishing programs.

We might expect that any Church which believes that the world may end at any minute would concentrate on purely religious concerns. This is what Jehovah's Witnesses do; they have no hospitals, homes for the aged, orphanages, colleges, clinics. Their only interest seems to be to warn mankind of the impending battle of Armageddon.

Not the Adventists. Their urgent belief in the Second Coming has not dampened their commitment to education or medical care or service to others. No Church can boast a more impressive record of medical service than the Adventist, considering the number of Adventists in the world.

In 1971 more than 4,000,000 patients were treated in the 135 Adventist hospitals and 170 clinics and treatment rooms. Around the globe the Adventists employ 696 physicians and dentists, mostly Loma Linda graduates, and 19,571 other medical personnel. Included in the total of hospitals and sanitariums are 42 in the United States and Canada.

From their earliest days the Adventists have promoted health reform, the prevention as well as the cure of disease. An Adventist layman, Dr. J. H. Kellogg, invented corn flakes and changed the menus at millions of American breakfast tables. Adventists started the pioneer Battle Creek sanitarium for treatment of nervous disorders and introduced the techniques of hydrotherapy and physical therapy.

Respect for the human body has led Adventists to insist on total abstinence from liquor, tobacco, and narcotics. For similar health reasons, which may be debated, the majority of Adventists have adopted vegetarianism. If not vegetarians all Adventists observe the Old Testament prohibitions against eating of pork, ham, and shell fish. Nor do most drink coffee or tea. Comparative studies indicate that these health regulations make Adventists less susceptible to heart disease, lung cancer and other killers.

Adventist church services resemble those of the Methodist Church although Adventists do not recite any creeds. Every three months the congregations observe the Lord's Supper which is always preceded by the ordinance of footwashing. Men and women are separated during this service as each person washes the feet of the person sitting next to him or her. Adventists usually address fellow Adventists as "brother" and "sister" while the minister is called "pastor" or "elder." Their weekly church bulletins publish the times of sundown for the following Friday and Saturday to mark the beginning and end of the Sabbath.

Most Protestants as well as Catholics reject the Adventist interpretation of the Sabbath commandment as demanding the observance of Saturday. Meals are prepared on Friday so that food preparation need not take up the wife's time on the Sabbath. Saturday morning is devoted to simple family recreations such as nature walks, prayer, or discussing Bible topics with friends. The radio and TV are silent until the end of the Sabbath at sundown on Saturday.

Another area of high priority for Adventists is that of the missions. This Church sent its first foreign missionary to his assignment in 1874. He planted the faith in Switzerland and now four out of five Adventists live outside the United States. The Adventist takes seriously his personal duty to preach the gospel to all men and to aid those who are called to be full time missioners.

Only a few countries, among them Afghanistan and Vatican City, lack a contingent of Adventist missionaries. Even tiny Pitcairn Island settled by the Mutiny on the Bounty seamen has been visited by the indefatigable missionaries and today all the descendants of the mutineers are faithful Seventh-day Adventists.

With funds received from the regular offerings of members the SDA Church employs 58,427 men and women as missionaries, teachers, printers, medical personnel. This means that one Adventist out of every 29 is a full time salaried employee of the Church. The president of the Church receives about $175 a week and all other church workers, even college presidents, receive somewhat less.

Nor do the Adventists limit their evangelization to foreign countries. They offer free Bible correspondence courses which have already enrolled more than 3,500,000 students. Some Adventists follow the example of the Witnesses and Mormons and go door-to-door to interest householders in their doctrines.

Every medium of communication has been employed to present the Adventist message. This Church runs 44 publishing houses which print books, magazines, and tracts in 262 languages. The "Voice of Prophecy" program is carried in English and Spanish on 737 radio stations while "Faith for Today" is shown on 252 TV stations.

Generally Adventists rear small families of two or three children so that relatively little increase in church membership comes from the birth rate (unlike the Mormons). Nevertheless the SDA Church reports six times as many members today as were reported in the 1906 federal census. Their evangelistic methods do win converts and their educational system cements the loyalty of Adventists to their Church and minimizes leakage.

While the Mormons administer a huge welfare program they limit their assistance to fellow Mormons in good standing. The Adventists extend their help to people of any or no religious faith. They are usually on the spot whenever a disaster occurs such as a tornado, earthquake, flood, or explosion. The Church owns mobile disaster relief units which can be dispatched to the scene. Within the community the Adventists often sponsor free first aid classes. From two large warehouses on each coast the SDA Church ships relief materials to help stricken areas overseas.

Each Adventist congregation organizes a "Dorcas" welfare society whose members engage in activities somewhat like those undertaken by the St. Vincent de Paul Society and the Salvation Army. The Dorcas members meet regularly to repair clothing, collect food, make bandages.

Adventists do not believe in killing even in war but they do not seek classification as conscientious objectors. Instead the SDA Church trains its young men at its own expense to serve in the army medical services as noncombatants. One such Adventist soldier won the Congressional Medal of Honor for bravery on Okinawa during World War II.

The decision to become an Adventist would not be made lightly. The convert would be expected to tithe his income, attend Sabbath services every week, abstain from all unnecessary work on the Sabbath, give up liquor and tobacco, educate his children in parochial schools, avoid dancing, card playing, and movies, give up cosmetics and jewelry, sever any connection with a secret society. Yet the Adventists seem to be purposeful, contented people who derive a deep satisfaction from their religion.

The SDA Church traces its history to the excitement over the Second Coming generated by the preaching of William Miller in the early 19th century. Miller, a War of 1812 veteran, searched his Bible, especially the Books of Daniel and Revelation, and announced that the end of the world would come in 1843. Later he set the date on Oct. 22, 1844. When that day passed without incident most of his following melted away.

Before his death Miller wrote:

"On the passing of the published time, I frankly acknowledged my disappointment. We expected the personal coming of Christ at that time; and now to contend that we were not mistaken is dishonest. We should never be ashamed frankly to confess our errors. I have no confidence in any of the new theories that grew out of the movement, namely, that Christ then came as the Bridegroom, that the door of mercy was closed, that there is no salvation for sinners, that the seventh trumpet then sounded, or that it was a fulfillment of prophecy in any sense."

William Miller never became a Seventh-day Adventist nor did he ever endorse any of the groups which survived the disappointments of 1843 and 1844. He held to more orthodox positions regarding worship on Sunday, the immortality of the soul, and the doctrine of eternal punishment. Miller died in obscurity in 1849.

One group of adventists in Washington, N. H. continued to have faith in Miller's prediction. Eventually this group accepted the interpretation that the event on Oct. 22, 1844 was not supposed to be the end of the visible world but the cleansing of the heavenly sanctuary by Jesus Christ. Never again would the adventists set a specific date for the Second Coming but they remained convinced that history was drawing to a rapid close and that Christ would appear in the very near future.

To this basic doctrine of adventism the tiny New England congregation added the belief that Christians should observe the Old Testament Sabbath rather than Sunday which had been designated by an early pope. The role of the pope in changing the observance has given the movement an anti-Catholic orientation. Many Adventists seem to consider the pope to be the Anti-Christ.

The movement grew and the Adventists were able to establish a national headquarters in Battle Creek, Mich. This headquarters was moved to Takoma Park, a suburb of Washington, D. C., in 1903.

The highest administrative body in the Adventist Church is the General Conference which meets every four years. Local churches follow a congregational polity but belong to state conferences.

Pre-eminent in the SDA movement for nearly 70 years was Mrs. Ellen G. White who is considered a prophetess by the Adventists. She wrote 24 books and more than 4,500 articles many of which were based on visions. The role of Mrs. White as a prophetess has disturbed Protestant fundamentalists who would otherwise agree with many Adventist positions such as their literal interpretation of the Bible and sturdy opposition to the theory of evolution.

Born Ellen Harmon in 1827 she was raised a Methodist but accepted Adventism after hearing the preaching of William Miller. She reported her first vision in 1844. Throughout the rest of her long life she confirmed or established almost every distinctively Seventh-day Adventist position through her dreams and visions. Her most famous vision was that of the ark and the Ten Commandments with a halo of light surrounding the Sabbath Commandment.

Modern Adventists consider Mrs. White to have been a prophetess. Article 19 of the "Fundamental Beliefs of Seventh-day Adventists" affirms "That the gift of the Spirit of prophecy is one of the identifying marks of the remnant church. . . . They (the Seventh-day Adventists) recognize that this gift was manifested in the life and ministry of Ellen G. White." Adventists maintain that all her visions and dreams harmonized with the Bible and deny that Mrs. White ever fell into error. Quotations from her writings are constantly employed to reinforce Adventist theological positions.

She married a young Adventist preacher, James White, in 1846 and bore four sons. Although she never held an official position in the SDA Church Mrs. White through her visions contributed more to the beliefs and practices of this denomination than any other individual. She died in 1915.

Unlike such cultists as the Mormons, Jehovah's Witnesses, and Christian Scientists the Seventh-day Adventists affirm an orthodox belief in the divinity of Jesus Christ and the Trinity. Their "Fundamental Beliefs" declares:

"The Jesus Christ is very God, being of the same nature and essence as the Eternal Father. While retaining His divine nature He took upon Himself the nature of the human family, lived on the earth as a man, exemplified in His life as our example the principles of righteousness, attested His relationship to God by many mighty miracles, died for our sins on the cross, was raised from the dead, and ascended to the Father where He ever lives to make intercession for us" (Article 3).

Like other Protestants the Adventists hold the Bible to be the "sole rule of faith and practice for Christians." At the same time they accord an honor to the inspired writings of Mrs. White which has led some Protestant scholars to doubt the Adventists' sole reliance on the Bible. Their rejection of the doctrine of predestination puts the Adventists in the anti-Calvinist theological camp.

In a number of other doctrines the Adventists differ sharply from Protestants as well as Catholics. For example, the Adventists deny the existence of a soul which survives the death of the body. They teach that ". . . Man was endowed at creation with conditional immortality; we do not believe that man has innate immortality or an immortal soul" (*Questions on Doctrine*, p. 23).

In the Adventist theological system the term soul refers to the entire man rather than to the spiritual part as distinguished from the material body. Thus they would say that man does not *have* a soul but man *is* a soul. Immortality is a gift which God bestows on the righteous. What happens at death? Article 10 of the "Fundamental Beliefs of Seventh-day Adventists" explains "That the condition of man in death is one of unconsciousness. That all men, good and evil alike, remain in the grave from death to the resurrection."

This belief is sometimes called "soul-sleep" but actually the Adventists do not accept the idea of a separate soul. At death man enters a deep state of sleep; if he has been a righteous believer God will bestow immortality at the Second Coming. The wicked too will be raised from the dead at the end of the millennium but only to be annihilated. Obviously the Seventh-day Adventists reject the doctrine of eternal punishment; the wicked are annihilated rather than punished.

In another important respect the Adventists part company with other Protestants. They believe that the Seventh-day Adventist Church constitutes the remnant church mentioned in the Book of Revelation 12:17, "And the dragon was wroth with the woman, and went to make war with the remnant of her seed, which keep the commandments of God, and have the testimony of Jesus Christ." That all the other major denominations worship God on Sunday rather than on Saturday convinces the Adventists that they alone observe all the commandments as God wishes them to be observed.

Nevertheless the Adventists do not claim to be the only true Christians. Those who mistakenly worship God on Sunday may still be counted as followers of Christ: "We fully recognized the heartening fact that a host of true followers of Christ are scattered all through the various churches of Christendom, including the Roman Catholic communion" (*Questions on Doctrine*, p. 197). Again the author of *Questions on Doctrine* explains: "We respect and love those of our fellow Christians who do not interpret God's Word just as we do" (p. 193).

The details of eschatology outlined by the Adventists would be familiar to Jehovah's Witnesses and some Protestant fundamentalists but would be strange to most other Protestants and Catholics. The end of the world is near—but Adventists no longer attempt to set a date for the end. History will be brought to a climax at the Battle of Armageddon which will be fought on the plain of Megiddo in Palestine.

Allied against God in this battle will be the evil powers of the world and the devotees of false religions. The war will end with the appearance of Jesus Christ who will vanquish the wicked. The unrighteous will be destroyed and the true believers will be taken to heaven. Satan and his cohorts will roam about a desolate earth for 1,000 years.

Now the righteous dead are resurrected and taken to heaven to reign with Christ for a millennium. At the end of these 1,000 years Christ will return to earth. The wicked are resurrected and join Satan in one last effort to defeat God. Satan, his demons, and the resurrected wicked people are defeated and annihilated. Finally the saints will occupy a restored and renewed earth and spend eternity praising God.

Not all Adventists belong to the Seventh-day Adventist Church. A number of other Churches stem from the preaching of William Miller. Largest of these is the Advent Christian Church, organized in 1860 and reporting 30,000 members in 405 congregations in the U. S. and Canada. These Adventists worship on Sunday instead of Saturday and do not accept the visions of Mrs. White. The Advent Christian Church supports two colleges and undertakes missionary work in Mexico, Malaya, Japan, India, and the Philippines.

The Church of God (Abrahamic Faith), the Church of God (Seventh Day), and the Primitive Advent Christian Church also belong to the adventist movement. They differ from the Seventh-day Adventist Church on minor doctrinal points.

Worldwide more than 2 million men, women and children live in what they firmly believe to be the latter-days of this world and make enormous sacrifices to bring this message to the rest of mankind.

FURTHER READING

Froom, L. R. E., *The Prophetic Faith of Our Fathers* (Washington, D. C., Review and Herald, 1946-54, 4 vols.).

Herndon, Booton, *The Seventh Day* (New York, McGraw-Hill, 1960).

Nichol, Francis D., *The Midnight Cry* (Washington, D. C., Review and Herald, 1945).

Seventh-day Adventists Answer Questions on Doctrine (Washington, D. C., Review and Herald, 1957).

The Baha'is
🔲🔲🔲🔲🔲🔲🔲🔲🔲

AT FIRST GLANCE the tenets of the Baha'i World Faith seem beyond criticism. The estimated 2 million members of this faith (mostly Iranians but including perhaps 35,000 Americans) seek to eliminate racial prejudice, end war, promote cooperation between science and religion, foster the unfettered search for truth, and erase the extremes of wealth and poverty.

They also believe in the equality of men and women, urge the adoption of an auxiliary international language, favor compulsory education for all, and propose the establishment of a worldwide tribunal to settle disputes. The theme of unity—of mankind and of all the world religions—pervades Baha'i literature.

Yet this catalog of beliefs and objectives, which might be embraced by millions of Christians as well as Baha'is, fails to reveal the basic nature of Baha'ism. As Anglican Bishop J. R. Richards explains: "Baha'ism is an off-shoot of an off-shoot of a Moslem faction." It bears about the same relationship to Islam that Mormonism bears to orthodox Christianity. Just as the Mormon bears witness to the prophethood of Joseph Smith, Jr. and the authenticity of the *Book of Mormon* the Baha'i gives his allegiance to a pair of 19th century Persian prophets and honors as divine and infallible the scriptures they produced.

In the Baha'i view the other religions of the world are not wrong but merely obsolete. Baha'ism is based on the idea of progressive revelation: God speaks to man through a series of prophets or "Manifestations" who are essentially one. These Manifestations have included Abraham, Moses, Jesus and Muhammed and even Zoroaster, Buddha, and Krishna. Each Manifestation revealed what religious truth was suitable for mankind at a particular stage of civilization and each delivered the same message which was later distorted by religious leaders.

The last great Manifestation appeared in Persia during the past century and took the name Baha'u'llah which means the Glory of God. No other Manifestation is expected for at least another 1,000 years.

A later head of the Baha'i faith explained its basic beliefs in these words: "The fundamental principle enunciated by Baha'u'llah, the followers of His Faith firmly believe, is that religious truth is not absolute but relative, that Divine revelation is a continuous and progressive process, that all the great religions of the world are divine in origin, that their basic principles are in complete harmony, that their aims and purposes are one and the same, that their teachings are but facets of one truth, that their functions are complementary, that they differ only in the nonessential aspects of their doctrines, and that their missions represent successive stages in the spiritual evolution of human society" (*The Faith of Baha'u'llah,* by Shoghi Effendi).

To understand the origin of Baha'ism we must take a look at the Islamic world from which it sprang. Like Christianity Islam has been plagued by divisions. Most of the people of Iran (Persia) belong to an Islamic sect known as the Shi'ite sect. They asserted that the ruler of Islam should be a descendent of Muhammed's son-in-law; these descendents known as Imams were actually supernatural beings, free from sin and imperfections. They further believe that the Twelfth Imam never died but would re-appear to ascend the throne of Persia, conquer the rest of the world, and establish a reign of peace and justice.

Within the Shi'ite sect there arose a religious leader who proclaimed that someone on earth was always in contact with the Twelfth or Hidden Imam. Shaykh Ahmad al-Ahsa'i, who died in 1826, founded the Shaykhi sect which made this claim and several others which most Shi'ites rejected.

In 1844 a young merchant in the town of Shiraz an-nounced that he was the Bab (the Gate) through which mankind could come to a knowledge of the Imam. His followers went further and concluded that the young man, Ali Muhammad, was himself the long awaited mes-siah or Mahdi. Those who accepted this revelation were known as Babis while the majority of Persian Moslems dismissed them as absurd. Fierce battles were fought be-tween the Moslems and the Babis in which thousands died. The Babis were finally defeated and the Persian govern-ment publicly executed the Bab in 1850.

Prior to his death the Bab spent his years in prison setting down the details of the new world order he ex-pected to head. The Shi'ites held that Allah had sent five prophets to guide mankind: Noah, Abraham, Moses, Jesus, and Muhammad and of these Muhammad was the final and greatest. The Bab denied that God had sent only five prophets or "Manifestations." In fact, the Bab revealed that he was the Manifestation who followed Muhammad and he in turn would be followed by another Manifestation but not for many centuries. The Bab expected that "He whom God will manifest" would appear between 1511 and 2001 years after the Bab's own lifetime.

The Bab devised a catalog of rules to guide the lives of his followers. Babi men were to shave their beards and Babi women to discard the veil. Instead of praying five times a day like the Moslems the Babis would pray three times. Traditional Moslem customs of prayer, fasting, and uncleanness were abrogated.

The Bab was fascinated by spiritual numerology and favored the number 19. He appointed a hierarchy of 19 men, devised a calendar of 19 months of 19 days, wrote the *Bayan*, the Babi Bible, which was supposed to be divided into 19 units of 19 chapters. Babi families were asked to entertain 19 visitors each 19 days. The dead were to be washed five times and buried in stone coffins; friends and relatives were required to visit the grave for 19 days.

The Babi planned to set up a Babi theocracy in Persia. After their property had been confiscated all non-Babis would be exiled. Foreign travel would be forbidden and all non-Babi books burned. Naturally the Shah of Persia viewed the Bab's ambitions with concern.

Before his execution the Bab appointed one of his disciples to head the movement: Mirza Yahya Subh-i-Ezel. When several hot tempered Babis sought to revenge the Bab's death by trying to assassinate the Shah the government cracked down on the Babis and killed thousands. The new leader along with many of his followers fled to Baghdad which was under Turkish control.

The leader's older half brother, Mirza Husayn-Ali, also arrived in Baghdad after a short prison term and the exiled Babis continued to challenge the beliefs of the Moslem majority in Persia and to represent a threat to the Persian authorities. At the request of the Persian government the Turks banished the Babi leaders to Constantinople and then to Adrianople.

Here in 1866 the older brother, Mirza Husayn-Ali who was also known as Baha, startled the Babi community by announcing that he was really the Manifestation predicted by the Bab. His younger but weaker half brother rejected the claim reasoning that God would not have inaugurated the elaborate Babi system to last only 21 years.

The fight for leadership by the half brothers was bitter and murderous; at least 16 Babis loyal to the appointed head were assassinated. Finally the exasperated Turks dispatched Mirza Yaya Subh-i'Ezel and his family to the island of Cyprus and sent Mirza Husayn-Ali, his wives, children and about 70 associates to Acre near Haifa. The older brother persuaded most of the Babis to accept his claims and he took the name Baha'u'llah which means the Glory of God. A minority remained loyal to the younger brother.

Baha'u'llah spent the rest of his life developing his own religious system on the ruins of Babism. He spent about two years in a prison barracks in Acre but in 1880 he rented a palace outside of the city and was supported by gifts from his adherents. Like the Bab he set down rules and regulations for the Baha'is, which in Arabic means a follower of Baha. Baha'u'llah did not cut all ties with Islam; he lived like a Moslem, observed the fasts and holy days of Islam, and finally was buried as a Moslem.

He downgraded the Bab to the role of a forerunner instead of a Manifestation and likened the Bab to John the Baptist, a herald of a greater one to come. He wrote enough books and tracts to fill a five foot shelf but by far the most authoritative book was the *al-Kitab al-Aqdas* or The Most Holy Book.

Baha'u'llah sent a series of epistles to world leaders including the Czar of Russia, Queen Victoria, Emperor

Napoleon III, the Shah of Persia, and even the Pope calling upon them to acknowledge his divine leadership. He scolded the "King of Austria" for ignoring him when he visited the Holy Land.

In describing himself Baha'u'llah declared: "In my person is nothing seen but the Person of God; in my beauty nothing but the beauty of God; and in my Being nothing but the Being of God." He also advanced the claim that he was "the source of the light of the names of God, and the manifestation of all the attributes of God." Baha'u'llah maintained that his reign as "He whom God will manifest" would last 1,000 years; anyone who claimed to be a Manifestation during this millenium was an imposter.

Baha'u'llah had at least three wives, all of whom survived his death in 1892. The Most Holy Book allows polygamy but Baha'is now advocate monogamy.

Two of his sons vied for control of the Baha'i community after his death. The successor appointed in the will, Abdul-Baha (the Slave of Baha) was challenged by his half brother, Muhammad Ali, but won the allegiance of most Baha'is. This did not include Baha'u'llah's family who preferred Muhammad Ali. Abdul-Baha excommunicated everyone in his family except his sister, his four daughters, and an uncle. As executor of his father's will he dispossessed his younger brothers.

Abdul-Baha was allowed to leave the country after the Young Turks revolution in 1908 and visited many Baha'i communities including the United States. While here he dedicated the grounds at Wilmette, Illinois, on which the imposing Baha'i temple would be built. The handful of American Baha'is, operating on a pay-as-you-go basis, were not able to finance and complete the temple for several decades.

Abdul-Baha drew Baha'ism further from Islam and Babism and closer to Western thought. He enunciated general principles of unity and peace which most men of goodwill could accept. Yet these principles did not encompass the full range of Baha'i beliefs or indicate the unquestioning obedience that members of the sect owed to Baha'i authorities in Haifa.

Knighted for his relief work during World War I, Abdul-Baha died in 1921 and received a Moslem burial next to the grave of the Bab on Mt. Carmel. He had appointed his grandson, Shoghi Effendi, to succeed him as head of the faith. The grandson had attended the Jesuit school in Haifa and the University of Beirut and was a 24-year-old student at Oxford when his grandfather died. He became "The Guardian of the Cause" and the final interpreter of Baha'i scriptures.

Shoghi centralized the Baha'i movement and set up a number of committees, task forces, public relations programs, etc. He severed the remaining ties with Islam and stopped going to the mosque. In 1937 he married a wealthy Canadian, Mary Maxwell of Montreal, but the couple had no children.

Like his grandfather he freely excommunicated his enemies which included all the members of Abdul-Baha's family and his own parents. Shoghi Effendi supervised the building of the Baha'i "Vatican" on Mt. Carmel which includes the gold-domed Shrine of the Bab and the Baha'i Archives building. In the latter are housed some of the Bab's nail clippings as well as relics of Baha'u'llah (strands of hair, dried blood, prayer beads, his snuff box, and his tea strainer).

Only one schism developed during his tenure as Guardian. Dissidents founded the New History Society in New

York City in 1929 with the backing of an American Baha'i who had been lieutenant governor of New York. The rival group is still active under the name "The Caravan of East and West."

When he died in London in 1957 he had not designated anyone to take his place. A cardinal belief of the sect had always been that a Guardian of the Cause would direct the activities of the Baha'i communities. The failure of Shoghi Effendi to nominate such a leader forced a reinterpretation of Baha'i polity. Control of the movement has now passed to an elected nine-member Universal House of Justice. A minority of Baha'is, unwilling to accept the absence of a Guardian, has acknowledged the claims of an American Baha'i, Charles Mason Remey, to be the new Guardian. Remey was once president of the Baha'i International Council. He lives in Florence, Italy, but is ignored by most Baha'is.

With or without a living Guardian of the Cause, the Baha'i World Faith has registered impressive membership gains in recent years. By 1971 the Baha'is were reporting 46,000 local assemblies (groups with nine or more adult members) in 317 countries, territories, and islands. Most of the world's Baha'is live in Iran and India but the number of local assemblies in the U. S. rose from 200 in 1958 to 839 in 1971. Wilmette spokesmen said the movement gained 20,000 converts in 1970 alone and most of these were rural blacks, American Indians, and Spanish-speaking Americans. Baha'i clubs have been set up on 230 American college campuses.

In their personal lives Baha'is must abstain from alcohol and narcotics but may use tobacco. They must observe a 19-day fast each spring which corresponds to the Islamic Ramadan; on these fast days the faithful eat no food or drink from sunrise to sunset. Other requirements are obligatory daily prayers, contributions to the cause, participation in a local assembly.

The Baha'i faith has no ordained clergy. At public worship members of the assembly read from Baha'i scriptures as well as from the Bible, Koran, and other sacred writings. Local assemblies usually meet in private homes or hotel rooms.

The number nine has a special significance for Baha'is. Nine members are required to form a local assembly, nine people constitute the National Spiritual Assembly, and nine leading Baha'is form the Universal House of Justice. Members observe nine major feasts during the year such as the Ascension of Baha'u'llah on May 29 and the martyrdom of the Bab on July 9. Baha'i temples are always built with nine sides to represent nine world religions.

The consent of the living parents of both the bride and groom is essential in a Baha'i marriage. If the marriage does not work out the couple must wait for one year before seeking a divorce in an effort to reconcile differences.

Every Baha'i is expected to wash his feet every day in the summer and once every three days in the winter; a weekly bath is also prescribed. Men may not shave their heads. At the end of every 19 years a Baha'i household should renew its furnishings.

Partisan politics is ruled out for the devout Baha'i. Shoghi commanded the Baha'is to "shun politics like the plague and be obedient to the government in power in the place where you reside." In practice this means that no Baha'i may belong to any political party, vote in a primary election, or accept political office. Young men must register as noncombatants in the draft.

Of all the books or "tablets" composed by Baha'u'llah

the most authoritative is undoubtedly the Most Holy Book. As the Baha'i writer George Townshend explains: "It contains the statutes and judgments which are to be the law of the Kingdom of God during the New Era. These ordinances are designed to meet the needs of every land and to ensure the continual progress of every people. They are universal in their scope, preserve the liberties of the nations, and are to lead to the harmonization of all interests and the establishment of enduring concord among the classes and the peoples of the world" (*The Promise of All Ages*, p. 129).

Oddly enough no authorized version of The Most Holy Book has been made available to Western Baha'is. Bishop Richards explains: "It has not been translated and put into their hands because it would prove an embarrassment and a hindrance, and would not commend itself to them." For example, Baha'is now teach monogamy and the equality of the sexes while the *Aqdas* clearly espouses polygamy and male superiority.

Recently the Royal Asiatic Society published a translation of the *al-Kitab al-Aqdas* from the Arabic by the noted Orientalists Dr. Earl E. Elder and Dr. William McE. Miller. We can now compare the original teachings of Baha'u'llah with those proposed by contemporary Western members of the sect.

For example, Baha'u'llah wrote: "God has ordained marriage for you. Beware lest you go beyond two (wives) and whoever is satisfied with one of the handmaidens, his soul is at rest and so is hers, and one does no harm in taking a virgin into his services." As in Islam a Baha'i husband may divorce his wife but not vice versa. The *Aqdas* warns, "The wives of your fathers are unlawful to you."

All sorts of rules are set down in the *Aqdas* and have the binding force of divine law for devout Baha'is. The penalty for arson or murder is severe: "Whoever burns a house intentionally, burn him" and "Whoever kills a person with intent, kill him." A corpse must be buried within one hour's distance from the scene of death; embalming and cremation are forbidden unless required by law. God has exempted women from worship and fasting whenever they find blood (in menstruation) since they are considered ceremonially unclean. An adulterer or adulteress must pay a fine (nine mithqals of gold or about $21) to the Baha'i House of Justice; the fine doubles for a second offense. Such are samples of the laws of God which should prevail during the New Era of 1,000 years.

Baha'ism was brought to the United States by a Lebanese Baha'i, Dr. Ibrahim Kheiralle. He helped set up assemblies in Chicago and Kenosha, Wisconsin, but later renounced Abdul-Baha and joined forces with Muhammad Ali. His action threw the tiny communities into turmoil and Abdul-Baha tried to strengthen his position by sending three of his ablest missionaries to this country. Eventually two of the three left the Baha'i movement and the third was excommunicated.

Abdul-Baha visited the United States in 1912 and preached the message of the unity of mankind, of religion, and of all nations. At the time he emphasized, "The Baha'i Cause is not an organization." Some of his listeners seemed to get the impression that one could be a Baha'i while remaining a Christian, Jew, or Moslem. This was not true then nor now.

The foundation for the Wilmette temple was started in 1921 but the building was not dedicated until 1953. Each year some 125,000 people tour the $3 million temple and hear an introduction to Baha'ism from the guides. The only decorations allowed in the building are geometric designs, symbols of the major world religions, and quotations from the writings of Baha'u'llah. About 1,200 people can be accommodated in the main auditorium. A Baha'i home for the aged has been built next to the temple.

The first Baha'i temple was built in Russia early in this century but it was confiscated by the Communists and turned into a museum; after heavy damage by an earthquake it was razed. Other temples have been built at Frankfurt, Germany; Sydney, Australia; and Uganda in Africa. (Remey was architect for the Ugandan and Australian temples). The next temple will be built in Panama and sites for 60 future temples have been chosen.

About 7,000 Baha'is attended a World Congress in London in 1963 and elected the nine-member Universal House of Justice which directs Baha'i activities. The nine included four Americans, three Persians, and two Englishmen.

The Baha'is actively seek converts. They hold small meetings in their homes which they call "firesides" to which they invite anyone interested in learning more about Baha'u'llah. They also run ads in daily newspapers, donate Baha'i books to public libraries, sponsor public lectures, operate summer schools in Maine, California, and Michigan. More than 500 American Baha'is serve as unsalaried missionaries in foreign countries.

Racial equality, a cornerstone of Baha'i teaching, has attracted thousands of black Americans. Shoghi Effendi wrote: "Freedom from racial prejudice, in any of its forms, should be adopted as the watchword of the entire body of American believers, in whatever state they reside.

It should be consistently demonstrated in every phase of their activity and life, in public or private. It should be deliberately cultivated in their homes, their business offices, their schools and colleges, their social parties and recreation grounds." Not only blacks but American Indians have been special targets of Baha'i convert campaigns; to date Indians from 54 tribes have accepted the message of Baha'u'llah.

Prominent converts have included Queen Marie of Rumania, movie actress Carole Lombard, singer Vic Damone, jazz musician Dizzy Gillespie, and painter Mark Tobey. The Baha'is refuse to furnish membership statistics to the *Yearbook of American Churches* but list the number of local spiritual assemblies and the number of towns and cities (now 2,100) in which Baha'is reside. To join the faith the convert makes a declaration of belief before another Baha'i or group of Baha'is. He receives a signed registration card and his name goes on the rolls at Wilmette. Full members must be at least 21 but a young person can declare his intent to affiliate at the age of 15.

Baha'is are confident that their faith will one day become the religion of mankind and they resist inclinations to be discouraged by the relatively slow growth of the movement in the United States and other Western nations. They like to quote Arnold Toynbee who made reference to the Baha'i religion in his *A Study of History*, Vol. VII: "In a Hellenizing World early in the second century of the Christian Era the Christian Church loomed no larger, in the sight of an Hellenically educated dominant majority, than the Baha'is . . . were figuring in the sight of the corresponding class in a Westernizing World midway through the twentieth century."

William Sears, an American high in the Baha'i hierarchy, states his optimism: "We think it (the Baha'i World Faith) will attract a majority of humanity. We believe we are building something exciting and wonderful. It's a minority religion now, but it won't be for long the way it is progressing."

Wilmette officials report that U. S. membership has been increasing at the rate of 15% a year but took a dramatic upturn in 1970 and 1971. Potential converts often turn away in bewilderment after dipping into Baha'u'llah's voluminous writings but no extensive study is required of new members. Even though the Baha'i faith appears to many as just another Islamic splinter group it boasts a band of dedicated devotees, a handsome temple, attractive literature, a liberal racial attitude, and a confident attitude toward the future.

FURTHER READING

Baha'u'llah, *Al-Kitab Al-Aqdas or The Most Holy Book* (London, Royal Asiatic Society, 1961).

Esslemont, J. E., *Baha'u'llah and the New Era* (Wilmette, Ill., Baha'i Publishing Committee, 1962).

Gaver, Jessyca Russell, *The Baha'i Faith: Dawn of a New Day* (New York, Hawthorn, 1967).

The Black Muslims
🔲🔲🔲🔲🔲🔲🔲🔲🔲

EQUALITY OF THE RACES characterizes the religion of Islam and has been an important factor in the spread of this faith in black Africa. Yet the hybrid form of Islam led by the Hon. Elijah Muhammad proclaims that all Caucasians are devils whereas the black man is the favored creation of Allah and is destined to rule the world in the near future. Those who accept the claims of Elijah Muhammad say they belong to the Nation of Islam; they are popularly known as Black Muslims.

Their leader declares: "By nature the black man was created good and by nature the white man was created evil." His followers are anti-white, anti-Jewish, and anti-Christian. "Christianity is a religion organized and backed by the devils for the purpose of making slaves of black mankind," says the American-born Prophet.

The movement seeks strict racial separation and wants no part of the efforts of groups such as the NAACP to foster integration. The Nation of Islam also advocates economic self sufficiency for blacks, total abstinence, thrift, cleanliness, and marriage only within the black race.

Elijah Muhammad, who is also known as the Messenger of Allah, asks that several states be given over to blacks so they can set up their own nation. The land must be "fertile and minerally rich" and the "former slave masters are obligated to maintain and supply our needs in this separate territory for the next 20 to 25 years—until we are able to produce and supply our own needs."

How many full fledged members belong to the 47 mosques around the country is unknown. Perhaps 10,000 would be the current estimate but thousands of others in the black ghettoes of Northern cities sympathize with the aims of the Nation of Islam, read the cult's newspaper, attend rallies, etc.

Most converts to the Black Muslims have been fairly recent immigrants from the rural South who find nothing but poverty, unemployment, crime and filth in the inner cities. Successful recruiting drives have been carried on in state and federal prisons. Without marketable skills or education these blacks see no possibility of ever escaping from the ghetto.

To them the Nation of Islam offers some glimmer of hope and pride of race. Elijah Muhammad urges them to abandon Christianity and "return" to the religion of Islam which is said to be the only proper faith for the colored races.

A prosperous string of businesses has been purchased with the contributions of members of the cult. The Black Muslims already operate grocery stores, a printing plant, dry cleaning establishments, restaurants, and bakeries. The sect owns a 1,430-acre farm in Albany, Ga. and a 1,000-acre farm in Cassopolis, Mich.; the Messenger of Allah says he will try to acquire 2 million acres within 10 to 15 years.

Purchase of the largest Greek Orthodox church building in the country by the Black Muslims was announced in 1971. The Muslims paid $4 million for the 1,500-seat church of Ss. Constantine and Helen on Chicago's South Side and converted it into a mosque.

Elijah Muhammad did not start the cult which he now heads. The founder was a mysterious silk-peddler-preacher who gathered a small band of devotees in Detroit in the early 1930's. He was known as W. D. Fard, Professor Ford, Walli Farrad and Mohammed Ali. He had served a three-year term in San Quentin prison and had been arrested on such charges as narcotics, assault with a deadly weapon, and bootlegging. Turning to religion he drew upon such sources as the Koran, the Bible, Freemasonry, and the literature of Jehovah's Witnesses to fashion his doctrines. Several hundred Detroit blacks belonged to his Moorish movement at the time of his disappearance in 1934. Today the Black Muslims revere him as Allah incarnate, the expected Mahdi, and the Christian Messiah.

Control of the cult passed to Elijah Muhammad, born Elijah Poole in Sandersville, Ga. on Oct. 8, 1897. His father was a Baptist farmer-preacher with 13 children. Elijah quit school after completing the 4th grade, drifted north and worked at odd jobs before affiliating with Fard's cult. One of his first steps after Fard disappeared was to move headquarters of the Nation of Islam to Chicago.

At various times the tiny cult was courted by the Communists, Trotskyists, and Japanese agents during World War II. Elijah Muhammad himself was jailed between 1942 and 1946 on charges of sedition and urging his followers to dodge the draft. After the war he bought an abandoned synagogue on Chicago's South Side and launched a membership drive. Other mosques were opened in Milwaukee, Cleveland, and Washington, D. C. A University of Islam enrolled 350 youngsters from the first grade through high school.

Black Muslims seek new citizens for their Nation in prisons and pool halls as well as among Christian congregations. Their biweekly newspaper, *Muhammad Speaks,* claims a circulation of 385,000 copies and is sold on street corners in black neighborhoods. A Muslim radio program is broadcast by 35 stations.

A former convict and dope addict who took the name Malcolm X brought considerable national publicity to the cult and became the popular minister of the New York City mosque. His charisma posed a threat to the control of the cult by Elijah Muhammad and his family.

Shortly after the assassination of President Kennedy, Malcolm X told the press that the murder was a case of "the chickens coming to roost." The Messenger of Allah took this occasion to suspend Malcolm X as minister of the New York mosque. The deposed minister launched his own Black Nationalist organization but was shot to death on Feb. 21, 1965 as he was about to address 400 followers in a Harlem ballroom. Three Black Muslims were convicted of the slaying.

Criminals and ex-convicts may be attracted to join the Nation of Islam but they must follow a strict moral code or risk excommunication. All Black Muslims must give up liquor and tobacco, extra-marital sex relations, gambling, drugs, dancing, sports, motion pictures. They may not vote, socialize with whites or Christians, serve in the armed forces, salute the American flag, straighten their hair, use more than a minimum of cosmetics, or act in a boisterous or loud manner. They must watch their eating habits. Elijah Muhammad has revealed that pork contains 999 specific germs and must never be eaten. Also on the list of forbidden foods are black-eyed peas, cornbread, rabbit, possum, collard greens, pinto beans, squirrel, coon, carp, and catfish. Muslims are urged to limit themselves to one meal a day; members with excess weight are expected to diet until they reach the desired weight.

Fornication or adultery are grounds for immediate dismissal. The cult insists that all women wear modest clothing which covers their arms and legs. Men outnumber women in the Nation of Islam who have no positions of authority but they are treated with great respect.

Elijah Muhammad retains full control of the organization; his wife, six sons, and two daughters are active Muslims. He lives in an 18-room mansion in the Hyde Park section of Chicago but also spends time at his home in Phoenix. He usually wears an embroidered fez, white bow tie, and conservative suit.

Not only does orthodox Islam repudiate black (or white) supremacy but it knows nothing of the peculiar myths propagated by the Black Muslims. One of the cult's basic beliefs is that the white man was created by a black genius called Yakub rather than by Allah. The first inhabitants of the earth were all black, belonged to the Tribe of Shabass, and built the city of Mecca. Many millions of years after the creation of the black man, Yakub appeared on the scene and started the mischief which has led to the recent subjugation of the black man to the white in Africa and America. Yakub was bright but a troublemaker. He started to experiment with mutations and came up with the red, yellow, and finally white race. This happened about 6,000 years ago according to Fard and Elijah Muhammad.

Allah allowed the white devils to run the world for some 6,000 years but this time was up in 1914. The whites made slaves of the blacks, imposed an inferior religion—Christianity, and deprived the blacks of their cultural heritage. Finally Allah appeared in human form in the person of Fard and appointed the Hon. Elijah Muhammad as His Messenger to bring the blacks back to their ancestral religion.

The white devil even took away the black man's name and gave him a slave name instead. Converts to the Nation of Islam get new names. He keeps his proper name and uses X for his last name. If there is more than one person in a mosque with the same first name the others become Robert 2X or George 3X.

Muslims must attend services at the mosque two or three times a week. Only blacks may enter a mosque and everyone must submit to a thorough search. Contraband articles such as knives, guns, liquor or cigarettes are checked at the door.

At the start of the service the minister gives an Arabic greeting "As-Salaam-Alaikum" and the congregation responds with "We-Alaikum-Salaam." The minister may then spend a few minutes in Arabic language instruction. The Hon. Elijah Muhammad neither speaks nor reads Arabic but hopefully all Black Muslims will some day learn to read the Koran in its original language.

The main feature of the service is the address by the minister which may last two hours or more. This sermon is essentially a recapitulation of the teachings of the Messenger of Allah.

Each mosque sponsors several auxiliary organizations. The men who make up the Fruits of Islam serve as the Messenger's bodyguard, drill, maintain order at meetings. They vow to lay down their lives in three situations: an assault on a black woman, an invasion of a mosque, or an attack on the Hon. Elijah Muhammad. The Fruits of Islam carry no weapons but become skilled in judo and karate. Black Muslim women belong to the Moslem Girls' Training and General Civilization Class.

Whether the Black Muslims with their distinctive racial views and creation myths should be considered real Muslims is debatable. Elijah Muhammad was allowed to make a pilgrimage to Mecca and many Muslims believe that anyone who declares his faith in Allah, Muhammad, and the Koran must be taken at his word. The few orthodox Muslims in this country and the Islamic Center in Washington, D. C. ignore the Black Muslims.

Membership has probably gone down during the past decade. The loss of an articulate spokesman such as Malcolm X has been felt. Another famous convert has been Cassius Clay (Muhammed Ali) who was stripped of his heavyweight title because he claimed exemption from the draft as a Black Muslim. Because Muslims are not supposed to participate in professional sports he has been suspended from membership by Elijah Muhammad but maintains he still believes in the principles of the Nation of Islam. Black intellectuals, militants, and members of the middle class have never responded to the message of the Messenger of Allah nor sought citizenship in the Nation of Islam.

FURTHER READING

Essein-Udom, *Black Nationalism*. (Chicago, University of Chicago Press, 1962).

Lincoln, C. Eric, *The Black Muslims in America* (Boston, Beacon, 1961).

Lomax, Louis E., *When the Word is Given*... (New York, World, 1963).

The Christadelphians
🔲🔲🔲🔲🔲🔲🔲🔲🔲

In MANY RESPECTS the Christadelphians resemble Jehovah's Witnesses but their movement was founded several decades earlier and has never attained the membership of the Witnesses. Founder of the Christadelphians was Dr. John Thomas (1805-1871), an English physician who was shipwrecked en route to the United States in 1832. He promised God to abandon medicine and turn to religion if he survived.

Dr. Thomas joined the Campbellite movement but soon got into arguments with his brethren. He believed that Baptists who joined the Campbellites should be baptized again by immersion. He parted company with Alexander Campbell when he began to teach that man does not have an immortal soul.

Seeking to recapture the spirit of primitive Christianity, Thomas elaborated his own theological views between 1844 and 1847. He did not lack confidence: "I flatter myself that I shall not have laid before my readers the results of my humble efforts, without having substantiated my claim to the discovery or solution of certain problems in the Apocalypse, which have hitherto baffled the ingenuity and learning of the most celebrated illuminati of the religious world."

He rejected the Trinity and the divinity of Jesus Christ. Jesus was a sinless man and had no existence before his birth. Yet Thomas taught that God was manifested in him.

Only Christadelphians are eligible to receive the gift of immortality; all others will remain in the grave. To be saved an individual must accept the Christadelphian gospel, submit to baptism by immersion, and keep the commandments. Baptism must be preceded by intensive Bible study and an oral examination.

All Christian Churches, Catholic or Protestant, were apostate. Although the sect has reserved its choicest condemnation for Roman Catholicism it has no sympathy for Protestantism. One of its publications in 1866 declared that all Christian denominations are branches of the "depraved, corrupt, iniquitous, tyrannical and murderous Church of Rome . . . whose cunning art of simulated kindness and ornaments of learning and fascinations of venerable pedigree are . . . entrapping thousands." The years have mellowed the Christadelphian assessment only slightly.

The sect is adventist. Jesus will soon return and the climactic battle of Armageddon will be fought on the plains of Israel. Jesus will ascend David's throne and rule the world for 1,000 years. The return of the Jews to the state of Israel is thought to fulfill Bible prophecies; even in the 19th century the Christadelphians contributed funds to Jews in Palestine.

The estimated 15,000 Christadelphians in the United States do not vote, serve in the armed forces, seek public office, join labor unions, attend the theatre or movies, dance or play cards. The sect frowns on smoking and drinking but does not insist on total abstinence. Any member who marries outside of the group subjects himself to excommunication. Christadelphians are expected to confine their friendships to co-religionists and to remain aloof from Christians and secularists.

England has more Christadelphians than the United States. Thomas went back to England on three occasions and spread his views among English Campbellites and Millerites. The chief organization is the Central Fellowship in Birmingham but there are many schismatic groups as well. There are 12 congregations in the city of Birmingham alone. More than 15,000 Christadelphians recognize the Central Fellowship and another 5,000 belong to splinter groups. Small groups of Christadelphians can be found in New Zealand and Australia.

Each local congregation, called an ecclesia, chooses its leaders who are known as "serving Brethren." They hold secular jobs and serve the church without pay; women hold no official position in the movement. Members usually meet in private homes or rented halls. They do not tithe their incomes but, in fact, the expenses of the ecclesia are not burdensome. The highpoint of the week is the celebration of the Lord's Supper each Sunday.

Christadelphians engage in no organized foreign mission work. They operate no charitable, educational, or medical institutions but sponsor a few summer Bible institutes and public lectures. Bryan Wilson reports: "In particular Christadelphians are violently opposed to those organizations which seek to ameliorate human life by political or legislative action. Men are seen as too inherently wicked to make such organizations of any avail" (*Sects and Society*, p. 286).

The Christian Scientists
🔲🔲🔲🔲🔲🔲🔲🔲🔲

JUST ABOUT 100 years ago a frail, middle aged lady slipped on the ice returning from a temperance meeting in Lynn, Massachusetts. "The Fall at Lynn" on that February evening in 1866 is taken as the date of the founding of the Christian Science movement by the woman known to us as Mary Baker Eddy.

During the past century the world has witnessed an orgy of sin: mass murder, adultery, blasphemy, torture, theft, lies, rape. Almost everyone alive in 1866 has since died. And during these intervening 100 years medical science has made more progress than during the preceding millennium even though many diseases elude conquest.

Yet hundreds of thousands of Americans deny the very reality of sin, sickness, and death. Following the teaching of Mary Baker Eddy they maintain that murder, leprosy, cancer, death and dismemberment are but illusions of mortal mind.

These Christian Scientists who deny the reality of what others take for granted are not ignorant people. Their educational level probably surpasses that of the general population. Their numbers include professors, scientists, editors, lawyers, astronauts, artists. They publish what is acknowledged to be one of the finest daily newspapers in the United States.

Basically Christian Science teaches that Jesus came not only to save man from sin but from sickness and death. The methods He and His disciples used to heal the sick and raise the dead can be used in modern times. Everyone can use these same methods to heal himself and others since the methods have been revealed in this era by Mrs. Eddy.

If a Christian Scientist is true to his beliefs he will never avail himself of drugs. Mrs. Eddy declared: "A metaphysician never gives medicine, recommends or trusts in hygiene, or believes in the ocular or the post-mortem examination of patients" (*Science and Health*, p. 269, 1881 edition).

When Mrs. Eddy's followers carry out their beliefs they sometimes make news. A California school teacher who had refused to take the required X-ray examination is discovered to be an active tubercular. A campaign to add flourides to a city water supply to prevent tooth decay is opposed by a committee of citizens who turn out to be mostly Christian Scientists and right-wing extremists. A child hurt in an automobile crash cannot be treated in a local hospital because the parents oppose medical treatment.

In the opinion of Dr. Abraham N. Franzblau, a psychiatrist and author of books on psychiatry and religion, the Christian Scientists hold "a thoroughly ludicrous and untenable position." He adds, "it negates bacteria, the degenerative process, viruses and all other diseases that have been the scourge of mankind" (*Wall Street Journal*, July 31, 1967).

We do not know exactly how many people subscribe to the theories of Christian Science. The Church of Christ, Scientist, is the only denomination in the United States which forbids any tabulation of membership. We do know that there are about 3,300 branch churches and societies reporting to the Mother Church in Boston. A few branch churches in metropolitan areas enroll as many as 1,000 members but many of the smaller branches and societies have only a handful. The last federal census which asked information on religious affiliation was the 1936 census; at that time 268,915 Americans identified themselves as Christian Scientists. Perhaps as many as 350,000 men and women in 1971 would so identify themselves.

Of course, thousands of others attend Christian Science meetings, read *Science and Health,* and visit practitioners but do not appear on the church rolls. Perhaps they still rely to some extent on medicine or refuse to give up tobacco or liquor which makes them ineligible for full membership. Scientists also frown on the use of coffee and tea.

Most Christian Scientists are women and most of these live in the larger cities. The top administrative officers of the Church are often men but women predominate in the ranks of the fulltime practitioners (healers). Some Christian Scientists are well known names in American homes: Senator Charles Percy of Illinois, box office queen Doris Day, party-giver Perle Mesta, columnist Roscoe Drummond; Kay Kyser who once led one of the nation's most popular bands has become a practitioner in North Carolina.

The great majority of Christian Scientists live in the United States but there are constituencies in England, West Germany, Canada, Australia, and New Zealand. Smaller groups of Scientists can be found in Switzerland, France, the Netherlands and some of the nations of Asia, Africa, and South America.

Consistent with its beliefs this Church operates no hospitals or clinics. Nor does it maintain any orphanages, welfare programs, or other charitable institutions outside of two sanitariums for those relying on Christian Science treatments. It has one home for aged Scientists. The Principia, a liberal arts college in Illinois, was founded and is staffed by Christian Scientists for Christian Science students but it has no direct connection with the Church. Christian Science organizations on college campuses have doubled during the past decade to a total of 445. The Church is spending $80 million to expand its headquarters in Boston and seems to enjoy a substantial income, especially from gifts and bequests from wealthy Christian Scientists.

Unlike most Protestant denominations the Christian Science Church steers clear of involvement in social action programs such as the civil rights and peace movements. It ignores the ecumenical activities to which most Protestant Churches give support.

Mrs. Eddy established a by-law for her Church which "ordained the Bible and *Science and Health* as pastor on this planet of all the churches of the Christian Science denomination." Two elected Readers conduct Sunday and Wednesday services in branch churches; they serve three year terms.

Closest counterpart to an ordained minister is the Christian Science practitioner. Supposedly anyone may apply the principles of Christian Science to regain health or solve any personal or financial problem but many devotees turn to the professional practitioners for help in difficult cases. Practitioners receive special training and must be authorized by the Mother Church. The number is declining; in 1941 there were 11,200 practitioners and today there are fewer than 7,100. They support themselves by the fees charged for their services. Many practitioners maintain offices and office hours, go out on house calls, and bill their clients for their services just as would a physician or dentist.

In many ways Christian Science has won legal recognition of its unusual beliefs during the past century. Christian Scientists can deduct the cost of practitioner's fees on their federal income tax forms as medical expenses. Some insurance companies pay for Christian Science treatment and care in lieu of medical treatment. Members of the Church often obtain exemption from medical examinations and vaccinations. Christian Scientists can qualify for commissions as Protestant chaplains in the armed forces.

The founder of this movement was born Mary Baker, in Bow, New Hampshire, on July 16, 1821. She was a frail and nervous child afflicted with a spinal weakness which brought about "fits" and seizures. Her education was sketchy and her acquaintance with medicine was limited to the homeopathic physicians who tried to treat her various illnesses.

She joined the Congregational Church when she was 17 but always objected to the stern Calvinism to which she was exposed. In 1843 she married a building contractor, George Washington Glover, and moved to South Carolina. In a few months her husband was dead of yellow fever and she was left expecting a child. She gave birth to a son but he was raised by a family in Minnesota and did not see his mother again until he was 34, married with two children of his own.

Mrs. Glover again entered marriage in 1853. This time the groom was a philandering dentist by the name of Dr. Daniel Patterson. He carried on his dental practice in various communities and apparently extracted both teeth and endearments from his lady patients. While touring a Civil War battlefield the doctor was captured and spent the rest of the war in a Confederate prison camp. After his release he decided against resuming housekeeping with his emotionally mercurial wife. Eventually Mrs. Patterson obtained a divorce on grounds of desertion. Dr. Patterson died years later a penniless hermit while the wife he abandoned was revered by tens of thousands of followers as the discoverer of the healing methods of Christ.

Afflicted by various nervous and mental ailments Mrs. Patterson sought help from many sources. She tried mesmerism and spiritualism and finally discovered a faith healer in Portland, Maine, with the quaint name of Phineas P. Quimby. Quimby believed that he had discovered the methods by which Jesus and His disciples had healed the sick. He was convinced that these were not miracles but simply the application of natural rather than supernatural means. He sometimes called his system of healing "Science of Health" and "Science of Christ" and "Christian Science." Quimby recorded his conclusions in ten bound volumes which were loaned to patients. (*The Quimby Manuscripts* edited by Horatio W. Dresser were finally published in 1921).

Mrs. Mary Baker Glover Patterson first visited Quimby in 1862 and seemed to obtain some relief from her troubles. She became one of his enthusiastic patients and students. Today Christian Science apologists try to minimize her debt to Quimby.

When Quimby died in early 1866 Mrs. Patterson wrote a eulogy in the form of a poem entitled "Lines on the Death of Dr. P. P. Quimby, Who Healed with the Truth that Christ Taught in Contradistinction to All Isms." Later when she had won fame as the "discoverer" of Christian Science she would explain her devotion and gratitude to Quimby as the result of a mesmeric spell he had cast on her.

A month after Quimby's death Mrs. Patterson slipped on the ice and took to her bed. On the third day in bed she opened her Bible to Matthew 9:2-8 which relates the story of the healing of the palsied man. She got out of bed, dressed, and began to tell others of her healing. She later declared that her physician had judged that she would never walk again.

Nevertheless, from then on Mrs. Patterson devoted her energies to developing and propagating her "discovery" and organizing her cult. She worked on her book *Science and Health* for the next four years; it has become the textbook of the movement. She added a section entitled "With Key to the Scriptures" which metaphysically interpreted the Books of Genesis and Revelation.

Science and Health was published in 1875 under the authorship of Mary Baker Glover (she had resumed the name of her first husband). The book sold for $3 a copy and as revised editions appeared all Christian Scientists in good standing were expected to purchase new copies.

Mrs. Glover practiced healing herself and accepted pupils for a standard fee of $300 for 12 lessons; this amounted to about half a year's wages for the Lynn shoe workers who made up most of her classes. She told her graduates they could soon recover the tuition by setting up healing practices of their own. She also expected to receive a royalty on all fees collected by her graduate healers.

In the same year which saw publication of her book a group of her students rented a hall in Lynn and employed Mrs. Glover as their pastor. One of her most devoted pupils was a mild mannered, former sewing machine salesman, Asa Gilbert Eddy. He became her third husband in 1877.

A revolt by eight of her faithful students in Lynn who charged Mrs. Eddy with "frequent ebullitions of temper, love of money, and the appearance of hypocrisy" induced her to transfer her activities to Boston. The Church of Christ, Scientist, received its charter in 1879. Mrs. Eddy was pastor and from the beginning held tight reins on her Church. Over a period of years she deposed all pastors of branch churches, forbade any conference of Christian Science churches, limited readings at church services to the Bible and her own textbook, prohibited public discussion in church after lectures, excommunicated any who disagreed with her, and drew up by-laws which could never be changed without her written consent (and thereby frozen since her death).

She established the Massachusetts Metaphysical College in 1881 of which she was the entire faculty. During its eight years of operation some 4,000 students had paid $1,200,000 in tuition. It was chartered to teach "pathology, ontology, therapeutics, moral-science, metaphysics, and their application to the treatment of diseases." Students could not only take the introductory $300 course but could also elect advanced courses taught by Mrs. Eddy such as "Metaphysical Obstetrics" ($100).

When she was 68 she legally adopted Dr. Ebenezer J. Foster, a 41-year-old homeopathic physician. His name was added to the faculty of her college although she continued to do most of the teaching. E. J. Foster Eddy was considered the heir apparent of the movement until he was dismissed by Mrs. Eddy in 1896. In 1909 he received $50,000 in a legal settlement.

Mrs. Eddy out-maneuvered her rivals in the cult.

She deposed Augusta Stetson, head of the large New York City branch. The limited terms of First and Second Readers prevented anyone from establishing a strong following which might challenge Mrs. Eddy's complete control.

By the time she had completed the organization of her Church and consolidated her control Mrs. Eddy was an old woman. Prof. Anthony Hoekema states: "Because her teeth had to be extracted, she resorted to artificial dentures; she also began to wear glasses; and, when her pain would not yield to purely metaphysical healing methods, she used to call in a doctor to administer morphine" (*The Four Major Cults*, p. 177).

Dominating her last years was growing fear of Malicious Animal Magnetism, or MAM. She reasoned that if mental methods could overcome disease and death even at a distance the misuse of these natural methods could cause illusions of sickness and evil. She surrounded herself with a corps of faithful Scientists who were responsible for shielding her from such invisible powers.

Mr. Eddy died in 1882 of heart trouble but his wife had another explanation. In a letter to the Boston *Post* she wrote: "My husband's death was caused by malicious mesmerism. . . . I know it was poison that killed him, not material poison, but mesmeric poison. . . ."

A regular feature in Christian Science publications for many years was a column of letters from Scientists who described the evil forces of MAM. Misfortunes, deaths, business reversals, failure of healings were regularly attributed to the power of MAM. In her *Church Manual* she wrote: "Teachers shall instruct their pupils how to defend themselves against mental malpractice." This MAM column has been discontinued since her death and the only testimonials which now appear relate to healings and other successful applications of Christian Science methods. MAM is still mentioned but it has become something of a skeleton in Mother Eddy's closet.

Compared to Christian Science the Roman Catholic Church takes on the appearance of a freewheeling debating society. The area of free theological discussion allowed to members of the Mother Church is very small. Each local congregation must sponsor one public lecture a year but copies of all such lectures must be submitted to Boston for approval. Even though the audience is usually made up 90 percent of Christian Scientists there is no question and answer period. Only the Bible, *Science and Health* and other approved books and tracts may be shelved in Christian Science Reading Rooms. Deviation from standard doctrine may bring excommunication by the Board of Directors of the Mother Church.

Mrs. Eddy set up a "Committee on Publication" which "shall be responsible for correcting or having corrected a false newspaper article which has not been replied to by other Scientists, or which has been forwarded to this Committee for the purpose of having him reply to it. If the correction by the Committee on Publication is not promptly published by the periodical in which it is desirable that this correction shall appear, this Committee shall immediately apply for aid to the Committee on Business" (*Church Manual XXXIII.*)

Dissident Christian Scientists have organized the Farallon Foundation of Los Gatos, California and direct most of their attacks on the board of directors of the Mother Church. A former practitioner, Arthur Corey, heads the Foundation. Another Farallon official, F. C. Lee, states: "The Mother Church is more dictatorial, for instance, than the Roman Catholic hierarchy."

To preserve the belief that the discoverer of Christian Science had indeed overcome the fate of all mankind Mrs. Eddy's associates shielded her and her infirmities from her followers in her last years. Death finally overtook Mary Baker Eddy on December 3, 1910. A penniless grass widow at the age of 45 who moved from one rooming house to another, she died leaving an estate of $3 million and a following of at least 100,000 men and women who revered her as the greatest religious figure in history next to Christ.

Since her death the Church of Christ, Scientist, has been governed by a self-perpetuating Board of Directors. They wield absolute authority and have resisted all attempts to liberalize church practices. In a sense they can follow no other course since the practices and administration of the denomination have been frozen by the *Church Manual* which cannot be amended.

Technically there is only one Christian Science church in the world: The First Church of Christ, Scientist, in Boston. All other congregations are simply branches of this church where members of the Mother Church may gather to worship and deliver testimonials.

Most active Christian Scientists belong to both a branch church or society and to the Mother Church in Boston. Authorized teachers may accept 30 pupils a year in the Primary class which prepares practitioners. The teachers themselves comprise an elite group within the Church since only one class for teachers is given every three years in Boston and only 30 may enroll in this Normal class.

Each branch church holds a Sunday morning worship service as well as a Wednesday evening meeting which features testimonials. The order of service is prescribed by the *Church Manual* and is the same around the world on any Sunday morning. After an organ prelude and a hymn from the *Christian Science Hymnal*, there is a reading from the King James version of the Bible. The Lord's Prayer is recited and includes Mrs. Eddy's metaphysical interpretation:

Our Father which art in heaven, Our Father-Mother God, all-harmonious, hallowed be Thy Name, Adorable One. Thy kingdom come. Thy kingdom is come; Thou art ever-present. Thy will be done on earth,—God is omnipotent, supreme. Give us this day our daily bread; Give us grace for today; feed the famished affections; and forgive us our debts, as we forgive our debtors, and Love is reflected in love; and lead us not into temptation, but deliver us from evil; and God leadeth us not into temptation, but delivereth us from sin, disease, and death. For Thine is the kingdom, and the power, and the glory, forever. For God is infinite, all-power, all Life, Truth, Love, over all, and All.

This is followed by another hymn, announcements, and solo selection. The Lesson-Sermon is the heart of the service. The First and Second Readers alternate in reading from *Science and Health* and the Bible. There are 26 subjects so that each is repeated twice a year. There is no sermon in the usual sense; no Reader is allowed to interject his or her own thoughts into the service. After a final hymn the service is concluded with the recitation of the "scientific statement of being" from p. 468 of *Science and Health*:

"There is no life, truth, intelligence, nor substance in matter. All is infinite Mind and its infinite manifestation, for God is All-in-all, Spirit is immortal

Truth; matter is mortal error. Spirit is the real and eternal; matter is the unreal and temporal. Spirit is God, and man is His image and likeness. Therefore man is not material; he is spiritual."

The Christian Science Church does not baptize members and observes only two spiritual communions a year; at these communion services there is no bread or wine but the worshippers spend a few moments in silent prayer. Mrs. Eddy prepared no ritual for marriage in her Church; Christian Scientists seek the services of Protestant ministers or civil officials when they wish to be married. Of course, the Church prescribes no burial ritual since this would imply the possibility of death.

The Church basks in the prestige of the award winning *Christian Science Monitor* founded by Mrs. Eddy in 1908 when she was 87. She declared that the object of this daily newspaper would be "to injure no man, but to bless all mankind." Its editors observe certain taboos of the cult but the paper carries only one frankly religious article in each issue. Its 224,000 subscribers receive editions published in Boston, Los Angeles, and London; most subscribers belong to the Mother Church but the *Monitor* also reaches many opinion makers, congressmen, business leaders. All top editors and most staff members are Scientists.

The official organ of the Church is the *Christian Science Journal;* other periodicals include the weekly *Christian Science Sentinel,* the *Herald of Christian Science,* and the *Christian Science Quarterly.*

Through its publications, reading rooms, literature racks, and 4,500 public lectures a year the Church seeks converts but its growth has slowed drastically in recent years. Recently a spokesman for the Board of Lectureship asked: "When 85 percent of the people out there are gray-haired and non-haired you begin to ask yourself 'What's going to happen to Christian Science?'"

Some 700 radio stations carry "The Bible Speaks to You" produced by the Mother Church. Along with the Vatican, Protestants, and Mormons the Christian Scientists erected a pavilion at the recent New York World's Fair. Yet while many people may harbor a vague distrust of doctors and a suspicion that people take too many pills, they hesitate to deny themselves and their children all medical care which is what full membership in the Christian Science Church demands.

Most people recognize the benefits of new surgical techniques, vaccines, drugs, X-rays and the like as so obvious that they cannot understand the faith of the Christian Scientist. They would have to discard a whole catalogue of beliefs they have held since childhood.

In practice even the devout Christian Scientist avails herself of what the average person would call medical care. She will patronize the optometrist, dentist, and obstetrician. Mrs. Eddy herself conceded: "Until the advancing age admits the efficacy and supremacy of Mind, it is better for Christian Scientists to leave surgery and the adjustment of broken bones and dislocations to the fingers of a surgeon, while the mental healer confines himself chiefly to mental reconstruction and to the prevention of inflammation" (*Science and Health*, p. 401).

Science and Health is considered an inspired work; Mrs. Eddy herself declared: "No human pen nor tongue taught me the Science contained in this book, *Science and Health*; and neither tongue nor pen can overthrow it" (*Science and Health*, p. 110). She declared: "In the year 1866, I discovered the Christ Science or divine laws of

Life, Truth, and Love, and named my discovery Christian Science. God had been graciously preparing me during many years for the reception of this final revelation of the absolute divine Principle of scientific mental healing" (p. 107).

In another book Mrs. Eddy exclaimed: "I should blush to write of *Science and Health with Key to the Scriptures* as I have, were it of human origin, and were I, apart from God, its author. But, as I was only a scribe echoing the harmonies of heaven in divine metaphysics, I cannot be super-modest in my estimate of the Christian Science text-book" (*The First Church of Christ, Scientist, and Miscellany*, p. 115).

She maintained that the Bible was full of errors due to faulty translations and could not, in any event, be understood except through the application of her own allegorical interpretations.

Despite thorough doctoring and editing Mrs. Eddy's book remains one of the most obscure scriptures ever penned. One of Mrs. Eddy's critics—Mark Twain—said of *Science and Health*: "For of all the strange and frantic and incomprehensible and uninterpretable books which the imagination of man has created, surely this one is the prize sample."

What does Christian Science teach? What are the principles which Mrs. Eddy formulated in 1866? In Christian Science there is no such thing as evil or sin. These are real only in the sense that they seem real to human beings until God reveals their unreality.

"The cause of all so-called disease is mental, a mortal fear, a mistaken belief or conviction of the necessity and power of ill health . . ." (p. 377). Again Mrs. Eddy writes: "Man is never sick, for Mind is not sick and matter cannot be" (p. 393). In reality there is no such thing as cancer or TB or multiple sclerosis or any disease catalogued by medical science. The cure for all these illusions lies in following the principle of Christian Science which denies their reality.

Finally, death itself is an illusion. Mrs. Eddy wrote: "Any material evidence of death is false, for it contradicts the spiritual facts of being" (p. 584). The death of the founder of the Church of Christ, Scientist, as well as many of her followers is explained by the fact that men have not yet attained the spiritual state which enables them to overcome death although such a conquest is quite possible.

Most of the traditional Christian dogmas of original sin, the sacraments, heaven and hell are repudiated by Christian Science. Mrs. Eddy dismissed the Trinity as polytheism: "The theory of three persons in one God (that is, a personal Trinity or Tri-unity) suggests polytheism, rather than the one ever-present I Am." The usual reference to God in Science churches is not as Father but as Father-Mother.

Christian Scientists draw a distinction between Jesus and the Christ. Jesus was a man who lived about 1900 years ago; Christ is defined as "the true idea of God." Jesus therefore was simply a man who demonstrated the Christ principle to a greater degree than anyone else. By demonstrating the Christ, Jesus effected the various healings described in the Bible.

Mrs. Eddy was explicit about her belief regarding the divinity of Jesus: "The Christian who believes in the First Commandment is a monotheist. Thus he virtually unites with the Jew's belief in one God, and recognizes that Jesus Christ is not God, as Jesus himself declared, but is the Son of God" (p. 361). This aspect of Christian Science has attracted a number of converts from Jewish backgrounds.

All signs indicate that the growth of Christian Science has slowed. Relatively few people seem willing to forego medical treatment and rely exclusively on metaphysical healing. Nevertheless Christian Science will probably remain as an influential minority religion.

FURTHER READING

Braden, Charles S., *Christian Science Today* (Dallas, Southern Methodist University Press, 1958).

Dewitt, John, *The Christian Science Way of Life* (Englewood Cliffs, N. J., Prentice-Hall, 1962).

Eddy, Mary Baker, *Science and Health With Key to the Scriptures* (Boston, Christian Science Publishing Society).

Peel, Robert, *Mary Baker Eddy: The Years of Discovery* (New York, Holt, Rinehart and Winston, 1966).

The Doukhobors
□□□□□□□□□□

AMERICAN HUSBANDS who "get mad" at their wives are likely to put on their hats and coats and leave the house. The Sons of Freedom sect of Doukhobors who "get mad" at the government are likely to take off all their clothes and burn down their houses.

For more than 40 years the Sons of Freedom have battled the Canadian government. Trouble started when the government seized some Freedomite land as payment for fines incurred when the members of the sect refused to send their children to school.

In 1962 the Sons of Freedom outdid themselves in arson and bomb attacks. They climaxed their series of destructions by blowing up a 366-foot power transmission tower on the east bank of Kootenay Lake, throwing 1000 people out of work because of the power loss. A few weeks later the Royal Canadian Mounted Police rounded up all the Freedomite leaders, charging some with terrorism and 70 others with masterminding the raids and with "conspiring to intimidate Parliament."

While the Sons of Freedom languished in jail their wives and daughters set out on a scorched earth policy at their main village of Krestova. They reduced the 110 houses to fewer than a dozen tar-paper shacks.

Another protest device of the Sons of Freedom is nudity. They maintain that nudity simply expresses their religious view that man is a naked child, but they also know that such demonstrations embarrass the authorities and bring attention to their cause. Freedomites have paraded in the nude, danced in the nude while setting fire to their buildings, and ridden 35 miles in a railroad box car to jail— in the nude. When 50 Sons of Freedom were convicted of public nudity in 1950 they quietly listened to the reading of the sentence and then proceeded to remove their clothes in the packed courtroom.

We should understand that the Sons of Freedom is only one sect of the Russian mystical movement known as Doukhoborism. Only 2000 or so of the estimated 18,000 Doukhobors in British Columbia and other Canadian provinces belong to this fanatical wing.

Most of the minority religions described in these chapters developed within Roman Catholicism or Protestantism. Doukhoborism arose as a protest against the Orthodox Church of Russia, as did such other sects as the Raskolnki, Khlysti, Skopsti, Molokani, Stundists, and Pashkovites which are generally unknown to Western Christians.

Doukhoborism began in Kharkov and the villages of Dnieper in eighteenth-century Russia when groups of peasants rejected the authority of the established Orthodox Church and appealed instead to the authority of the "inner light." In this and some other respects they resembled the Quakers and they would later be befriended by English and American Quakers.

The Doukhobors believed in God but denied the Christian doctrine of the Trinity. Jesus was simply a man who lived many years ago and who possessed wisdom and virtue to an unusual degree. Neither Bible nor the Church was a reliable guide to spiritual perfection; only the inner voice could lead man to this goal.

Their name—Doukhobors—means Spirit Wrestlers. The Orthodox priests and civil authorities insisted that the dissidents were wrestling against the spirit of God, whereas the believers maintained they were wrestling for the spirit. They turned their backs on the priests, icons, rituals, and sacraments of Russian Orthodoxy. They likewise spurned the schools, the taking of oaths, and military service. They would follow the dictates of their consciences and the direct guidance they received from God. Their plain board altars held only a pitcher of water, a dish of salt, and a loaf of bread. They greeted each other with "Slava bohu" (The Lord be praised).

A basic contradiction in Doukhoborism has been their firm assertion of the freedom and independence of the individual coupled with their eager acceptance of spiritual dictatorship. Often the dictator was far from spiritual himself. One of their early leaders was Saveli Kapustin who was acknowledged as such in 1790. He had declared: "As truly as the heaven is above me and the earth beneath my feet, I am the true Lord Jesus Christ."

From the beginning of their revolt the Doukhobors were hounded by the czar's officials who wanted them to serve the usual terms as conscripts in the Russian army. They refused to bear arms and threatened, if conscripted and pressed into battle, to shoot their rifles into the air above the enemy's heads.

Czar Alexander I, a more liberal ruler, allowed the Doukhobors to settle in the Milky Waters area bordering the Black Sea. Here they prospered, established model villages, and paid their taxes. Only occasional brushes with the authorities over suspected proselytizing among the Orthodox marred their efforts to build a utopia. In 1817 the Doukhobors reported the death of Kapustin but many believed that he simply went into hiding and continued to direct the sect for several years from his refuge.

Kapustin's son, Vasili Kalmikoff, succeeded to the leadership of the sect but became a drunkard and died in 1832. His son, Illarion Kalmikoff, was also dissolute and let the apostles and elders manage the affairs of the community. He was a bachelor but the elders desired a male heir to the spiritual throne so they supplied him with six virgins. Two sons were born in this experiment.

While Illarion loafed, cavorted with his mistresses, and drank vodka the elders instituted a reign of terror. Debauchery, secret murders, feuds rent the Doukhobor settlements. The government finally declared, "In the name of your religion and by the command of your pretended teachers, you put men to death, conceal crimes committed by your brothers, and hide information from the government." They were banished to the Wet Mountains of the Caucasus.

Illarion's son, Peter Kalmikoff, assumed the role of "Christ" after his father's death and following family tradition spent most of his hours drinking, hunting, and sleeping. He married a 16-year-old girl, Lukeria Vasilivna Hubanova, and passed the spiritual leadership to her before he died. "I give you to Lukeria. The spirit of Christ will pass from me to her," he told his faithful Doukhobors. At 28 he was dead. By this time the number of Doukhobors had risen to about 10,000.

The son of a well-to-do Doukhobor family, Peter Vasilivich Verigin, had caught the eye of Lukeria many years before when he was just a lad. In the meantime he had married another girl by the name of Dunia. Lukeria was annoyed at his marriage and induced him to divorce his young bride and live with her. A month after Peter left his wife she gave birth to a boy, Peter Petrovich Verigin, who would one day assume the leadership of the Doukhobors in Canada—with disastrous results.

Conditions in the Doukhobor villages did not improve. Superstition, magic, dream interpretations were prevalent. The government began to draft Doukhobors for three-year army terms, considerably shorter than the usual 25-year period for other conscripts. When Lukeria died, Peter Vasilivich tried to take over control but not all Doukhobors recognized his authority. The villages divided into the so-called "Mad Doukhobors" and the "Bad Doukhobors."

In 1886 Peter was arrested for agitating against the state and was exiled to Archangel province, about 1500 miles from the main Doukhobor settlements. He continued to direct Doukhobor affairs by letter although his power was unknown outside the Doukhobor communities. The Doukhobors had learned to use evasion and deceit in talking to outsiders. They answered all questions about their organization by repeating: "We have no leader, none among us is greater than another. We are all brothers and sisters in Christ."

In exile Peter absorbed the writings of Leo Tolstoy and incorporated these into Doukhoborism. He became a vegetarian and by letter directed the Doukhobors to follow suit. He directed them to redistribute their wealth and establish a communal system. He advised against the use of tobacco and liquor and finally forbade sexual intercourse. Hundreds left the movement when they heard of this latest regulation. The government moved Peter further from the Doukhobor faithful by sending him to Siberia.

Tolstoy encouraged the Doukhobors and protested their persecution and Peter's exile to authorities. His naive assessment of the real nature of the sect indicates he knew little about the true role of Peter Vasilivich Verigin:

> The Doukhobors are a most remarkable people. They work with their hands, exploiting no one, producing more than they consume. They reject authority of both church and state, acknowledge no human authority, yet live together peacefully in their community with no guidance other than their own reason and conscience. Among these dignified, confident, yet illiterate peasants, is the germination of that seed sown by Christ himself 1800 years ago.

One letter from Peter told the believers: "Christ wants you to burn your guns!" They collected all their rifles, pistols, and swords, poured oil and fat on the mountain of weapons and set them afire on June 29, 1895. This angered the Cossacks who descended with whips and clubs on the hymn-singing Doukhobors gathered around the bonfire. Now the government broke up the Doukhobor settlements, sending some to the swamps of Batum while others wandered about the Russian countryside. Many died of whippings, disease, and malnutrition.

Verigin and his Doukhobor counselors decided to seek refuge in some other country. Assisted by English and American Quakers they negotiated an arrangement with Canada which was looking for immigrants. The first boatload of Doukhobors arrived in 1898; the Canadian government has had difficulties with the Russian mystics ever since.

The Russian Government refused to allow Peter Vasilivich Verigin to accompany the Doukhobors to their new homeland. He continued to send letters but his advice was typically vague and ambiguous. He never rescinded his ban on marriage and sexual intercourse but the Doukhobors resumed their old habits in Canada.

When Verigin finally managed to leave his Siberian exile and reached Canada in 1902 he saw clear evidence of disintegration of the Doukhobor movement. Some Doukhobors in Saskatchewan had left the communal living plan and obtained land of their own. They were known as Independents. Another group, forerunners of the Sons of Freedom, objected to the Canadianization of their children or any compromise with the state. Verigin's own Christian Community of Universal Brotherhood faced serious problems brought about by mismanagement, excesses, indecision.

The arrival of the exiled leader boosted the morale of all the Doukhobors. He managed to obtain loans for land and equipment. In 1909 and 1910 he led most of the Doukhobors from Saskatchewan to British Columbia where they are concentrated to this day. Here they planted thousands of fruit trees, irrigated the land, built sawmills and brick factories. They started a jam factory at Brilliant and soon B. C. Jam was well known in Canadian pantries. (Eventually the jam factory, pride of the Doukhobor community, would burn to the ground, the object of an arsonist's torch.)

Peter sent for his divorced wife Dunia and his 24-year-old son, Peter Petrovich Verigin. The young man—foul-mouthed, arrogant, cruel, and lewd—spent his days in Canada discrediting his father's claims to religious leadership. The Doukhobors accepted his abuse and vices with the thought that God works in mysterious ways. After a few months his father sent him back to Russia.

On October 28, 1924, Peter Verigin boarded a Canadian Pacific train with one of his many mistresses. Both were blown up in the middle of the night when a dynamite bomb went off under Verigin's seat. Seven other passengers were killed in the explosion. The crime was never solved. More than 10,000 Doukhobors attended his funeral; his grave remains a shrine although it too has been the object of bombing attacks.

Peter Petrovich Verigin returned to Canada from the U.S.S.R. and his arrival split the Doukhobors into further schisms. His gambling, drunkenness, and stupidity combined with the economic effects of the Great Depression and the expensive arson and bombings dragged the settlements into bankruptcy.

More than 600 Sons of Freedom were tried for nudity, arson, and perjury in 1932 and were confined on Piers Island, two miles off the coast of Sidney, Vancouver Island. The government had to put the prisoners on the island since the jails were already full of Freedomites. They also imprisoned Peter Verigin.

Verigin died in 1939. Despite his conduct he had managed to hold the allegiance of some Doukhobors. World War II further disorganized the Doukhobor community. High wages and good prices for lumber and farm products drew the Doukhobors from the communal system and today no Doukhobors are living under the original, Tolstoyan plan. Most Doukhobor children now attend public schools and a few have even gone on to college and entered the professions. Another Verigin, John, directs the heirs of the Christian Community of Universal Brotherhood which is now called the Union of Spiritual Communities of Christ. His authority is less secure than that of the two Peters because of the possible existence of an uncle in the U.S.S.R. The uncle has not been heard from in years and has become a mythical character.

The Sons of Freedom display the most intense reaction to Canadian life. They still resist the education of their children in public schools and continue their protest by nudity, arson, and bombings. Several years ago the Sons of Freedom threatened to go back to Russia to which the Canadian government replied in effect: "Wonderful. Can we help you pack?" But the Sons backed down and the problem for the Canadians remained. Recently many of the Freedomites have accepted the leadership of one Stefan Sorokin who came from Uruguay and has since returned to self-exile in South America. He sends regular proclamations and directions to the Freedomites. Should he attempt to return to British Columbia the police have warrants for his arrest on a number of charges. Sorokin's followers call themselves the Christian Community and Brotherhood of Reformed Doukhobors.

In recent years nine other countries besides Russia have turned down proposals to accept the cantankerous Sons of Freedom: Cuba, Turkey, Peru, Chile, Colombia, Brazil, Uruguay, Venezuela, and Argentina. Commented Robert Bonner, attorney general of British Columbia: "We don't want to unload our troubles on another country, but I don't know what to do with these people."

Plagued by dissolute leaders, schisms, and the fanaticism of the Sons of Freedom the Doukhobors have been unable to maintain their communal way of life in Canada. The materialistic attractions of Canadian life and the democratic attitude of the Canadian government do not provide the same soil for growth as did the oppressive czarist regime of eighteenth and nineteenth century Russia. Doukhoborism seems to lack the ingredients to guarantee survival and the sect is unlikely to see the twenty-first century.

FURTHER READING

Hawthorn, Harry B., ed. *The Doukhobors of British Columbia* (Vancouver, B. C., University of British Columbia and J. M. Dent, 1955).

Wright, J. F. C., *Slava Bohu*: *The Story of the Doukhobors* (New York, Farrar & Rinehart, 1940).

The Hutterites
🔲🔲🔲🔲🔲🔲🔲🔲🔲

POPULAR INTEREST in communal living is evidenced by the many magazine and newspaper articles describing these alternate life styles. The history of most communes is short whether they are organized by hippies or religious enthusiasts. But the oldest and largest communes have been those of the Hutterites. For more than 400 years these devout, ascetic, German-speaking Christians have successfully combined communal living, pacifism, and isolation from the world.

All of the estimated 20,000 Hutterites live in 170 colonies in North America. Two thirds live in the prairie provinces of Alberta, Manitoba, and Saskatchewan in Canada and the other third live in South Dakota and Montana.

In many ways the Hutterites (sometimes called Hutterians or Hutterian Brethren) resemble the Amish but unlike the Amish they accept modern technology while rejecting the idea of privately owned property. To the Hutterites the community of goods is one of the basic principles of Christianity. They base their belief on the Bible: "And all who believed were together and had all things in common" (Acts 2:44) and consider private property the root of many moral evils.

Each Hutterite colony consists of between 60 and 150 men, women, and children. When a particular colony approaches a population of 125 or so the leaders set procedures in motion to start a branch colony. The parent colony looks for a suitable plot of land—6,000 or more acres—on which to settle the new group. The mother colony finances the purchase of land, building materials, and equipment and selects half its membership to man the new outpost.

Both the Zero Population Growth exponents and the Women's Lib advocates would shudder at Hutterite customs. Without a doubt the Hutterites report the highest birthrate in the hemisphere, if not in the world. The average completed family includes nine or ten children; the Hutterite birthrate of 45 per 1,000 is about three times the general American birthrate. As a result each colony doubles in size within 16 to 20 years. A University of Alberta professor estimates that if the Hutterites continue to grow at their present rate they will number 20 *billion* by the year 2303. The present world population is approximately 3½ billion.

The only career open to Hutterite women is that of wife and mother. All major decisions are made by the baptized men of the community while the women raise children, cook, sew, and take care of their households. If large families and female domesticity are destructive of personal values the statistics do not bear this out. In more than 100 years in America only one divorce among the Hutterites has been recorded. No Hutterite has ever committed suicide, none has ever been jailed except for pacifism, and hardly any Hutterite has been known to suffer from a mental disorder.

Apparently the fundamentalist Christian faith and the cradle-to-grave security of communal living provide all the support needed to maintain an unusually stable society. Contact with the outside world is minimized.

Colonies are located off the beaten path although members will go to town to sell produce or buy necessities they are unable to provide for themselves. No radio, television, or secular publications are allowed.

While the Amish reject electricity, automobiles, tractors, and modern farm machinery the Hutterites distinguish themselves by innovative farming techniques which call for a high degree of mechanization. If the prolific Hutterites did not achieve an above average yield from their agricultural operations they could not support such large families or save enough to finance branch colonies.

Through the centuries the peaceful Hutterites have endured persecution and harrassment and hundreds have died for their religious faith. They consider 1528 as their founding date. This was the year in which a small group of Anabaptists in Tyrol decided to adopt collective farming. They were soon joined by Jacob Hutter, a traveling hatmaker, whose name they came to bear.

To the Anabaptists the Protestant Reformation did not go far enough. They rejected the established churches, refused to bear arms or swear oaths, and insisted that only adults could receive a valid baptism. The largest body of surviving Anabaptists, the Mennonites and the strict Mennonites known as Amish, did not question the propriety of private property.

Hutter was burned at the stake as a heretic at Innsbruck in 1536. His successor, Peter Rideman, drew up the basic Confession of Faith which Hutterites follow to this day.

Because of their farming skills the Hutterites were tolerated in Moravia where they expanded to 70 colonies of some 20,000 members. The Thirty Years War, the Turkish raids, and religious persecution drove them from Moravia in 1622. Some went to Slovakia and some to Transylvania. Many returned to the Catholic or Protestant beliefs of their ancestors but a remnant settled in the Ukraine in 1770 at the invitation of the Empress Catherine.

For a century the Hutterites lived in Russia under the protection of the Czarist government even though Russian nationalists objected to this German enclave. In the early 19th century many Hutterites abandoned the communal way and chose to live on family-owned farms. These usually affiliated with Mennonite congregations. Eventually the government changed its policy and threatened to conscript Hutterites for military service and to Russianize the children. The Hutterite elders in the three Russian settlements resolved to emigrate again, this time to the United States.

The entire Hutterite community of 800 people resettled in South Dakota in 1874 but about half of these gave up the communal way of life. The remaining Hutterites prospered until World War I when their pacifism and German culture brought them into conflict with the larger society. By 1915 they had grown to 1700 in 17 colonies. Draft boards refused to honor the claims to conscientious objector status of young men from the colonies; two young Hutterites died in military prisons for refusing to put on uniforms. Once again the Hutterites decided to move. They headed across the border to Canada where most Hutterites now live. Only one colony remained in the United States but in the succeeding years others have been re-established in South Dakota and Montana.

Daily life in a Hutterite colony has not changed much over the centuries except for the appearance of new inventions. A bell awakens the community about 6:15 a.m. Meals are served in a common dining room where the men, women, and children eat separately and in silence. Farm work occupies the men while the women handle house-keeping and other chores. Each evening the people gather for a half hour worship service and on Sunday for two hours. The minister does not prepare his own sermons but reads sermons written and handed down from the pioneer days of the movement. The congregation sings German hymns a capella.

The minister is chosen by lot from those nominated. He and his family eat alone apart from the community dining room. In the larger colonies there must be two ministers so that one can accompany the half which sets up the branch colony.

Hutterite children attend German school where they learn the language and religious customs. State laws re-quire attendance at English public schools until they reach the age of 14. All Hutterites are tri-lingual. In ordinary conversation they speak a German dialect, in church they use High German, and in dealing with the Gentiles outside the colony they use English.

Their homes lack wallpaper, pictures, or mirrors but are kept spotless. The colony does not allow cameras, tele-vision, radios, card playing, tobacco, dancing, or musical instruments but will install a telephone to communicate with the town or other colonies. Hutterites are not tee-totalers and enjoy beer and wine in moderation.

Most Hutterites request baptism between the ages of 18 and 20. They finish a long instruction period and are baptized on Palm Sunday or Pentecost, not by immersion, but by pouring of water. At one time the Hutterites were zealous missionaries but now they make no concerted effort to win converts; they have their hands full taking care of the growth due to their birthrate. Outsiders who seek to join a colony must give their adherence to Hutterite theology and customs and sign over all their material goods to the colony they join.

The values of the Hutterite community stand in sharp contrast to those of the outside world. Cooperation rather than competition characterizes the community. Each person has assigned responsibilities and would not know what anyone means by an "identity crisis." The object of life is to attain holiness through Christian faith, work, and self denial rather than self development or achievement of a higher standard of living. Each Hutterite accepts the idea of order inculcated by his religion: man over woman, old over young, parent over child. He gets along with the bare necessities of life and sees only disorder and covetousness resulting from private property. The colony may scrimp to pay for a new combine or milking machine but it has no plans to spend its money on a color TV set or carpets or an oil painting.

Not only asceticism but practicality demands a standard of frugality. A colony must set aside at least $10,000 a year for 20 years to have enough funds to buy land for its branch.

Although few converts join the colonies, few Hutterites leave the community for the world. Those who do, usually young men who have not been baptized, often return after a few weeks or months of life in the world.

Because hardly any Hutterites receive baptism before the age of 18 and only the baptized members can marry with Church sanction there are no teen age marriages. If there were, the birthrate might be even higher. Young men will typically choose a wife from another colony which might be 30 or more miles away. The Church forbids marriages between first cousins. The bride leaves her family and colony to live in her husband's colony.

During World War II draft boards treated the Hutterites with more compassion. Some 276 Hutterites served in workcamps as conscientious objectors. The clannishness and growth of the colonies have antagonized some of their neighbors and relations between the Hutterites and Gentiles are not always cordial. The province of Alberta limits the size of colonies to 6,400 acres and similar attempts to control Hutterite growth have been made in other provinces and states.

Desirable plots for branch colonies are increasingly hard to discover and finance but the birthrate demands such expansion. Perhaps a move to some other area such as South America or Australia will be required during the coming decades. No relaxation of the Church's absolute ban on birth control seems to be likely in the near future.

A related movement founded in the 20th instead of the 16th century is the Society of Brothers. Dr. Eberhard Arnold (1883-1935) started a small commune in southern Germany in 1922. He heard about the Hutterite communities and visited Canada where he was well received and ordained by a group of elders. When his own commune was shut down by the Nazis the group moved to England. They tried to emigrate to Canada but were turned down by the authorities and instead 350 Brothers went to Paraguay.

Fraternal relations were maintained for some years between the Society of Brothers and the Hutterites but eventually a split took place. The Brothers accused the Hutterites of losing missionary zeal and abdicating any chance to witness to the world. The Hutterites scolded the Brothers for allowing folk dancing, motion pictures and smoking in their Paraguayan colonies.

Today the Society of Brothers operates communes in Paraguay as well as three in the United States, one in England, and one in Germany. The 1500 Brothers represent 20 nationalities and are more intellectual and less rigid than the Hutterites. They engage in publishing, teaching, and toy making as well as agriculture and their colonies include libraries, hospitals, and excellent schools.

FURTHER READING

Hostetler, John A., and Huntington, Gertrude Enders, *The Hutterites in North America* (New York, Holt, Rinehart and Winston, 1967).

Peters, Victor, *All Things in Common: The Hutterian Way of Life* (Minneapolis, University of Minnesota Press, 1965).

The I AM Movement

DURING ITS HEYDEY in the 1930's the I AM movement drew thousands to its rallies. Many others devoured violet-hued I AM publications and attended classes at I AM centers around the country. Since the death (ascension) of founder Guy Ballard and the charges of fraud sustained by a United States court, the once powerful I AM cult has dwindled to a devoted few.

Ballard's widow, Edna, now in her 80's, maintains homes in Santa Fe and in Chicago where the I AM cult owns a 12 story Loop office building and a publications center on the South Side. Mrs. Ballard is considered the only Accredited Messenger who can receive messages from the Ascended Masters including Beloved Daddy Ballard. Their son Donald handles the movement's business affairs.

Guy Ballard was born in 1878 in Newton, Kansas. He became a spiritualist medium in Chicago but also cultivated an interest in mining. He married Edna Wheeler, a professional harpist and medium, in 1916. A son was born two years later.

The Ballards dabbled in Christian Science, Theosophy, Unity, Rosicrucianism and other occult groups. Ballard claimed to have spent two years in the Orient between 1919 and 1929 but this is doubted by former associates. Guy ran into difficulties when he was indicted by a Cook County grand jury on March 25, 1929 on a charge of "obtaining money and goods by means of a confidence game." Warrants were never served because he slipped away to the West coast where he lived for two years under the alias of Dick Gilbert.

With her husband thousands of miles away, Edna Ballard got a job in a Chicago book shop known as the Philosopher's Nook. It specialized in occult literature. Edna also edited two periodicals, *American Occultist* and *The Diamond*.

Meanwhile Guy Ballard entered mining engineering in northern California. Through his study of Theosophy he had heard about the Brotherhood of Masters, or Great Souls, who were said to dwell in mountain haunts.

One morning, he related, he hiked up the side of Mount Shasta and stopped at noon near a mountain spring. He was about to scoop up a cup of cool water when a young man appeared from nowhere and addressed him: "My brother, if you will hand me your cup I will give you a much more refreshing drink than spring water."

Ballard's cup was magically filled with a creamy white liquid. After drinking this potion he experienced an electric-type shock which induced a wonderful sense of well-being. The young man turned out to be the Master St. Germain. He revealed to Ballard that in previous lives Ballard had been a famous musician in southern France and a temple priest in ancient Egypt. Then he disappeared.

A few days later, Ballard relates, he received a thin gold card inviting him to revisit the mountain rendezvous. This time his host treated him to some marvelous cakes and he was transported to the Sahara desert as it existed 70,000 years ago.

On a third occasion a dove delivered a gold invitation. This time Guy left his physical body and flew with St.

Germain to a mountainside. St. Germain pushed aside some boulders and revealed rooms filled with precious jewels and metals. A special vault held treasures from the sea which had been lost on sunken Spanish galleons. In a sort of mystic movie theater Guy Ballard sat with 70 Masters and watched the history of the world unfold on a mammoth screen. They witnessed the civilizations of the Gobi and Sahara deserts, the Roman empire, the life of Christ, the story of the lost continents of Mu and Atlantis.

These excursions to the mountain monastery of the Great White Brotherhood continued as Ballard absorbed the principles of the Mighty I AM. On one holiday they were entertained by a visit by seven guests from Venus.

Mrs. Ballard began to instruct I AM classes in her Chicago home. The Bible of the movement, *Unveiled Mysteries,* was published by the St. Germain Press under Guy Ballard's pen name of Godfre Ray King. He shrugged off charges that his book was simply a rewrite of a book which had appeared 50 years before entitled *Dweller on Two Planets.*

As the movement spread the Ballards staged several large rallies in Detroit and Cleveland and managed to fill the 6,000-seat Shrine auditorium in Los Angeles in 1935. The cult's artist-in-residence Charles Sindelar announced that Jesus had agreed to sit for 21 days for his portrait. This portrait along with Ballard's books, phonograph records, and ritualistic paraphernalia was sold in the lobby.

Guy Ballard wore only white suits with pink bow ties. Edna swirled onto the stage in a pink evening gown with a diamond wreath, pink cape, and white ostrich feather. Ballard explained to his audiences that he could make himself invisible at will and could dip into lakes of jewels and riches anytime he wished. He urged his followers to call on the purifying Violet Consuming Flame but reminded them to remove their hats because otherwise the cosmic light could not penetrate below the chin.

The cult established centers and reading rooms in New York, Philadelphia, Washington, and Los Angeles. The Ballards traded their battered Ford for four cream-colored limousines. By 1938 the couple was traveling with an entourage of 14 people.

Contributions were called "I AM Love Gifts." The *Los Angeles Times* estimated that the Ballards averaged $1,000 a day from their class tuition and books sales. And these were Depression dollars.

A new policy was announced in 1939. Secrecy was to be the order of the day. The days of the auditorium rallies were over. This policy continues to this day as any visitors to an I AM center soon discover.

The personal lives of I AM devotees were strictly regulated. An elite class, the Hundred Percenters, agreed to abstain from all meat, onions, garlic, tobacco, liquor, card playing and sex activity. Married members are asked to live like brother and sister since the use of sex chains one to an endless series of rebirths.

On Dec. 29, 1939 Guy Ballard died of hardening of the arteries. Edna declared: "Our Blessed Daddy Ballard made his Ascension last night at 12 o'clock from the Royal Teton Retreat and is now an Ascended Master."

But the I AM followers who had often heard Guy Ballard boast that he had finally conquered death and disease were not all satisfied with the widow's statement. Many became disillusioned and quit the movement. The new policy of secrecy made it difficult to replenish the I AM ranks. Ballard's death marked the beginning of the end of the cult as a major American religious body.

Six months later another blow fell. A grand jury indicted Edna and a score of associates on 18 counts. In part, the indictment charged that the defendants "did unlawfully, knowingly, and willfully devise and intend to devise a scheme and artifice to defraud, and for obtaining money and property by means of false and fraudulent representations, pretenses, and promises from a large number of persons." Ballard was said to have taken in $3 million during the seven years in which the cult operated under his direction.

A hostile press reported the sensational trial and by the time the verdict was delivered the I AM movement was thoroughly discredited. Mrs. Ballard was found guilty and sentenced to concurrent terms of one year on each of seven counts and fined $8,000. The sentence was suspended. In 1946 the Supreme Court voided the sentence because women had been excluded from the grand jury panel.

Nevertheless the damage to the image of the cult had been done and the cult is still denied the use of the U. S. mails and must ship its literature by express.

The I AM movement has always considered itself to be superpatriotic. During the trial the defendants bemoaned the ingratitude of the government since they said the I AM-ers by means of powerful mental waves had annihilated three Nazi submarines heading for the Panama Canal, had disposed of 346 enemy spies, and had rendered harmless the Japanese incendiary balloons sent over the West coast.

The I AM theology embraces a pantheon of gods and demigods. Of these the greatest is St. Germain but there are many other Ascended Masters, now including Guy Ballard.

Each human being possesses an electronic body which abides about 12 to 50 feet above the physical body. This electronic body pours light and energy by means of a ray of white light into the top of the head. This light centers in the heart.

To purify the body I AM students are asked to call on the Violet Consuming Flame. Only this flame can destroy the residue of evil thoughts and desires which prevent a man from escaping the series of reincarnations.

The movement has always stressed the importance of colors. Some colors are beneficial and others destructive. Favorite colors are lavender and violet which are worn by both men and women.

The main devotional exercise in an I AM temple is the recitation of "decrees." These are affirmations which are repeated again and again in a fast tempo. There are hundreds of printed decrees for various purposes such as the Purity Decrees, the Electronic Circle Decrees, and the Great Silence Decrees. Every I AM session also features a recorded message by Guy Ballard; at the conclusion the congregation declares "Thank you, precious Daddy."

No current membership statistics are available. The 1961 edition of *Purpose of the Ascended Masters "I AM" Activity* booklet, which is an introduction to the cult, speaks of 3 to 5 million followers. A more realistic estimate would be about 5,000. The two main temples in Chicago and San Francisco may each serve constituencies of 500 with smaller groups at the I AM centers in Calgary, Alberta; Vancouver, British Columbia; Boston; and Portland.

I AM owns some valuable property, possesses an extensive cultic literature, and continues to hold the allegiance of a small number of followers. Younger converts are not taking the place of older members who pass on. The cult will have to face the trauma of Edna's death. It seems safe to predict that the mighty I AM will never again reach the success it enjoyed in the 1930's.

FURTHER READING

Bryan, Gerald B., *Psychic Dictatorship in America* (Los Angeles, Truth Research Publications, 1940).

King, Godfre Ray (Guy Ballard), *Unveiled Mysteries* (Chicago, St. Germain Press, 1934).

The Jehovah's Witnesses
🔲🔲🔲🔲🔲🔲🔲🔲🔲

HARDLY ANYONE READING these words has not at one time or another been approached by a Jehovah's Witness seeking converts. Every square mile in the United States has been assigned to some member of this cult and he is expected to call on the householders in his territory once or twice a year. Other Witnesses stand on busy street corners trying to sell copies of *Watchtower* or *Awake!* magazines.

Do such tactics actually win converts or do they merely antagonize people? Certainly many people are annoyed by the persistent Witnesses who ring their doorbells and take up their time. But the membership statistics indicate that all these hours of doorstep preaching are not wasted. The worldwide membership of the cult passed the 1,500,000 mark during 1971; in 1938 there were fewer than 50,000 Witnesses.

The Witnesses flatly deny the doctrine of the Trinity. They assert that Jesus was once known as Michael the Archangel, became a perfect man, and is now "Chief executive Officer of Jehovah." Jesus Christ is not God but a creature inferior to God. Any references in Scripture to the Holy Spirit are understood to mean only the power of Jehovah God. They might well be classified as fundamentalist unitarians.

To their unitarianism they add an urgent belief in the imminent end of the world. The final battle of Armageddon—between the forces of God and Satan, good and evil —may start today, next week, next month, certainly within the next decade. The chief duty of faithful Witnesses is to warn non-members to join the New World Society in order to escape annihilation in this climactic battle. Only by joining the cult can people survive the battle and live to repopulate a paradise on earth which will be established after Jehovah's victory. The survivors, and certain righteous dead who will be resurrected, will live forever in a world without death, sickness, disease, sin, or crime. This materialistic heaven is the most that the average Witness can hope for. Only a tiny fraction of mankind—144,000—will reign as spirit creatures with Jehovah and Jesus Christ. This quota has been filling up since Pentecost so that only about 11,000 of this remnant are still alive; they are all Jehovah's Witnesses and only they may partake of the bread and wine in the annual Memorial Service.

Denial of the doctrine of eternal punishment was one of the first distinctive beliefs preached by the founder of the cult. The wicked will not suffer the torments of hell. They will simply be annihilated.

Since Satan rules the world and especially organized religion, business, and politics, the committed Witness will withdraw from any involvement with the secular world. He resigns from society and takes refuge in the New World Society. Jehovah's Witnesses will not serve in the armed forces of any nation, salute the flag, stand for the national anthem, vote, hold public office, become active in a labor union or other secular organization, or form close ties with non-Witnesses. He enters a world of his own centering around the local Kingdom Hall (parish). He may have to hold a secular job to support himself and his family but his main interest in life is to warn his neighbors of the impending battle of Armageddon.

The catalog of things which the cult opposes is impressive: Catholicism, Christmas trees and observances, Communism, evolution, higher education, liquor, lodges, Protestantism, Mother's Day, Sunday Schools, tobacco, the United Nations, the YMCA. His children will generally avoid birthday parties, Christmas and Easter celebrations, school organizations, college. Increasingly the cult has built a mystique around blood; since blood is supposed to contain the life principle the devout Witness will never eat blood such as blood sausage or meat which has not been properly prepared, as in the Kosher ritual. Their objection to blood transfusions has led to unfavorable publicity and various law suits. The Watchtower Society also objects to psychiatry and the use of hypnosis in medicine.

Founder of this cult was a Pittsburgh, Pa. haberdasher, Charles Taze Russell (born 1852). Originally a Presbyterian, he later joined the Congregationalist Church but continued to be disturbed by certain traditional Christian doctrines such as that of hell. An Adventist preacher convinced him as early as 1872 that the end of the world was near. Russell began to teach small classes of Bible students and started a magazine, the *Watch Tower and Herald of Christ's Presence,* in 1879. He began to warn his followers that the Bible clearly pin-pointed the end of the world in 1914. This date was also confirmed by a mystical analysis of the dimensions of the Great Pyramid of Egypt.

Russell assumed the title "Pastor" by which he was known to his supporters. He traveled around the world preaching his novel Biblical interpretations and prophecies. From his pen flowed a stream of books, tracts, and magazine articles. In 1908 he moved his headquarters from Pittsburgh to Brooklyn.

Some of his followers left after his highly publicized divorce. Mrs. Russell, who was also active in the movement and helped edit the publications, sued for divorce on grounds of "his conceit, egotism, domination, and improper conduct in relation to other women." The Pastor was later returned to court several times when he tried to avoid alimony payments. Other disciples turned away when he tried to promote $60-a-bushel "Miracle Wheat," a fake cancer cure, and a marvelous "Millennial Bean."

The year 1914 came and passed and the end of the world had not yet come. Russell went back to his study of the Bible and announced that what was expected to be a visible event had really been invisible. Christ and Satan had battled in heaven and Satan had been thrown down to the vicinity of the earth to continue his mischief. This was said to account for the wars and revolutions, famines, earthquakes, epidemics and other disasters since 1914. Pastor Russell died in 1916 on a Pullman car while returning from a preaching trip to the West coast. At this time his followers numbered only a few thousand, including the mother of Dwight D. Eisenhower.

In 1917 a small town lawyer, who had joined the movement in middle age and had become its legal advisor, succeeded to the presidency of the Watchtower Bible and Tract Society. J. F. Rutherford (born in 1869) had taken his turn as a presiding judge in his home county and was thereafter known to the cultists as "Judge" Rutherford. At first he could not say enough about Pastor Russell: "When the history of the Church of Christ is fully written, it will be found that the place next to St. Paul in the gallery of fame as expounders of the Gospel of the great Master will be occupied by Charles Taze Russell."

In a few years, however, the new president set out to destroy the cult of personality which had grown around Russell. Rutherford let Russell's books go out of print. He discarded some of the Pastor's pet theories such as that centering around the Great Pyramid. Today the name of Russell is barely known among Jehovah's Witnesses and many of his teachings have become only a source of embarrassment to the cult's hierarchy.

Not long after his election to the presidency of the Society, Rutherford and six other officials were sentenced to terms in Atlanta Penitentiary on charges of sedition. After the armistice they were released and the charges were dropped. This action almost wiped out the organization and Rutherford had to expend his full energy to rebuild the movement after his release from prison. What is more, some of Russell's staunch followers went into schism and founded the Dawn Bible Students, the first of several schisms in the movement.

The Judge introduced the use of the portable phonograph as a basic missionary technique. He recorded a series of sermonettes which even his most bashful and tongue-tied followers could play in a householder's living room. In 1931 he gave the movement a new name: Jehovah's Witnesses. Before this the members were known as International Bible Students, Russellites, Watchtower people, etc. During Russell's era the movement was organized along congregational lines. Rutherford abolished this policy in 1938, and since then all officers are appointed by and directly responsible to the Brooklyn hierarchy.

Rutherford displayed a particular hatred toward Catholicism and intensified his attacks on the Church by means of radio sermons and lurid pamphlets. The reputation for orneriness which still plagues the movement is largely a legacy of Rutherford's 25 years as president. Since his death the Watchtower Society has undergone a considerable face lifting which has eliminated some of the crude attacks on the Catholic and Protestant Churches, although the basic hostility of the movement toward organized religion remains.

Judge Rutherford spent most of his declining years in a mansion near San Diego which had been purchased as a home for the Old Testament princes who were soon to return to earth. He seldom appeared at rallies or meetings but continued to compose numerous scripture-laden books and pamphlets. He died in 1942.

An organization man succeeded Rutherford as head of the Witnesses. Nathan Homer Knorr (born in 1905) joined the movement as a lad of 17 and worked his way up the hierarchy in Brooklyn. Like Rutherford, he attempted to erase the influence of his predecessor. The judge's books are no longer in print. His name seldom appears in any Watchtower publication. All articles and books are now published anonymously. Even letters from headquarters bear no signature—only a rubber stamped "Watchtower Bible and Tract Society."

Most of the growth of Jehovah's Witnesses has taken place under Knorr's leadership. He established a systematic training program for missionaries at the Gilead Bible School. This school, now in Brooklyn, offers intensive theological and missionary training to dedicated Witnesses, who may then be assigned anywhere in the world. The worldwide activities have expanded from 54 countries in 1942 to 200 in 1970. No longer do Witnesses lug phonographs from door to door; each Kingdom Hall conducts its own public speaking and apologetics program designed to train members to present their own sermonettes and Bible instructions.

The actual number of people who are influenced by this sect far exceeds the 1,500,000 active members. More than 7,400,000 people receive copies of the *Watchtower* magazine twice a month; it is translated into 73 languages. Attendance at the annual Memorial or communion service is sometimes double the number of Witnesses carried on the official rolls. Hundreds of thousands of people consider Kingdom Halls as their spiritual home, read Watchtower literature, attend Bible classes and public lectures without being counted as full-fledged, baptized Witnesses.

About 401,000 active members live in the United States. Other concentrations of Witnesses are 62,000 in England, 48,000 in Canada, 39,000 in France, 51,000 in Mexico, 75,000 in Nigeria, 52,000 in Zambia, 54,000 in the Philippines, and 87,000 in West Germany. During the Nazi regime many Witnesses were sent to concentration camps for refusing to serve in the German army or to give the Hitler salute; an estimated 2,000 Witnesses died in these camps. The movement is banned today in all Communist countries.

The annual increase in membership seems to have leveled off at about 3 percent; during the 1930's membership gains of as much as 25 percent a year were reported.

There is no provision in Jehovah's Witnesses for passive membership—for members who simply want to have their names on the roster. Every baptized member is considered an ordained minister. Even those who are invalids or elderly try to carry on their missionary work by telephone or mail. The average Jehovah's Witness in the U. S. will log 11 hours a month in door-to-door preaching.

Anyone who shirks this responsibility is considered weak in his devotion to Jehovah. The many hours spent in this evangelistic activity are in addition to attendance at the five regular meetings each week in Kingdom Hall.

Worldwide, the Watchtower Society reports a staggering total of more than 180 million hours of such personal preaching during a typical year. Each Witness—man or woman, adult or child—knows he is expected to become a missionary; he cannot fulfill this obligation by paying someone else to seek converts or relying solely on prayer. He must set up priorities in his personal life which will reserve first place to missionary work.

Allied with the willingness of Jehovah's Witnesses to sacrifice spare hours seeking converts is their willingness to suffer ridicule and abuse for their beliefs. They know that this is an age of television, family togetherness, and backyard living; if they want to reach people in the 1970's they will have to reach them in their homes. But this also means that the Witness will be met with slammed doors, insults, and rebuffs.

Their aggressive tactics have often brought the Witnesses into conflict with the law. So far the Watchtower Society has taken 50 cases involving civil liberties to the Supreme Court; of these it has won two-thirds. These decisions have established the rights of all Americans to distribute religious literature on the street, to go door-to-door to try to interest others in a particular cause, etc.

The legal hassles are not over. In 1970 a U. S. district court judge in Sacramento, Calif, denied citizenship to two women who were Jehovah's Witnesses. The judge declared that he did so because "they are not attached to the principles of the constitution." The women told him they would not vote, serve on any jury, support any war, or participate in any governmental activities.

Many, if not most, Jehovah's Witnesses come from limited educational backgrounds. The number of college graduates in their ranks is low and many can produce nothing more than a grade school diploma. Nevertheless the Witnesses know that they cannot participate in the weekly Kingdom Hall discussions, carry on fruitful doorstep preaching, or be accepted as dedicated Witnesses by their peers unless they set aside time to read the Bible and the various Watchtower magazines, tracts, and books. Many Witnesses acquire a formidable knowledge of the Bible texts by following a systematic study plan.

The Watchtower Society has always stressed the printed word as a basic means to win converts. Its semi-monthly magazine *Watchtower* reports a circulation many times that of the largest Catholic or Protestant periodical. Its companion publication *Awake!* emphasises less doctrine and includes more popular articles; it claims a circulation of 7,000,000.

The standard doctrinal text, *The Truth That Leads to Eternal Life,* has been distributed to 40 million people in 50 languages. The Society has produced its own translation of the Bible called the New World Translation of the Hebrew Scriptures and Christian Greek Scriptures. It reflects many of the beliefs of the Witnesses. For example, instead of "Lord" or "God" the New World translation uses "Jehovah." Witnesses use their own version in Kingdom Hall classes and Bible studies but will use a Protestant or Catholic version to instruct householders.

The average Kingdom Hall in this country includes fewer than 65 people. Once a congregation passes the

250-member mark plans are made to split it into two congregations. The congregational servant (pastor) knows everyone in his flock. Every member knows everyone else and most members are eager to welcome a stranger. The fellowship of the congregation becomes a strong cement in the solidarity of the cult. Throughout the world there are now almost 25,000 congregations.

No collections are ever taken up at Kingdom Hall meetings or public rallies; members contribute according to their means by placing their offerings in inconspicuous boxes in the rear of the halls.

The simplicity of life of most Witnesses is an appealing feature. For example, at Bethel House in Brooklyn the 724 residents from President Nathan Homer Knorr down to the rawest recruit in the bindery all receive the same recompense: room, board, and $14 a month. All eat the same plain food, much of which is grown on Witness-operated farms in New York and New Jersey.

The Witness is encouraged to give his employer an honest day's work for an honest dollar, keep his needs modest, take care of his family, do his part as a missionary, and contribute to the upkeep of his Kingdom Hall and the Watchtower Society. Some 88,000 Witnesses have become Pioneers who devote full time or almost all of their time to evangelism; they receive the same nominal living allowance as the Bethel residents.

Most living Jehovah's Witnesses are converts, often fairly recent converts. Time will tell whether the impressive growth of the Watchtower Society since the 1930's simply demonstrates the zeal of religious converts or whether such converts will be able to transmit their enthusiasm to the next generation. The growth does seem to have reached a plateau in recent years.

FURTHER READING

Pike, Royston, *Jehovah's Witnesses* (New York, Philosophical Library, 1954).

Stevenson, W. C., *The Inside Story of Jehovah's Witnesses* (New York, Hart, 1968).

Stroup, Herbert H., *The Jehovah's Witnesses* (New York, Columbia University Press, 1945).

Whalen, William J., *Armageddon Around the Corner: A Report on Jehovah's Witnesses* (New York, John Day, 1962).

The Mennonites
🔲🔲🔲🔲🔲🔲🔲🔲🔲

A BEARDED MAN in a broad-brimmed black hat jogs along a country road in his buggy. In a few minutes he will turn into his farmyard and greet his wife and seven children. His bankbook would arouse the envy of many executives and professional men but he lives in a house which lacks electricity, a radio, indoor plumbing, and even pictures on the walls. He and his family are known as "plain" people around Lancaster, Pennsylvania. They are Amish.

A few hundred miles away a young doctor skillfully removes the appendix of a patient. He won his bachelor's degree in biology at Goshen College and completed his medical training at the state university. After two more calls in the hospital he will drive back to his office in his late model Ford.

Both the Amishman and the physician belong to the religious family known as the Mennonites. They are the spiritual descendants of the Anabaptists of the Reformation who were hunted down and persecuted by Catholics, Lutherans, and Reformed. To other Christians the Anabaptists were heretics and to the state officials they were traitors and rebels.

Around the world some 480,000 adults belong to the Mennonite family of Churches and of these the largest number are North Americans. But this is a spiritual family which has been plagued by schisms since its earliest days.

Over the years Mennonites have quarreled over whether a second band of suspenders constitutes worldly luxury and whether one or two individuals should wash and wipe the feet in the foot-washing ceremony. In the United States alone the estimated 170,000 baptized Mennonites belong to at least 19 different Church bodies.

Many of the most serious divisions have sprung from the practice of the ban or "shunning." The Anabaptists have always sought to establish a voluntary Church of saints in contrast to the state Churches which embraced saints and sinners, children and adults, believers and mere conformists. In order to preserve the exclusive character of their congregations the Mennonites have resorted to excommunication of members in a far stricter sense than others.

The Amish, for example, enforce the ban to the extent that an excommunicated husband cannot eat at the same table or engage in sex relations with his wife. He is completely ostracized from the community and his own family.

Moderate and progressive Mennonites still enforce excommunication and discourage marriage outside the religious family but do not apply the ban as the Amish do.

Over the centuries the Mennonites have divided over other issues as well. They have set up rival congregations and churches over the use of hooks and eyes instead of buttons, the foot-washing ceremony, the introduction of Sunday Schools and missions, the use of English, automobile ownership, and the length and parting of hair. As in the rest of Christendom the Mennonites have tried to reverse the trend toward fragmentation in recent years.

An apostate Dutch priest, Menno Simons, gave his name to the movement but he was not the founder of the Mennonites. The movement began in Switzerland among followers of the reformer Zwingli. These Zwinglians wanted a complete separation of church and state rather than a "reformed" state church envisioned by Zwingli himself. They also insisted that baptism was based on faith and that since such faith was impossible for a child, only adults should be baptized after confession of faith. When Zwingli and most of his followers rejected these positions, the dissenters organized in 1525 and were soon known as Anabaptists, that is, people who rebaptized those who had received the sacrament in infancy.

These early Anabaptists became the object of intense persecution by state and church officials. The first martyr in 1527 was bound hands to knees, rowed to the middle of a lake, and dumped overboard to drown. Later thousands of others throughout Europe would be broken on the rack, left to rot in prison, beheaded, and burned.

The Anabaptists attempted to restore what they believed to be the character of the primitive Christian Church. They taught nonresistance to evil which meant that they refused to serve in the army. They preferred an untrained and unsalaried ministry chosen by lot. The Church should be a brotherhood with no hierarchy or titles. They would not swear any oaths or hold any public office. Perhaps the closest modern day parallel would be Jehovah's Witnesses.

Menno Simons was born about 1496 and ordained a Catholic priest at the age of 28. He became pastor of the parish church in his father's village. Like most priests of his day he had received a sketchy preparation which included just enough Latin to be able to say Mass and administer the sacraments.

His first doubts about Catholicism concerned belief in the Real Presence and transubstantiation. Although he continued to offer Mass he came to an understanding of the Eucharist which approached that of the "memorial meal" concept of the Anabaptists. When he heard of the beheading of a tailor in a neighboring village who had denied the validity of infant baptism the priest began a study of baptism and again arrived at the Anabaptist position. Finally, Menno Simons became disturbed by the massacre of a group of 300 Anabaptists by a provincial governor. In 1536 he left the priesthood and accepted baptism by an Anabaptist leader. For the rest of his life he was a hunted and hounded man.

Menno Simons' qualities of leadership were soon recognized by the peaceful Anabaptists and he was elected an elder. He married and had at least three children. A price was put upon his head and any who sheltered him or his family were warned that they would forfeit property and life.

He and his followers disassociated themselves from the violent Anabaptists in other parts of the continent but usually failed to convince the state authorities. Some of these other Anabaptists fomented peasant revolutions, practiced communism, tolerated sexual excesses, etc.

Although Menno Simons did not found the sect he became its most influential and capable leader at a critical time. As early as 1544 the peaceful Anabaptists were being called Menists. He did not formulate the beliefs of the Mennonites and in some doctrinal positions such as his teaching that Jesus did not receive his body through the flesh of Mary the great majority of Mennonites parted company with him.

He lived to see the issue of the ban disrupt Mennonite communities in several countries. Under pressure he agreed to side with those who called for a strict enforcement of the ban but later regretted his action. Menno Simons died in 1561.

Persecution of the Mennonites ceased in the low countries after 1600. In the land where Anabaptism was born, Switzerland, the Mennonites were almost annihilated except in parts of the canton of Bern. They were forbidden to practice their religion and commanded to attend the state church, have their children baptized, and their marriages solemnized by the state clergy. The Mennonite movement survived in the Netherlands and parts of Germany and eventually in the United States and Canada.

The most serious schism was precipitated by a young minister in Alsace. Jacob Amman thought that the Church was not strict enough in enforcing the ban. The zealous preacher visited churches throughout Switzerland, Alsace, and southern Germany and demanded a yes or no answer on the matter of strict shunning. His action polarized Mennonite churches in these areas into two rival groups.

He also introduced the foot-washing ceremony and instituted communion twice a year instead of only once a year. He urged his followers, now called Amish, to resist change and to cling to the old ways of dress and customs. His followers began to withdraw from the main body in 1693. No Amish remain in Europe; the bulk of the Amish now live in Pennsylvania and several Middle Western states.

In Holland the number of Mennonites declined from 160,000 in 1700 to fewer than 30,000 in 1820. There are only 38,000 in that country today but they have an influence far out of proportion to their numbers as do the Jews, Quakers, and Unitarians in the United States. In the Netherlands Mennonites sit on the boards of the largest banks, serve in the cabinet, furnish a large number of professors and physicians. One Mennonite became Governor General of the East Indies. Recently out of 100 members of the Royal Academy of Sciences 11 were drawn from the Mennonite community.

This community has become far more secularized than the American Mennonites of even the more liberal branches. Dutch Mennonites have partially given up such traditional positions as pacifism and avoidance of public office. A Dutch Mennonite has even been appointed Minister of War. Their doctrinal stand is considered unorthodox by many American Mennonites since some of the Dutch question such basic Christian doctrines as the trinity and incarnation. Most Dutch Mennonites prefer to be known as Doopsegezind.

Czarina Catherine II of Russia promised more land and freedom to the Mennonites. Many German Mennonites accepted her offer and migrated to Russia between 1788 and 1824. Descendants of these Russian-Germans came to the United States in the late 19th century and to Canada after the Bolshevik Revolution.

Outside of North America and the Netherlands the largest bodies of Mennonites can be found in Soviet Russia (an estimated 40,000), India (30,000), the Congo (40,000), Germany (12,500), Indonesia (21,000), and Mexico (11,500). Only 2,000 Mennonites remain in Switzerland where Anabaptism originated.

Persecution drove thousands of Mennonites from Europe to American shores. The first permanent Mennonite settlement was in Germantown, Pennsylvania in 1683 at the invitation of William Penn. Descendants of these pioneer Mennonites have included Samuel Cunard of the steamship line; Surgeon General William G. Gorgas, who discovered the yellow fever mosquito; and David Rittenhouse, who was appointed first director of the U. S. Mint by Washington.

A visitor to a Mennonite church 100 years ago would see a simple meeting house. Inside the men and boys sat on one side of the aisle and the women on the other. The latter wore a small "cap" or veil and the men wore dark suits without lapels. The biweekly worship service, conducted in Pennsylvania German dialect, included hymns, a sermon, silent prayer, testimonies, Bible reading, and the Lord's Prayer.

Today almost half of the Mennonites in the United States belong to the Mennonite Church which was once known as the Old Mennonites. This is essentially a continuation of the church founded by the Germantown immigrants although it has also absorbed some Amish groups. These 85,000 Mennonites occupy what might be considered a middle ground between the ultraconservative Amish and the progressive General Conference Mennonite Church. But all Mennonites in North America share a relatively conservative theology in the context of contemporary Protestantism.

The Mennonite Church finds its strength in Pennsylvania, Virginia, Indiana, Ohio, Iowa, and Ontario. This Church supports 11 high schools, three colleges (Goshen, Hesston, and Eastern Mennonite), a hospital, two nursing schools, three children's homes, and four homes for the aged.

Most members of this and other Mennonite branches are farmers, but a growing number have gone into other professions, especially teaching, medicine, and business. More than 220 physicians belong to the Mennonite Medical Association.

Membership in the Mennonite Church has quadrupled

since 1900, mostly through a high birth rate. The Church does not win many converts but about one-fourth of those who do join come from Amish families. This does not mean that the Church does not seek converts. The Mennonite Hour is carried by several hundred radio stations. Some 220 missionaries work in 17 countries, especially in Africa, India, Japan, Puerto Rico, and South America.

Although this Church like other Mennonite bodies insists on the concept of a church set apart from the secular society, the Mennonite Church does not limit its charity to its own people. The Mennonite Disaster Service has rebuilt Negro churches in the South which have been destroyed by racists. This Service also responds to appeals for help in cases of flood, tornadoes, and fires.

This Mennonite Church teaches that only believing adults should receive baptism and that pouring is the scriptural mode. The bread and wine in the semiannual communion service are "symbols of the body and blood of Christ." Foot-washing and exchange of the "kiss of charity" are observed along with communion. The sick are anointed with oil.

The bishop, sometimes called the elder, supervises the local congregation. Under the bishop are the ministers or teachers and the deacons. At one time ministers were ordinarily chosen by lot. As many books were placed on the pulpit as there were men in the congregation. One of the books held a slip of paper appointing the man who drew it to be minister. Nowadays the trend is to engage seminary graduates.

A statement of doctrine declares that "mixed marriages between believers and unbelievers are unscriptural, and marriage with divorced persons with former companions living constitutes adultery." Yet the Mennonite who enters a mixed marriage in this denomination is not excommunicated or avoided as he or she would be among the Amish. These Christians believe it is unscriptural to "follow worldly fashions, engage in warfare, swear oaths, or join secret societies."

A somewhat more progressive stance characterizes the General Conference Mennonite Church which was organized in Iowa in 1860. This Church has always sought the union of all Mennonite believers and has promoted foreign missions, publications, and seminary training for ministers. It employs instrumental music in worship and prescribes no distinctive garb.

This Church operates two liberal arts colleges, a junior college, a Bible college, a seminary, and a number of charitable institutions. It reports 36,000 members in the United States and almost 17,000 in Canada and has missions in Mexico, South America, India, Japan, Taiwan, and the Congo. About two-thirds of its American membership is of Dutch ancestry and the others are Swiss.

Russian-German immigrants who started to reach America in 1874 organized the Mennonite Brethren of North America. These immigrants had been influenced by a religious revival among the Mennonites in South Russia in 1845. Most U. S. members live in Kansas and Oklahoma but there are others in Nebraska, California, and several western states. There are slightly more (15,456) Mennonite Brethren in Canada than in the United States (13,425). This Church operates Tabor College in Hillsboro, Kansas. It seeks converts among the American Indians and Mexican-Americans and has sent missionaries to India, Central and South America, Europe, Japan, and Africa. Their missionary effort is impressive.

They maintain missions in 16 countries and assign 224 missionaries to this work. Of the total of 32,000 members in mission areas they report 20,000 in India and 8,700 in the Congo.

Most picturesque and conservative of the many Mennonite factions are the Old Order Amish. These 20,416 Mennonites of Amish persuasion impose a strict ban on backsliders, insist on dress regulations, refuse to compromise with the modern world, oppose all education beyond the 8th grade, choose their ministers by lot, worship in homes and barns instead of churches, speak a dialect known as Pennsylvania Dutch. They do not believe in Sunday Schools, missions, or church conferences.

Several dozen Amish came to America before the Revolution. Today their communities stretch from Lancaster, Pennsylvania in a line through Ohio, Indiana, Illinois, and Iowa. They occupy some of the best farm land in the nation.

In an age marked by progress the Amish set themselves firmly against change. They have no particular desire to improve the world or to make any contribution to it. Their motto is, "The old is the best and the new is of the devil."

Thirty to forty Amish families form a congregation. They take turns meeting for church services at the home of members. Although Pennsylvania Dutch is used for conversation, a form of High German is employed in their liturgy; the hymnbook used by the Amish dates from the 16th century and has never been revised.

The Amish take their children out of school as soon as the law allows. Some have gone to jail rather than send their children to a consolidated high school. In 1966 a group of Amish prepared to leave the United States for Central America; they claimed they were being persecuted for not sending their children to the public schools. Amish children who persist in seeking a high school education face possible excommunication.

Within the Amish communities great respect is given to age. Children take care of their parents and would never think of asking for public relief or committing aged parents to state homes. The family is dominated by the father.

An Amish father or mother considers life successful if all the children have married Amish, live on farms, and remain within the Amish faith.

Amish leaders have gone to Washington to ask exemptions from the provisions of social security, unemployment insurance, and medicare. Life insurance ownership also violates Amish values.

Young people join the Church through baptism in their late teens and subscribe to the *Ordnung* or regulations of the particular Amish branch to which they belong. In general these regulations forbid electricity, telephones, central heating, automobiles, tractors with pneumatic tires, buttons, higher education. Many Amish groups also forbid silk clothing, bright colors, a man's hat with a brim smaller than three inches, high heels for women, pressed trousers, parted hair, overstuffed furniture, napkins or doilies, mirrors, pictures on the walls, photographs, and membership in any secular associations.

The Amish have no objections to receiving the best medical treatment available or to using drugs but naturally they do not number any physicians in their ranks.

A few non-Amish join the Church to escape the pressures of modern society but far more leave the Amish communities. A Church which excommunicates anyone who buys an automobile, attends high school, or marries outside of the faith is bound to lose some young people. An Amishman who joins another Mennonite sect is considered to have lost the faith and succumbed to the lures of the world. The Amish sect grows year by year because the average family includes 7 to 9 children. When one Amishman in Indiana died in 1933 he had 565 living descendants.

Even though the Amish resist change some change seems inevitable. For example, many Amish will now use a tractor provided it does not use pneumatic tires. The state of Pennsylvania now insists that buggies be equipped with head and tail lights and turn signals—operated by electricity. When Amish farmers rent farms they sometimes put up with the electricity and plumbing since the owner prefers that these conveniences not be ripped out.

These four major bodies—the Mennonite Church, General Conference Mennonite Church, Mennonite Brethren Church of America, and Old Order Amish Mennonite Church—claim 85 percent of the Mennonites in the United States but there are at least 15 small Mennonite bodies.

The Church of God in Christ, Mennonite Church broke with the Mennonite Church in 1859 because it judged the parent body to be apostate. This group keeps the beard and the ban but allows the use of farm machinery and automobiles. Baptism of the Holy Spirit is preached by this body of Mennonites. Its 5,419 members support missions in Mexico and it has an additional 1,811 adherents in Canada.

The Old Order (Wisler) Mennonite Church traces

its history to the preaching of Jacob Wisler, a Mennonite bishop who left the larger body in 1872. He protested the use of English in church services and the introduction of Sunday Schools. This group reports 5,213 members in the United States and 2,091 in Canada.

Bishop Moses M. Beachy led a group out of the conservative Amish Church in 1927. This group gains converts from Amish who want to own automobiles. It is also more liberal in that it worships in church buildings and supports Sunday Schools and missions. Their discipline, especially in the use of the ban, is less severe than the Amish. Beachy died in 1946. In 1971 there were 4,000 members of the Beachy Amish Mennonite Church.

Descendants of Russian Mennonite immigrants form the bulk of the membership of the Evangelical Mennonite Brethren. This body was once called the Conference of Defenseless Mennonites of North America. In proportion to their numbers they support an ambitious missionary program involving 100 overseas missionaries. There are 1,682 adult members in this country and 1,300 in Canada.

No Mennonite body belongs to the National Council of Churches; the Mennonites and, of course, the Amish generally stand apart from the modern ecumenical movement. Representatives of all major Mennonite bodies met in Amsterdam in July, 1967, to attend the Mennonite World Conference. Founded in 1925, the World Conference meets every five years.

Since 1920 most Mennonite groups have cooperated in a worldwide program of relief and humanitarian service called the Mennonite Central Committee. The MCC was founded to aid victims of the Russian Revolution but has spread around the world. It maintains offices in such strategic locations as Vietnam, Leopoldville, Atlanta, Seoul,

Berlin, Hong Kong, and Jordan. Conscientious objectors from Mennonite Churches may volunteer for overseas service in the Pax program or TAP (Teachers Abroad Program) of this Committee.

The Amish and other Mennonites invariably win the respect of their neighbors for their honesty, simple living, and industriousness. Their witness for peace is no doubt needed today as much as in any past century.

Mennonites are asking themselves what their message may be to a world facing problems of technology, urbanization, race, population, competing political and social ideologies. The historic Anabaptist posture has been one of retreat from the world rather than confrontation.

Moderator Harold E. Bauman of the Mennonite General Conference declared recently: "Mennonites no longer are protected by their closed communities, and because of this they face a new era of responsibility and mission when their deeds must say more than their words." He also predicted that non-whites will soon form a majority of the world's Mennonites since far more converts are joining the Church in Africa and Asia than in white nations.

Some evidence is seen in such bodies as the Mennonite Church and the General Conference Mennonite Church that the Christian has a greater responsibility for the world and his neighbor than to ignore them. Such involvement coupled with efforts at Mennonite unity could give new meaning to this centuries-old religious movement.

FURTHER READING

Horsch, John, *Mennonites in Europe* (Scottdale, Pa., Herald Press, 1950).

Hostetler, John A., *Amish Society* (Baltimore, Johns Hopkins Press, 1963).

Mennonite Encyclopedia, 4 vols., ed. by Harold S. Bender, Cornelius Knahn, and Melvin Gingerich (Scottdale, Pa., Mennonite Publishing House, 1955-59).

Smith, C. Henry, *The Story of the Mennonites,* 4th ed. (Newton, Kansas, Mennonite Publication Office, 1957).

Wenger, J. C., *The Mennonite Church in America* (Scottdale, Pa., Herald Press, 1966).

The Moravians
🔲🔲🔲🔲🔲🔲🔲🔲🔲

LONG BEFORE Martin Luther nailed his 95 theses to the church door and launched the Protestant Reformation there were thousands of "Protestants" in Bohemia. By 1517 there were 400 Moravian congregations with about 175,000 members; these Protestants had their own bishops and clergy, catechism, printing plant. Along with the Waldensians of Italy the Moravians claim to be the oldest Protestant denomination.

They trace their history to John Hus, a priest and rector of the University of Prague, who was burned at the stake for heresy in 1415. Hus disputed the spiritual authority of the pope and bishops and appealed to the Bible only. He exposed the corruption of the Catholic Church of his day and pleaded for reform. While bound to the stake he cried: "I shall die with joy in the faith of the Gospel I have preached!"

After his martyrdom his followers squabbled among themselves for several decades. Finally in 1457 a small group of Hussites formed the Unitas Fratrum or Unity of the Brethren; this group rallied the Hussites into a powerful religious force while the other Hussite sects disappeared.

By the end of the 16th century the Unitas Fratrum had become the largest Protestant Church in Bohemia but the Thirty Years War destroyed its power. The organized Church was defeated in the battle of White Mountain in 1620 and the remaining Hussites were forced to practice their religion in secret.

For a century the Unitas Fratrum remained an underground movement. Small groups met deep in the forests or in private homes. Nominally Roman Catholics, the Hussites often hid Bibles and hymnals under the floors of their houses. Bishop John Amos Comenius (1592-1672) provided the leadership that enabled the movement to remain alive.

In 1722 a group of Moravians accepted the invitation of a Saxon count, Nicholas von Zinzendorf, to settle on his estate. Zinzendorf, a devout member of the state Lutheran Church and a Pietist, envisioned the Moravians as a leaven in the state Church. The Moravians themselves never gave up the idea of re-establishing the Unitas Fratrum and resisted efforts to be incorporated into the Lutheran establishment. Their village on Zinzendorf's land was called Herrnhut and was organized on a communal basis with separate social organizations known as choirs for single men, single women, children and widows.

Although the Moravians accepted the Apostle's Creed they preferred a mystical to a doctrinal religion. Their theological views differed in only minor respects from evangelical Lutheranism but they emphasized a particular devotion to the crucifixion and the wounds of Jesus on the cross.

One unusual Moravian practice was the use of the lot to decide community or personal problems. By this method the church leaders believed they were giving God an opportunity to provide divine guidance. The lot might be used to decide who would go on a mission assignment, who would marry whom, what law would be adopted in Herrnhut. After prayer an individual would draw one of three slips of paper; the slips read "yes", "no" and "no decision." By the end of the 19th century the lot had fallen into disuse.

Moravians initiated the modern Protestant missionary movement; they were the first Protestants to go to foreign countries to seek converts under the auspices of a Church. In the 1730's the Moravians were sending missionaries to South America, Greenland, and South Africa. The first missionaries landed on the island of St. Thomas in the West Indies in 1732 and three years later a group of Moravian missionaries went to Georgia. Their conduct and spiritual life on board ship exerted a powerful influence on John Wesley who would later found the Methodist movement. The Georgia mission was unsuccessful but other Moravians came to Pennsylvania in 1740 and founded the cities of Nazareth and Bethlehem.

Count Zinzendorf came to Pennsylvania in 1741 and tried to unite all the German Protestants in the area into one Church but failed. The Moravian settlements were closed to outsiders but missionaries brought the gospel to the Indians; even today the Moravians support an all-Indian congregation in California and work among the Eskimos in Alaska. While Bethlehem was being developed another group of Moravians founded Salem, N. C. in 1766; it is now known as Winston-Salem.

Eventually the control of Herrnhut over the American Moravian communities was loosened. Non-Moravians settled in Bethlehem and Winston-Salem and the Moravians themselves jettisoned their distinctive dress, communal forms, and pacifism. Moravians pushed on to Ohio, Indiana, and Illinois.

Today the Moravian Church in America includes two provinces. The 49 congregations in the Southern province are all within 120 miles of Winston-Salem and enroll 22,373 members. The Northern province embraces churches from New York to California and from southern Illinois to Edmonton, Alberta, Canada. It reports 38,270 communicants in 113 congregations.

Besides the two American provinces there are five others around the world. Total Moravian membership exceeds 300,000. American Moravians maintain missions in Alaska, Nicaragua, and Honduras while other Moravians staff missions in ten other areas. Herrnhut itself is now a village of 2,000 in East Germany while Bethlehem, Pa. is a steel city of 75,000. A General Synod which represents all Moravians meets every ten years.

The Moravian Church operates Moravian College in Bethlehem and Salem College in Winston-Salem as well as a seminary, junior college, and four secondary schools. A charter member of the Federal Council of Churches, the Moravian Church belongs to the National and World Councils of Churches and participates in many ecumenical projects.

This Church follows the church year and a liturgical form of worship but Moravian churches have no altars. They observe the Lord's Supper six or seven times a year. After offering the right hand of fellowship the communicants receive the bread and wine while standing; other Christians are welcome to Moravian communion services. The Church baptizes infants by both sprinkling and pouring but does not admit children to communion until they have been confirmed. A distinctive Moravian custom is the love feast which consists of coffee and buns. The Moravian liturgies for Christmas Eve, Holy Week, and Easter Dawn attract many people because of their beauty and solemnity.

The power of Moravian bishops is spiritual rather than administrative. Zinzendorf was elected second bishop of the Church and the Moravians claim an episcopal succession which goes back to the 15th century. The orders of the Church also include presbyters or elders, and deacons.

Besides the major body in the United States there is the 6,000 member Unity of the Brethren. Until 1962 this group was known as the Evangelical Unity of the Czech-Moravian Brethren in North America. It enrolls descendants of immigrants who began arriving in Texas in 1850 and shares positions identical with the Unitas Fratrum.

A small component of worldwide Protestantism the Moravians have made a significant contribution through their missionary programs, their influence on other Protestants such as Wesley, and their liturgy and hymns.

FURTHER READING

Gollin, Gillian Lindt, *Moravians in Two Worlds* (New York and London, Columbia University Press, 1967).

The Mormons
🔲🔲🔲🔲🔲🔲🔲🔲🔲

AT THIS MOMENT an army of 12,000 dedicated young men and women is carrying the gospel of Mormonism around the world. Most of these missionaries left for their assignments when they were only 19 or 20 years old; their families pay all expenses during their two-year stints. They are helping to make Mormonism a major religious denomination.

The Church of Jesus Christ of Latter-day Saints reports 2,815,000 members and most of these live in the United States. During the decade of the 1960's this denomination grew 74 percent.

As many as 105,000 adult converts have been baptized in a single year. These thousands of newcomers to the Mormon Church do not take their new allegiance lightly. They must give up tobacco, liquor, coffee, tea, and even cola drinks. They must agree to tithe their gross income. They must attend church services regularly and pledge loyalty to the Mormon hierarchy.

Evidence of the growing prestige of the Mormon Church and of individual Mormons is abundant. President Nixon appointed two Mormons to his cabinet: former Gov. George Romney and David Kennedy, a Chicago banker. Other Mormons have made the headlines in recent years: Ezra Taft Benson, President Eisenhower's Secretary of Agriculture and one of the 12 apostles of the Church, financier Marriner S. Eccles, Secretary of the Interior

Stuart Udall in the Kennedy administration. Among its members are an estimated 300 millionaires. Four Latter-day Saints sit in the U.S. Senate and five in the House of Representatives.

The Mormon Church has become the dominant financial institution in the Rocky Mountain area. Its daily income from tithes and business investments exceeds $1 million. The Church owns hotels and motels, a daily newspaper, cattle land in Florida, two insurance companies, a mortuary, scores of farms, factories, and office buildings, Salt Lake City's largest department store, a publishing house, sugar refineries, a sugar plantation in Hawaii. Through its Bonneville International corporation, the Mormon Church operates seven radio and TV stations; its newest acquisition is KBIF in Hollywood.

The Church runs what has become the largest church-related university in the nation: Brigham Young University in Provo, Utah. It enrolls three times as many students as, say, Notre Dame and 97 percent of these are Latter-day Saints. This Church claims to enroll a higher percentage of its young people in colleges and universities than any other denomination.

Once confined mainly to the intermountain states, especially Utah, the Mormons are busy establishing new wards (parishes) in Eastern, Midwestern, and Southern states. Utah remains 70 percent Mormon but in Salt Lake City itself the Latter-day Saints are now outnumbered by the non-Mormon "Gentiles."

Things have changed for the Mormon Church whose members were once massacred and driven out of Missouri and whose founder and first prophet was murdered in the Carthage, Illinois, jail by an enraged mob. Now noted for their sobriety, honesty, and industriousness, the Mormons were once branded from pulpits and political platforms as barbarians and lechers. After the Civil War the Federal government turned from the fight against slavery to the fight against polygamy and eventually forced the Mormon Church to suspend the practice of plural marriage.

A Federal army once entered Utah and threatened to depose Brigham Young but the Mormons vowed to burn their cities to the ground if the troops entered Salt Lake City. A compromise prevented a tragedy comparable to the burning of Moscow before Napoleon. For years American audiences were regaled by the stories of Mormon polygamy and alleged treason; one of the most popular lecturers was Young's 27th wife who had divorced him and joined forces with Gentile critics.

One basic reason for this persecution was the Mormon insistence that it was not *a* Christian Church but the one and only Christian Church. This claim infuriated frontier Protestants. The Mormon position has not changed much today. Mormonism teaches that all other Christian bodies lack any authority from God to teach or baptize and this includes all Catholic, Protestant, and Orthodox Churches. Without exception these Churches are considered apostate and counterfeit.

Mormonism claims to be a restored rather than a reformed Church. Founder Joseph Smith maintained that the Christian Church fell into apostasy shortly after the death of the last apostle. But he maintained that God the Father and Jesus Christ had appeared to him in person and restored the true Church and the authority of the priesthood in 1829. Acceptance of the claims of Smith and of the authenticity of the Book of Mormon and other Mormon scriptures is demanded of all members.

Smith was a barely literate young man in Western New York when he reported the discovery of a set of golden plates in the Hill Cumorah in 1827. An angel called Moroni revealed the hiding place of these plates which were said to reveal the history of the original inhabitants of the Americas. They were written in a language known as Reformed Egyptian but the angel furnished a device known as the Urim and Thummim which enabled Smith to translate the characters.

Actually Smith "translated" most of the 275,000 word book by peering at a seer stone in his hat. He employed several secretaries to take his dictation since he did not know how to write. When the book was completed the angel took back the plates.

He also told his followers that John the Baptist had appeared to him and a companion in 1829 and baptized them by immersion, ordaining them to the Aaronic priesthood. Later Peter, James, and John were supposed to have conferred the higher or Melchizedek priesthood on the pair.

Smith organized his new Church in New York with six members and began to distribute copies of the Book of Mormon. This remarkable volume relates how Jesus appeared to the American Indians after His crucifixion and established a second Church for the inhabitants of this hemisphere. He appointed a second set of 12 apostles. The Indians he visited were descendants of Jews who came by boat from Palestine about 600 B.C. Two great Indian nations arose—the good Nephites and the wicked Lamanites. In a great battle near the Hill Cumorah the last Nephite general, Mormon, buried the plates which recorded the history of his people.

Smith converted several members of his own family and a few friends but the reception he and his marvelous book received in the neighborhood was lukewarm. He decided to move his headquarters to Kirtland, a village which is now a suburb of Cleveland, Ohio.

A former Campbellite minister, Sidney Rigdon, threw in his lot with Smith and led most of his Kirtland congregation into the infant Church. Soon Smith had 1,000 followers. He ordered the building of a temple in Kirtland and elaborated the organization of his Church. But his involvement in the failure of a wildcat bank aroused his enemies. He and Rigdon found it wise to flee Kirtland in the middle of the night.

The Prophet headed for a Mormon outpost in Missouri but trouble with the Gentiles led to the murder of 40 Saints and the forced evacuation of the Mormons from that state in 1839. The Mormons purchased swamp land on the banks of the Mississippi River and Smith named the new settlement "Nauvoo" which he said meant "beautiful plantation" in Hebrew. In a few years Nauvoo reached a population of 20,000 while Chicago remained a village of only 5,000.

Nauvoo enjoyed a particularly liberal charter from the state of Illinois. Smith assumed command of a private army, the Nauvoo Legion; he wore the uniform of a lieutenant general and rode a white horse as he inspected his troops. As in Kirtland he started construction of a huge temple in which to perform the new rites such as baptism for the dead.

Before long the Gentiles in Illinois took a second look at their new neighbors and began to voice misgivings about the welcome they had extended. Tales about strange religious doctrines and rites, of thefts, of growing Mormon power, and of polygamy stirred the countryside. Smith sent missionaries to England and the Scandinavian countries and they began to return shiploads of converts to Zion. He even announced his candidacy for the presidency of the United States and directed his missionaries to seek votes.

Not everything was harmonious in Nauvoo. A number of Smith's cronies apostatized. Rigdon, who had been nominated for vice-president on the Mormon ticket, left Nauvoo for Pittsburgh. When ex-Mormons published a newspaper that confirmed the rumor that certain Mormon leaders were taking additional wives, Smith ordered his henchmen to destroy the printing plant.

The Prophet had overplayed his hand. For this and other alleged crimes he was arrested and taken to the jail in nearby Carthage. Before he could be brought to trial a mob painted and dressed like Indians stormed the jail and killed both the Prophet and his brother Hyrum. His career ended on June 27, 1844, when he was only 39.

Fortunately for the Mormon Church a remarkable leader, Brigham Young, took over the direction of the Church and organized the epic march to the mountains. Hundreds died along the way from disease, cold, and starvation but those who survived built the theocratic empire in the West. Not all the Latter-day Saints followed Young; Smith's wife Emma remained in Nauvoo and raised her family in the nearly deserted river city.

Once safely settled in the sanctuary the Mormons admitted that they had actually been teaching and practicing polygamy during the years in which the Church had denounced the charge as libel. From 1852 to 1890 the Mormon Church openly taught that a man might have many wives if he married them under the authority of the Church. Brigham Young himself married 27 women and his friend Heber Kimball supported 45. In some cases

Mormon patriarchs married mother and daughter sets or pairs of sisters. One Mormon sired 67 children. The best estimate seems to be that between eight and ten percent of Mormon families were polygamous.

Such a departure from traditional Christian morality would not be tolerated by the rest of the nation. The Republican party platform thundered against the "twin relics of barbarism: slavery and polygamy." Congress passed a series of laws aimed at abolishing the practice. Eventually the Federal government confiscated most Church property, jailed the leading Mormons, drove the others into hiding, and disfranchised the polygamists. The president of the Mormon Church yielded in 1890 and forbade future plural marriages, but the Church today still considers polygamy a suspended doctrine and has never denied its divine sanction. Mormon writers brand the laws against polygamy as unconstitutional and an infringement on religious liberty.

Today a Mormon who is discovered to have married more than one woman is quickly excommunicated from the main Mormon Church. Nevertheless, the Attorney General of Utah has estimated that as many as 20,000 people live in polygamy in that state. Polygamists often belong to one of the fundamentalist Mormon sects which hold that the Church should never bow to government pressure.

Several other religious bodies besides the Utah Church and the fundamentalists claim the name Latter-day Saints, revere Smith as a Prophet, and accept the Book of Mormon. Largest of these groups is the Reorganized Church of Jesus Christ of Latter Day Saints with headquarters in Independence, Missouri. It is headed by a grandson of the Prophet. To the embarrassment of the Utah Church all of the direct descendants of Joseph Smith, Jr., belong to the 182,000 member Reorganized Church, which rejects polygamy, secret temple rites, and polytheism. It now owns the Kirtland Temple.

The Reorganized Church maintains that leadership of the Church should have passed to the Prophet's son, Joseph Smith III. A group of Saints who had remained in the Middle West held the first meeting to "reorganize" the Church in 1852. The Prophet's son accepted the presidency of this Church in 1860 and held the post until his death in 1914. His mother, Emma Smith, also joined.

Closer to traditional Protestantism than the Utah Church the Reorganized Church ordains Negroes to its priesthood, sends salaried missionaries overseas to seek converts, allows members in good standing to contribute less than the full tithe. It reports almost five times as many adherents as it had in 1906. Recently the president of this Church received a revelation directing him to order construction of a temple.

Much smaller splinter groups are the Church of Christ (Temple Lot) with 3,000 members, the Church of Jesus Christ (Bickertonites) with 2,447 members including many Italian-Americans, and the fundamentalist Church of the First Born of the Fullness of Time.

The Utah Church maintains 12 temples in the United States, Canada, England, Switzerland, and New Zealand where it carries on secret rites. Only Mormons who can present a "recommend" from their bishop can gain admittance to a temple. To qualify they must tithe their incomes, attend church regularly, and observe the dietary prohibitions.

Joseph Smith went to Freemasonry for the materials for his temple ritual. He grew up in western New York during the anti-Masonic excitement following the Morgan affair. Although the Book of Mormon calls Masonry the work of the devil, Smith later joined the Masonic lodge in Nauvoo. His brother Hyrum, Brigham Young, and other Mormon leaders were also Masons. Because of certain irregularities the Grand Lodge of Illinois lifted the dispensations under which the Nauvoo lodges worked. Mormon-Masonic antagonism continues; the Grand Lodge of Utah still refuses to initiate any Mormon and the Mormons themselves discourage lodge affiliations.

Mormons are initiated into the esoteric aspects of the cult in a four-hour secret endowment rite. Those taking their endowments in one of the temples wear a special costume including the sacred undergarments, robe, moccasins, cincture, hat, and Masonic type apron. They observe playlets illustrating the Mormon concept of salvation and exchange secret grips, passwords, and signs. Devout Mormons wear their sacred undergarments throughout life. The garment resembles a union suit although it has been abbreviated in recent years. It bears mystic marks signifying the penalties attached to violations of secrecy.

Most of the ordinances performed in the temples are intended for the benefit of the dead rather than the living. Mormons undergo proxy baptisms for their dead ancestors. To discover their ancestors they may spend many hours a year searching out their genealogies.

Mormons worship a god who was once a man as we are but who has perfected himself through the ages to the exalted position he now holds. He is not the creator but the organizer of preexistent matter. God has a body of flesh and bones. But the god of this world is only one of many gods. Other gods rule other worlds.

If a man accepts the restored gospel of Mormonism,

is baptized by immersion by a Mormon priest, and is married for time and eternity in the temple, he too may aspire to godhood. He may be exalted so that he will rule over his own planet and procreate spirit creatures who will then worship him as their god. No aphorism is better known in Mormonism than "As man is, God once was, and as God is, man may become."

Mormons believe that all humans have preexisted with God before birth. When God revealed his plan of salvation about a third of these spirit creatures rebelled and followed Lucifer. Others preferred neutrality in the subsequent warfare between God and Lucifer and these neutrals were probably cursed by being born with a dark skin as Negroes. Each mortal agreed to erase his memory of life with God before entrance into mortality.

Almost every worthy Mormon male holds some rank of the Mormon priesthood. A Mormon boy is ordained a Deacon at the age of 12 and advances to Teacher and Priest in the Aaronic priesthood and to Elder, Seventy, and High Priest.

The Negro, who has been cursed by God, may not be ordained to any rank of the priesthood nor be married in the temple. A few Negroes have joined the Mormon Church despite their inferior status but Mormons do not seek converts among the Negroes in this country or in Africa.

The local unit of the Church is the ward. All bishops (pastors) are unpaid and usually hold secular jobs to support themselves. They do not receive the formal seminary training which Catholics, Lutherans, Presbyterians, Episcopalians, and others expect of clergymen. Sunday meetings at the ward chapel will include priesthood meetings for the various ranks of priests, Sunday School (attended by Mormons of all ages), and the weekly sacrament service at which bread and water are blessed and distributed.

Wards are grouped in units known as stakes of Zion of which there are about 500. At the head of the tightly organized church structure is the president who holds the titles of prophet, seer, and revelator. At the age of 93, Joseph Fielding Smith was elected to this position in 1970. Smith's father, cousin, and great-uncle (Joseph Smith, Jr.) occupied this post before him. The president is assisted by counselors and by the 12 apostles. He holds office for life and is usually succeeded by the senior apostle.

Mormonism has its strong and weak points. In its favor are a dedicated membership, a strong missionary impulse, a tradition of encouraging education, and a financial base which makes this Church the wealthiest per capita in the United States. Its members find a full and rich spiritual, social, and recreational life in its bosom. Participation in the priesthood gives each Mormon male a sense of direct involvement in his Church. Dietary regulations, the sacred undergarments, and secret temple rites remind the believer that he is set apart from the rest of the community. He knows too that his Church is interested in his temporal welfare and will come to his aid if he should become ill or unemployed.

The Mormon Church can look for a healthy increase in membership through births and conversions. Mormonism emphasizes family values and encourages the ideal of the large family. The present Mormon birthrate far exceeds the national average. The Mormon death rate is lower than the national average although it is not certain whether this is due to total abstinence, the climate and living conditions in the intermountain area, or the Church's programs in health education and recreation.

On the deficit side the Mormon Church stands or falls as a religious institution on the authenticity of the Book of Mormon. No non-Mormon archeologist accepts the Book of Mormon as of any value in his study of early life on this continent. Literary critics have little difficulty placing the writing of the Book in the early part of the 19th century. If Smith simply concocted the story of the golden plates and the historical romance known as the Book of Mormon, the claims of the Mormon Church as a restoration of the gospel must be abandoned. The Church is also saddled with a concept of race which teaches that God has cursed anyone with Negro blood. Except for the Black Muslims, the Mormon Church is the only American denomination to elevate race to the theological plane.

For millions of non-Mormons, the first encounter with Mormons may be the visit of two dark-suited men at their front door. They are missionaries trying to win converts around the world to the Church of Jesus Christ of Latter-day Saints.

Many of these fledgling missionaries make up in zeal and dedication what they may lack in theological sophistication. Outside of their Sunday School training or perhaps college religion course at Brigham Young University, their preparation for their evangelistic work may be limited to the two-week short course in mission techniques at Salt Lake City. They may not even know the language spoken by the people to whom they are sent but confidently expect the Lord to bestow the gift of tongues. The Church provides a step-by-step course of instruction for convert-making along with a kit of visual aids and publications; the volunteers are told to stick to the six lessons when they find a willing listener.

Not only does the Mormon Church gain tens of thousands of new members through this mission system but it cements the loyalty of the young people who respond to these calls. A man who has given two years of his life to his Church and who has personally instructed and baptized converts will probably remain a dedicated church member to his deathbed. Even if the calls on householders do not result in conversions, the missionaries, the cream of Mormondom, usually make a favorable impression on the Gentiles and help form a more favorable image of their Church.

One of the requirements which the Mormon missionaries make plain to every prospective convert is that of tithing. Every Mormon is expected to contribute 10 percent of his gross income to the Church and another 2 or 3 percent to the upkeep of his local ward (parish). If he does not tithe he is not considered a member in good standing. He will not qualify to enter a Mormon temple to perform the sacred ordinances for the living and the dead. He may not be married for time and eternity in a temple.

The vast sums collected by the Mormon Church from the tithes of faithful members enable that Church to engage in an extensive program of welfare, education, public relations, broadcasting, building, and missions.

No doubt one of the chief attractions of Mormonism for born members as well as converts is the extensive church welfare program. Although the boast that no Mormon has ever had to go on relief may be doubted, it is true that Mormons in good standing can usually count on receiving substantial help in the form of food, clothing, cash, and help in landing a job. Begun in 1936, the church-sponsored welfare program now embraces 600 church farms, canneries, storehouses, manufacturing firms, etc. Needy Mormons may apply for help in case of sickness, unemployment, or other personal difficulties.

By its emphasis on welfare activities the Mormon Church demonstrates its interest in the material as well as the spiritual welfare of its adherents. Those who have must share with those who have not; those who have been helped are asked to replenish the supplies when they are back on their feet. Like tithing, the welfare program provides a secondary benefit in drawing people away from a preoccupation with self needs and materialism.

One Mormon custom related to the welfare program is Fast Sunday. On the first Sunday of each month devout Mormons give up two full meals and contribute what they would have spent for this food to the church welfare fund. This money goes to buy food for those temporarily unable to pay for it themselves.

Material aid to the needy is not the only distinctive feature of Mormonism. The Church offers a full religious and social program for members of all ages. Every denomination sponsors youth groups and ladies' aids and men's clubs but none comes close to matching the Mormon organizations. The pioneer Mormons who went West were said to have first built a ward chapel and then a dance hall; they were never influenced by the Puritan disapproval of dancing and dramatics. The Mormon Church has always encouraged all types of wholesome recreation including scouting, discussion groups, crafts, singing, and sports.

Some Protestant Churches have tried to erase the distinction between clergy and laity by stripping the clergy of titles, special garb, etc. Mormonism broke down the distinction by ordaining all qualified males (except Negroes) into the priesthood. Each order of the priesthood is responsible for certain spiritual and material activities within the ward. This system fosters a deep and personal involvement in the work of the Church and a close identification with its objectives.

The hierarchy of the Church worries about some threats to family life. Salt Lake City has one of the highest divorce rates in the nation. A growing number of young Mormons are entering marriage with Gentiles. The general acceptance of contraception runs counter to Mormon views. A member of the First Council of Seventy, A. Theodore Tuttle, told church members at the October, 1969 general conference: "The Church speaks out boldly against the common evil of this day—deliberate limiting of families by birth control."

These problems do not mean that the growth of the Mormon Church is likely to slacken in the near future. The number of young missionaries has doubled during the past decade. The Church builds a favorable public image through the 350-voice Mormon Tabernacle choir, TV programs, exhibits at fairs, guided tours of Temple Square in Salt Lake City.

The one troublesome issue is that of race. In 1969 Stanford University severed all athletic ties with Brigham Young University because of the church's racial policies. These policies were then restated by the 96-year-old head of the Church, David O. McKay. Liberals within the Church hope for a reversal of the ban on ordination of blacks.

Residents of Utah, Arizona, Idaho, Nevada, Wyoming, New Mexico, and California know the Latter-day Saints as neighbors and the Mormon Church as a powerful influence in their states. New temples are planned for Washington, D.C. and Chicago. The Church of Jesus Christ of Latter-day Saints is fast becoming a national Church of size, wealth, and prestige.

FURTHER READING

Brodie, Fawn M., *No Man Knows My History* (New York, Knopf, 1945).

Hinckley, Gordon B., *What of the Mormons?* (Salt Lake City, Church of Jesus Christ of Latter-day Saints, 1953).

Hirshon, Stanley F., *The Lion of the Lord, a Biography of Brigham Young* (New York, Knopf, 1969).

O'Dea, Thomas F., *The Mormons* (Chicago, University of Chicago Press, 1957).

Turner, Wallace, *The Mormon Establishment* (Boston, Houghton-Mifflin, 1966).

Whalen, William J., *The Latter-day Saints in the Modern Day World* (Notre Dame, Ind., University of Notre Dame Press, 1967).

The New Apostolic Church

ALTHOUGH THE New Apostolic Church claims the allegiance of almost 500,000 adherents in Germany, it has only 21,000 members in 169 congregations in the United States. Most of these are Americans of German ancestry.

The beginnings of the movement go back to the Catholic Apostolic Church whose leading exponent was Edward Irving (1792-1834). Irving, a graduate of Edinburgh, had been ordained by the Church of Scotland and later pastored a small Presbyterian church in London. He joined a prayer circle which believed that the Second Coming would take place in 1864 and would be preceded by restoration of the college of 12 apostles. The Irvingites antedated the modern Pentecostal movement by encouraging speaking in tongues as evidence of a second baptism.

While seeking a restoration of the gifts of the apostolic church the new sect, called the Catholic Apostolic Church, began to incorporate elements usually associated with Roman Catholicism. The liturgy resembled the Mass and the Church introduced vestments, veneration of Mary, the tabernacle and sanctuary lamp, holy water, anointing of the sick.

The Catholic Apostolic Church sent missionaries around the world but received a warm welcome only in Germany. One by one the original apostles died but their places were not filled. By 1860 only six remained. When some German churchmen attempted to fill the vacancies in 1863 they began the schism which produced the New Apostolic Church. It was first called the Universal Christian Apostolic Mission but the present name was adopted in 1906.

At first the leader of the new church was Heinrich Geyer but he was supplanted by F. W. Schwartz. The Catholic tendencies of the parent church were reversed, a modified Calvinism was accepted, and the leadership of the movement was centralized in the office of chief apostle or Stamm-apostle.

Under the direction of Hermann Niehaus who took office in 1905 the movement reached a worldwide membership of 300,000. Instead of only 12 apostles the Church appointed an apostle for each administrative region. J. G. Bischoff succeeded Niehaus and membership almost doubled by the time Bischoff died in 1960. Twenty-seven apostles assembled to choose the present chief apostle, Walter Schmidt.

Under Schmidt is an elaborate organization of district apostles, deputy apostles, bishops, district elders, pastors, priests, deacons, and subdeacons. The 4,000 congregations of the New Apostolic Church are organized with Teutonic efficiency. Besides Germany and the United States there are churches in England, Canada, Switzerland, Holland, France, Australia, South Africa, and South America. Chicago is the main center in the United States; the first missionaries arrived in this country in 1901.

This Church confers baptism, communion and sealing (or confirmation) on the dead as well as the living. In this respect it resembles the temple work of Mormonism. Sealing is conferred only by an apostle and is also known as the baptism of fire. Only the sealed are believed to be eligible to share in the first resurrection and join with

Christ in ruling the world during the millennium. The Church fosters the gifts of the Holy Spirit including speaking in tongues and healing. The New Apostolic Church is authoritarian, anti-Catholic, adventist, and mission-minded.

Remnants of the Catholic Apostolic Church may be found in Germany but there were never more than a few hundred followers in the United States. Lacking apostles since 1901 the Church has been unable to have any ordinations or confirmations. A few elderly priests are still alive but the Church is moribund.

Eleven dissenting New Apostolic apostles broke away from the main organization in 1956 and claim to represent 50,000 members. They reject the sacraments for the dead and have restored some of the original Catholic emphasis. There are several splinter groups in Germany and Holland such as the "Apostolate of Jesus Christ" and the "Apostolisch Genootschap."

The New Thought Churches
🔲🔲🔲🔲🔲🔲🔲🔲🔲🔲

A VARIETY OF RELIGIOUS groups carry on the work begun in the mid-nineteenth century by the Portland, Maine healer, Phineas P. Quimby. Some are tiny bands meeting in rented halls and others such as the Church of Divine Science and the Church of Religious Science have become substantial denominations with scores of local congregations.

New Thought covers a wide spectrum of beliefs but all groups which may be identified by this term insist that man need not believe in sickness, evil, and poverty. They prefer not to draw a sharp line between God and man and their philosophies are often considered pantheistic. New Thought teaches that man can always apply a spiritual solution to his problems; in this way he can achieve health and happiness.

Most but not all such groups belong to the International New Thought Alliance. (Unity School of Christianity, an heir of Quimby's thought, prefers to remain outside of the INTA). The *Yearbook of American Churches* does not even list these many New Thought Churches, yet through their publications and lectures they influence millions of people who belong to Protestant and Catholic denominations.

Quimby, born in New Hampshire in 1802, claimed to have been cured of tuberculosis. He opened an office in Portland in 1859 and began to treat a stream of patients. At one time he practiced hypnotism but later he relied on mental healing. Quimby was critical of orthodox Christianity but nevertheless believed that Jesus had discovered the principle of spiritual healing. Among his many clients was Mrs. Patterson known later as Mary Baker Eddy, founder of Christian Science.

Horatio Dresser edited Quimby's writings in 1921; the original manuscript in the Library of Congress runs to 2,100 pages in 12 journals. Braden declares: "Carefully dated, they revealed beyond question to any but the most convinced Eddy disciples that Quimby had held the basic ideas of mental healing years before Mrs. Eddy sought healing at his hands in 1862" (*Spirits in Rebellion*, p. 57).

Warren Felt Evans left the Methodist ministry to become a Swedenborgian and later gave Quimby's ideas literary form. He is best known for his book *The Divine Law of Cure* published in 1881; he also wrote *The Mental Cure, Mental Medicine,* and *Esoteric Christianity.*

Quimby and the New Thoughters drew upon Transcendentalism, Swedenborgianism, mesmerism, Hinduism, Spiritualism and other systems. New Thought rejected the Calvinism of American Protestantism and proposed an optimistic, empirical faith. They invited inquirers to test the principles of New Thought to gain health and prosperity.

Most New Thought disciples believe in the divinity of man and the impersonality of God. They admire the moral teachings of Jesus but repudiate the dogmas of orthodox Christianity such as those of original sin and the atonement.

Quimby himself died in 1866 and founded no church. New Thought groups were organized in the 1890's and

later and often gained initial strength by absorbing dis-
affected Christian Scientists. New Thought is more syn-
cretic, less authoritarian and monolithic than Christian
Science. New Thoughters prefer spiritual healing but express less opposition to *materia medica* than do the followers of Mary Baker Eddy.

New Thought ideas have been popularized by such
authors as Ralph Waldo Trine whose *In Tune with the
Infinite* has sold more than one million copies. The books
of Emmet Fox have introduced thousands of Americans
to New Thought. For years Dr. Fox preached to the largest
congregation in New York City, first in the Hippodrome
and then in Carnegie Hall.

Four ladies participated in the founding of the Church
of Divine Science in Denver in 1898. They were Mrs.
Malinda E. Cramer, a healer in San Francisco, and Nona
L. Brooks and her two sisters. This Church teaches that
God is Spirit, Mind, Principle, Love, Truth, Substance,
Soul, Intelligence, Being, Omniscience, Omnipotence, and
Omnipresence. Ministers trained at the College of Divine
Science in Denver staff the several dozen autonomous
churches.

Dr. Ernest Holmes founded the Church of Religious
Science in 1952; previously he had formed the Institute
of Religious Science and Philosophy (1927). He wrote the
textbook of this movement: *Science of Mind*. This movement has split into two branches: about 30 churches in the
International Association of Religious Science Churches
and 70 in Affiliated Churches of the Church of Religious
Science. More than half of these congregations are in
California.

Many other groups fall into the New Thought category and can usually be identified by such names as Meta-

physical Science, Mental Science, Home of Truth. The importance of New Thought lies not in the number of adherents, although these number in the tens of thousands, but in its influence on those who never set foot in a New Thought church. William James once wrote that New Thought "together with Christian Science, constitutes a spiritual movement as significant for our day as the Reformation was for its time."

FURTHER READING

Braden, Charles S., *Spirits in Rebellion* (Dallas, Southern Methodist University Press, 1963).

Judah, J. Stillson, *The History and Philosophy of the Metaphysical Movements in America* (Philadelphia, Westminster, 1967).

The Occultists
🔲🔲🔲🔲🔲🔲🔲🔲🔲

FROM PARK AVENUE apartments to hippie pads interest in occultism has been enjoying a remarkable revival. Science and technology may rack up achievements which dazzle the imagination, but millions of Americans seem to prefer to poke around in the pre-scientific worlds of witchcraft, astrology, fortune telling, numerology, and other branches of the occult.

Almost everyone, astrology buff or skeptic, knows his sun sign and finds it hard to resist taking a peek at the horoscope in his daily newspaper. The ancient art of astrology is riding high. A corps of some 10,000 professional astrologers casts individual horoscopes for devotees willing to pay as much as $100 for this service.

Moviegoers thought they were getting a glimpse of modern day witchcraft in *Rosemary's Baby*, but the mixture of Satanism and witchcraft in the film bore little resemblance to the facts. Even sillier is the TV show *Bewitched* which features Elizabeth Montgomery as a nose-twitching witch married to an innocent.

But witchcraft is practiced in the 1970's; and, although certain aspects of the craft remain hidden to all but initiates, we can discover a great deal about the Old Religion also called Wicca, the Craft of the Wise.

Books about witchcraft and other occult arts have become so numerous that large bookstores reserve special alcoves for their display. One New York store specializing in occult titles reports sales are up 100 percent in three years. A book by Sarah Morrison entitled *The Modern Witches Spellbook* is advertised "For those who'd like to be witches and get their hands on a batch of castable spells." This book also includes a shopping guide for such necessities as bottled bat's blood. Another new book, *Today's Witches*, by Susy Smith, estimates there are about 60,000 active witches in the United States.

Fortunately for today's card-carrying witches, the climate of opinion in this country has become more tolerant than an earlier age; in 1662 and 1663 the good folks of Salem, Massachusetts hanged nineteen people found guilty of witchcraft. The last of the anti-witchcraft laws in England were not repealed until 1951. The British Medical Association says there are some 7,000 witches playing their trade, including healing, in England. They operate mostly in rural areas—or in cities where regular M. D.'s are reluctant to make house calls. In Africa the witch doctor retains his influence among the unsophisticated.

The best known witch on the contemporary scene, Sybil Leek, came to the U. S. from England where she said she could trace her witch ancestry back to 1134. She now lives in a Florida mansion, appears on TV talk shows, writes books about astrology, spells, ghosts, etc.

Witchcraft claims to be the continuation of the pagan religion which preceded and was generally supplanted by Christianity in Europe. Pockets of believers in the Old Religion passed along the secrets to their children and grandchildren. The most prestigious contemporary witches claim membership in these first families of witchcraft but thousands of recent converts have no such pedigree.

People dabble in witchcraft for a variety of reasons.

Some are attracted by the promise of witchcraft to endow the practitioners with the power to cast spells, win lovers, cure warts, discomfort enemies and otherwise accomplish their wishes by magical means. Young people sometimes take up witchcraft as a new kick, a way to "turn on" without drugs through mysterious rites, nudity, incantations, incense, dancing and such carrying-on. To "born" witches such conversions bring the satisfaction that witchcraft is being more widely propagated, but their enthusiasm is tempered by the realization that the kids usually do not engage in top-drawer witchcraft.

The basic unit or congregation of witchcraft is the coven of thirteen people. Led by a high priest or high priestess, the coven includes regular witches as well as initiates who may spend from six months to a year to gain full membership. With no accrediting body or denominational authority witchcraft cannot control the formation of covens. Anybody can start a coven; some organizers are serious students of the occult while others are sports who relish the idea of thirteen men and women cavorting in the altogether.

Coven members meet at the fortnightly Esbath or Witches' Sabbath on a Saturday night around midnight. They also gather for the Old Religion's four main holidays: February 2, April 30, July 31 and, of course, October 31 (Halloween).

Usually the high priest or priestess provides the meeting place in his home and prepares it for the esoteric rites. An altar is erected and covered with a white cloth. The ceremonies themselves are conducted inside a consecrated circle drawn in chalk or sand on the floor and about nine feet in diameter. Candles illuminate the room and four red candles are often placed in the corners. One object of worship is a reliquary which holds a semi-precious stone and the name of the god to whom a particular coven gives its homage. Other witchcraft paraphernalia include a wand and sword, a plate of salt, a goblet of water, incense, and the broom which is understood as the symbol of domestic cleanliness rather than the witches' mode of transportation.

Witches greet each other with "Blessed be." Clothes hamper their mystical vibrations so they usually shed their garments and conduct their activities in the nude or "sky-clad." The rituals themselves are recorded in the witchcraft bible called the Book of Shadows. Copies are transcribed by initiates and kept out of the hands of the profane.

In addition to the nudity the sexual element in witchcraft is obvious. At an initiation the high priest kneels in front of the candidate and bestows the fivefold kiss on the feet, knees, sexual organs, breasts, and lips. Much of the ritual of the Old Religion is simple phallic worship and fertility rites.

The candidate for full membership repeats the following oath:

> I,———, in the presence of the Mighty One, do of my own free will and accord most solemnly swear that I will ever keep secret and never reveal the secrets of the art, except be it to a proper person, properly prepared within a circle such as I am now in. All this I swear by my hopes of a future life mindful that my measure has been taken and may my weapons turn against me if I break this solemn oath.

Hans Holzer, author of *The Truth About Witchcraft*, and twenty other occult books, reports that the majority of witches he knows are former Roman Catholics. The high priest of a London coven which allowed him to witness an initiation is a defrocked, thrice married Catholic priest. Holzer comments: "I have never met a former Unitarian or other liberal Christian who sought out witchcraft, simply because the liberal Christian churches are close enough to the ideals of the Craft not to warrant it."

Witches do not believe in heaven, hell, or the devil but almost all accept the doctrine of re-incarnation. They view Satanism as a perversion of Christianity and have nothing to do with devil worship or black Masses. At least they don't if they consider themselves "white" witches rather than black witches who specialize in curses and mischief making.

The experienced witch has a spell for almost every situation. For example, if a burglar has broken into your house and you do not want him to return, you can ask your neighborhood witch to cast a spell. For this she (or he) needs three pieces of hog fat, three pieces of bread, and three pieces of salt. The witch throws these items into an open fire and recites the appropriate incantation. If the spell works, you will not be bothered by a burglar again.

But spells can work both good or evil. If you were the burglar you might consult your own witch, probably a black witch, who would cast a spell to facilitate your endeavor. She would ask the gods to muzzle the householder's watchdog, let the householder enjoy a deep sleep, or let you escape with your loot.

Ethical witches may disown black magic and Satanism but these do count some adherents. For example, Anton Szandor LaVey directs the First Church of Satan in San Francisco. A former circus lion tamer, LaVey wears a black robe and clerical collar; he has shaved his head but wears a mustache and goatee which gives him a resemblance to the Master he claims to serve. He frankly identifies himself as the devil's advocate.

Satan's clergyman schedules a black mass every Friday at his church. A genuine black mass calls for a defrocked priest, consecrated host, a prostitute, and a virgin whose body serves as an altar. LaVey's imitation falls short on most scores, as do the black masses of assorted underground groups who encounter difficulties in finding a qualified altar.

LaVey has conducted weddings and funerals at his "church" and apparently meets the legal requirements of the state as an ordained minister. He claims that more than 7,000 people in twenty-five grottos around the country pay a $13 membership fee in his Satanic denomination.

He maintains Satanism simply teaches that man should gratify every desire so long as he does not hurt anyone else. "It's just Ayn Rand's philosophy with ceremony and ritual added," explains the Reverend LaVey.

Under the category of the occult we would also include such movements as Theosophy, Spiritualism, and Rosicrucianism but these are examined at length in other chapters of this book.

To catalog all the occult phenomena and movements would take volumes. Evidence for the revival is abundant. An up-to-date gift shop will stock Tarot cards which are used to tell fortunes. Parker Brothers, Inc. sells about two million Ouiji boards a year. Before making important decisions in affairs of the heart or bank book, people consult astrologers, numerologists, and psychics. Others try to predict the future by consulting dice, dominoes, bumps on their head, and even moles and warts on their bodies.

The reading public devours books about Edgar Cayce,

the Baptist psychic who engaged in spiritual healing and prophecy. Police departments call in Peter Hurkos, the Dutch psychic, to try to solve murders and kidnapings. Psychic Jeane Dixon is the subject of the book, *A Gift for Prophecy,* which has sold 290,000 copies in hardback and millions of copies in paperback. She is probably best known for her prediction of President Kennedy's assassination. Holzer estimates he has chased away 500 ghosts from haunted houses and has requests for another 6,000 house-cleanings in his schedule book.

Someone called the sects the unpaid bills of the Churches. In a sense, the occult revival is also a judgment against the Churches. If the Churches were offering hearty spiritual food, perhaps fewer people would turn from the light of the gospel to the darkness of the occult. Of course, part of the explanation for the occult revival must also be an unhealthy search for the exotic and erotic.

The Catholic Church has traditionally warned the faithful against participation in Gnosticism, witchcraft, spiritualist seances, and the like. If any warning is necessary, she points out that belief in re-incarnation, magic, curses and such is incompatible with Christianity.

These warnings still hold even though there is a world of difference between the witch, Satanist, or occultist and the housewife who looks at her daily horoscope in the newspaper out of curiosity.

In spite of the Church's warnings, the occult, and one of its oldest, most popular forms, astrology, is enjoying a startling resurgence. Millions of Americans direct their daily activities according to their horoscopes, and many more satisfy their curiosity by checking the astrology column in their newspaper. Out of 1,750 daily newspapers in the country more than 1,200 carry an astrology feature.

For thousands of years men have looked heavenward and speculated that perhaps the stars had some influence on their lives and the fortunes of their communities. This systematic speculation known as astrology fell into disrepute in the eighteenth century. Now, in a time when men actually walk on the moon and make plans to journey to Mars, the ancient art of astrology has staged an amazing revival.

The professional astrologists in the United States can thank *their* lucky stars that business has never been better for them and their 150,000 colleagues who practice the astral art in their spare time. The professionals list their office hours in the Yellow pages, and get from $25 to $300 for preparing a horoscope. They can join a national professional organization and study astrology at several schools.

At least twenty magazines are devoted to the subject. The devotee can buy a wide assortment of books telling him how to cook by astrology, find a mate with compatible constellations, or make a killing in the stock market with the help of the stars.

Even the computer has been put to use by the astrologers. One firm provides a 10,000 word horoscope for $20. Date, time, and place of birth are fed into an IBM 360-40 computer. Another company mails a personalized horoscope prepared by a computer, every three months, and bills clients $9 for each one.

The hit musical *Hair* has popularized the common astrological belief that mankind has now entered the Age of Aquarius. The Piscean Age of sorrow and trouble ended in 1904, and we can now look forward to 2,000 years of peace and brotherhood. World Wars I and II did not get the Age of Aquarius off to a very good start, but true believers are sure the world has entered a new and promising cycle.

In a complex and often bewildering world, astrology promises some answers and some guidance for millions of people. Worldwide it probably claims more adherents than it has had at any time during the past 200 years. Some observers attribute its popularity to a general turn toward anti-scientism: the wonders of science have brought about not only material progress but also wars, pollution, and a general sense of frustration. Others see astrology and the occult occupying ground once held by institutional religion.

Although astrology held an honored place in Babylonian, Greek and Roman societies, it was discredited by the rise of science and new knowledge. A decade ago only a few enthusiasts continued to believe that the position of the sun, moon, and planets at the moment of an individual's birth exercised a powerful influence on his character.

For several millennia such ancients as the Chaldeans, Egyptians, Assyrians, Hindus, Babylonians and Chinese studied the heavens and devised systems which analyzed human character and foretold future events. Of these people the Babylonians undoubtedly made the greatest contribution to astrology.

Babylonian priests discovered visible planets: now known as Mercury, Venus, Mars, Jupiter. They kept careful records of the movements of these bodies as well as of the sun and moon. Of course, they lacked telescopes, but they lived in a part of the world blessed with clear skies—no smog. From towers built on flat lands they could scan the complete horizon.

At first the Babylonians taught that the planets themselves were gods, but later they came to believe that a god ruled each planet. As they elaborated their ideas they associated each planet with certain characteristics. Sometimes the apparent color of the planet gave them a clue: reddish Mars was identified with war and bloodshed.

From observation of the planets, and aided by a lively imagination, the ancients developed a complex lore which attributed meaning to the various positions of the heavenly bodies. At first their predictions concerned only nations, but eventually horoscopes were drawn for individuals. The first such personal horoscope was made about 263 B.C.

From Babylon, astrology was carried to Greece, where further developments took place. The Greeks reasoned that if the sun and moon had such obvious influences on the tides and temperatures, the other planets might well determine aspects of human life. Plato and Aristotle both believed that the stars were divine. Hippocrates declared: "The man who does not understand astrology is to be called fool rather than physician." (Despite the contemporary revival of astrology the subject has not been reintroduced into the medical school curriculum.)

Greek slaves brought astrology to Rome during the Punic wars and before long almost all the Romans took it for granted that the stars had a major influence on men and events. Early scientific writers such as Pliny and Seneca offered mild criticism of astrology, but assumed the validity of its basic principles.

Christianity alternated between toleration of, and bitter opposition to astrology. St. Augustine mounted the Christian attack on the basis that astrology negated man's free will. He used the argument of twins as conclusive proof that astrology was either hokum or the work of demons.

Astrologers tried to defend their art in an increasingly Christian culture by pointing out the role of their colleagues, the Magi, in the Christmas story. Christian apologists retorted that the Magi renounced their belief in astrology at the cradle in Bethlehem and, significantly, returned home by a different route.

The revival of Aristotelian and Arabian learning in the twelfth century gave a boost to astrology. The Arabs had developed not only mathematics and medicine far beyond European levels, but had paid considerable attention to the perfection of astrological arts.

St. Thomas Aquinas formulated the compromise which allowed the astrologers and churchmen to live in peace. The angelic doctor admitted that stars influenced the body, and the body influences the intellect and will:

"The majority of men, in fact, are governed by their passions, which are dependent upon bodily appetites; in these the influence of the stars is clearly felt. Few indeed are the wise who are capable of resisting their animal instincts. Astrologers, consequently, are able to foretell the truth in the majority of cases, especially when they undertake general predictions" (*Summa* I. I. 115).

The astrologers, eager to placate the Church, generally left a place for free will in their system. They argued that the stars exerted an influence on men, but that men could resist these influences. For example, a horoscope might reveal that a person has a strong tendency toward selfishness. Knowing this the selfishly-inclined man can make an extra effort to cultivate generosity.

Throughout the Middle Ages most people believed that the stars did influence human life. Astrology was taught at several leading universities between 1200 and 1600. Pope Julius II set the date for his coronation by astrology, and Paul III consulted his astrologers before setting the date for any consistory. Leo X founded a chair of astrology at the Sapienza. So long as astrology ruled out fatalism and made room for free will it got along all right with the medieval Church.

Astrology held its own until the middle of the eighteenth century. By then the advances in astronomy and the re-orientation of thought demanded by modern science had shaken the older world-view of astrology. Since 1781 three new planets had been discovered: Uranus, Neptune, and Pluto, and even unsophisticated people questioned the value of astrological calculations based on the wrong number of planets.

Until very recent years astrology was derided, and people found it hard to believe that earlier scientists had ever swallowed the myths and assumptions of astrology. Historians honored astrologers as the precursors of astronomy, as they acknowledged the debt of the chemists to the alchemists; but they gave no credence to astrological analysis. Even though popes and theologians had once pinned their faith on astrology, the Catholic Church again began to condemn all astrology as a form of divination.

Perhaps the one person most responsible for renewing interest in astrology in the United States was a Boston astrologer, Evangeline Adams. She polished her reputation by casting horoscopes for such famous personalities as financier J. P. Morgan, Enrico Caruso, and Mary Pickford. Through her efforts the courts removed astrology from the category of fortune-telling, which was a criminal offense.

Miss Adams explained: "It should be clearly understood that the stars only indicate what will come to pass if intelligence and free will are not used to change the natural course of events. The wise man cooperates with the stars, the fool thinks he rules them." She reaffirmed the old astrological saying: "The stars impel, they do not compel." People can assert themselves against the influence of the stars just as they can fight hereditary or environmental factors in their lives.

Evangeline Adams died in 1932; by this time she was conducting a popular radio program on astrology and was receiving 4,000 requests a week for horoscopes and personal advice. Her convert, Carroll Righter, has become the best known astrologer in the nation.

Righter attended the University of Pennsylvania and later received a law degree. Of independent means, he engaged in various philanthropic activities during the Depression and started to investigate astrology in order to disprove its claims. Instead he became an enthusiast, and emerged as a professional astrologer in 1939. Now his column is carried by more than 300 newspapers, with a circulation of some 30 million.

Some of his faithful clients in Hollywood have been Robert Cummings, Tyrone Power, Van Johnson, Marlene Dietrich, Peter Lawford, and Ronald Reagan. Many stars refuse to make any decision regarding their careers or love life without consulting their favorite astrologer. Jackie Gleason was once told he would risk death if he took a plane, and he has not flown since. A prominent actress was asked why she had not married. She solemnly told the interviewer: "To me marriage is a sacred state and as a Catholic I would never enter marriage unless I was sure it would last a lifetime . . . besides my astrologer told me not to marry until I was thirty years old."

During World War II the allies knew that Hitler retained a court astrologer and probably made some of his military decisions on the basis of the stars. The British hired Louis de Wohl, an astrologer and Catholic author, to cast Hitler's horoscope and try to guess what the German astrologers were telling the Fuehrer. Regardless of nationality or politics, any professional astrologers should reach about the same conclusions and offer about the same advice for a given set of birth data. Despite Hitler's patronage, German astrologers fell on hard times after the flight of Rudolf Hess to England. Hess, too, retained a personal astrologer and was believed to be under his spell.

Widespread interest in astrology in the United States and Canada is a recent phenomenon. In many parts of the world belief in astrology is taken for granted by almost all people. In countries such as India, Pakistan, Ceylon, and Burma, practically everyone checks with an astrologer about a proposed marriage, about the propitious date for an undertaking, or about business deals. An East Indian astrologer must study for twenty years before he is given a government license for public practice.

To gain more insight into the work of an astrologer I asked a professional to prepare my horoscope. Mrs. Frederick Geiger has been practicing astrology for twenty years, and belongs to the American Federation of Astrologers.

Besides astrological consultations and preparing horoscopes (sometimes for popular figures such as Bill Cosby and Phyllis Diller), Mrs. Geiger teaches a class in astrology for about fifty Purdue students enrolled in the so-called Free University. She insists that astrology rests on a firm scientific basis, but offers no explanation of how planets actually affect human lives.

Like all astrologers Mrs. Geiger works from basic information: the day, hour, and place of birth. She must adjust the birth time to Greenwich mean time, taking into account such complications as daylight saving time. To the conscientious practitioner the difference of even an hour can distort a horoscope. Using a book of ephemeris (a table of planetary positions) and computing the correct astral time, the astrologer begins to construct the horoscope. This is a sort of map which shows the position of the sun, moon, and planets in relation to the earth and the signs of the Zodiac at the moment of birth.

The ancients devised the twelve signs of the Zodiac which correspond to about thirty days on the calendar. The location of the sun in a particular sign is considered of prime importance. This sun sign determines whether a person is an Aries, Taurus, Gemini, Cancer (Moonchild), Leo, Virgo, Libra, Scorpio, Sagittarius, Capricorn, Aquarius, or Pisces. Another important factor is the sign which is ascending or rising at the moment of birth. In my case I was found to be a Capricorn (my birthday is January 1, and Capricorn covers those born between December 22 and January 19) with Sagittarius rising.

Capricorns, I was told, are thoughtful, serious, somewhat ambitious, economical, hardworking. They are blessed with good reasoning ability and make the most of opportunities. With Sagittarius ascending Mrs. Geiger told me I was also inclined to be jovial, bright, hopeful, generous, and charitable. My disposition was likely to be frank, fearless, impulsive, demonstrative, outspoken, nervously energetic, sincere, and quick to arrive at conclusions. My physical appearance was probably tall and slender; actually I am 5 feet 6½ inches and weigh 170 pounds.

Although the position of the sun and the ascending sign are of great importance, the position of the other planets is significant, too. The location of these planets in various "houses" and their relation to one another are studied. Like other professions, astrology revels in its own jargon—such as "cusps," "aspects," "houses," and "triplicities."

Mrs. Geiger loaned me one of the standard texts used by those who prepare horoscopes: *A to Z Horoscope Maker and Delineator* by Llewellyn George. The author of this 812-page volume promoted the study of "scientific" as opposed to occult astrology. He saw a bright future for the art: "It is only a question of time when the United States and other nations will find astrology indispensable for an orderly arrangement and the conduct of affairs in harmony with natural laws."

Most of the characteristics in anyone's horoscope will be traits people like to hear about. You would have to come up with an unusual combination of planets to produce a horoscope which indicated you were ornery, stingy, self-centered, and ugly.

The George book describes the particular influence of each heavenly body. We are told that the moon governs the brain, stomach, breasts, the left eye of the male, and the right eye of the female. This information has probably not changed since it was first revealed to the Babylonian wise men a few thousand years ago. It means as much today as it meant then.

Mrs. Geiger offered no explanation of how or why the planets at the moment I drew my first breath, in Michigan City, Indiana, should exert a force in my life. She did maintain that she had never drawn up a horoscope which did not accurately reflect the personality of the client.

Some astrologists do advance theories of causality.

George attributes the influence to "magnetic currents" set in motion at the time of birth. Someone might ask why other variables do not produce a similar influence. These variables might include the prevailing winds, pollen count, temperature, Dow Jones average, or barometer reading. Another astrologist, in a tentative explanation, points out that the moon causes the ebb and flow of tides; and since the human body is 70 percent water it too may be affected by the moon.

Perhaps most of the astrologists who offer any rationale fall back on the theory of the accumulated wisdom of the ages. They say if you take 1000 persons and discover that most tall people were born in July, and most short people arrived in December, and if you continue such an analysis for fifty centuries or so, you will build up the kind of lore on which the astrologers draw.

Most scientists and intellectuals scorn astrology. You cannot take an astrology course at Harvard or MIT. One of the few respected scholars in recent times to show any interest in astrology was the psychologist, Carl Jung. He often arranged to have horoscopes drawn up for his patients and was impressed by what they revealed. Jung urged closer examination of the claims of astrology, and commented: "Today, rising out of the social deeps, astrology knocks at the doors of the universities, from which it was banished some 300 years ago."

Critics of astrology say that horoscopes are so general they can apply to almost anyone. They say that astrologers crow about their rare bull's eyes and keep silent about the more numerous misses. Serious astrologers admit that the kind of astrology presented in the daily newspaper columns is practically useless. For one thing, these columns classify people only by the sun sign, which is important but accounts for only about 25 percent of the influences charted by professional astrologers.

The outlandish language and outdated concepts turn other sophisticated people away from astrology. They know that planets do not rise in the night sky; instead the earth turns toward the planet. Astrologers talk about the "conjunction" of planets; but at these points the planets are actually millions of miles apart. Finally, except for the light and heat of the sun and the effect on the tides by the moon, the changes in light, gravitation, and magnetism produced by other planets are so slight they can hardly affect human character. Someone might admit some influence by the moon, which is next door to earth, but hesitate to admit any influence by Jupiter which is 390,000,000 miles away when it is closest to us.

The "live and let live" compromise between the Catholic Church and astrology lasted for several centuries after Aquinas, but more recently the Church has returned to a general attitude of condemnation. The common teaching has been to discourage dabbling in astrology and the occult. Eager to protect the concept of free will, most moralists have agreed with the words of Cassius in Shakespeare's *Julius Caesar*:

> *The fault, dear Brutus, lies not in our stars*
> *But in ourselves that we are underlings.*

The Vatican magazine *Osservatore della Domenica* carried an article about astrology in 1961, written by Father Reginaldo Francisco. He stated: "If one really believes in the horoscope one commits a grave sin. One falls into heresy by denying free will and one violates the first commandment." Oddly enough the popular women's magazine, *Cosi,* published by Italian nuns, featured an astrology column on a regular basis for years.

Anyone is free to dismiss astrology as hokum but should this judgment be enough to merit ecclesiastical condemnation? Some people claim to be able to analyze character by studying handwriting, or by examining the bumps on a person's head, or by matching color preferences with personality traits. The scientific foundation for these methods is not much sounder than for astrology, but the Church has never become excited about such practices.

The average American who takes an interest in astrology is not rejecting free will or falling into heresy. His attitude is one of curiosity. He might be exhorted to spend his time more wisely, but so might the enthusiasts who devote every weekend to watching sports on TV or the inveterate bridge and bingo players, or the golf nuts.

Perhaps the wisest course for the Church is still that suggested by St. Thomas Aquinas. If a Christian accepts a theory of astrology which denies free will and puts men at the mercy of the stars, he rejects his religious faith. If he simply believes—with or without much scientific confirmation—that the position of the stars at the moment of his birth has an influence on his personality and fortunes he may be kidding himself but he contradicts no specific Christian belief.

FURTHER READING

Ford, Arthur, *Unknown but Known* (New York, Harper & Row, 1968).

Holzer, Hans, *The Truth About Witchcraft* (Garden City, N. Y., Doubleday, 1969).

Parker, Derek, *Astrology in the Modern World* (New York, Taplinger, 1970).

Rachleff, Owen S., *The Occult Conceit: A New Look at Witchcraft, Magic, and Sorcery* (Chicago, Regnery, 1971).

Somerlott, Robert, *"Here, Mr. Splitfoot": An Informal Exploration Into Modern Occultism* (New York, Viking, 1971).

Spence, Lewis, *An Encyclopedia of Occultism* (New Hyde Park, N. Y., University Books, 1960).

The Old Catholics
🔲🔲🔲🔲🔲🔲🔲🔲🔲🔲

OBJECTING TO THE definition of papal infallibility made by the First Vatican Council in 1870, small groups of Catholics in Germany, Holland and Switzerland organized the Old Catholic movement. Today the Old Catholics number 300,000 in these three countries as well as Austria, Czechoslovakia, Yugoslavia, and Poland. The 282,000-member Polish National Catholic Church in the U.S. and Canada also traces its priestly orders through Old Catholicism.

Literally scores of churches claim the Old Catholic label and the casual observer will be confronted by an almost hopeless task if he wishes to catalog them all. We will discuss four major categories. First, the legitimate Old Catholic Churches which are bound by the Declaration of Utrecht (1889) and honor the archbishop of Utrecht as primate. Second, the Polish National Catholic Church which is the only U. S. body recognized by Utrecht. Third, the assortment of tiny Old Catholic groups in this country which claim valid orders from various sources but which do not receive recognition from Utrecht. Fourth, the mixture of Catholicism and Theosophy known as Liberal Catholicism.

The roots of Old Catholicism in Germany go back further than 1870. A schismatic "German Catholic Church" came into being about 1845. The founders were two priests, Johannes Ronge and Johann Czerski. Later on, by way of protest against the latitudinarianism of the Ronge-Czerski schismatics, Dr. Pribil of Berlin founded the "Protestant Catholic Church." The 1864 encyclical *Quanta Cura* of Pius IX helped to increase the strong anti-papal mentality of many German Catholics. Then in the late 1860's Joseph J. Overbeck, a secular priest and professor of Syriac at Bonn, became a Lutheran. He tried to form a Western Orthodox Church, published many books, and continued his campaign until 1884, when the Holy Synod of Moscow finally rejected the scheme.

Schismatic bodies existed in France from 1801 when the "Petite Eglise" came into being. It consisted of bishops and clergy who refused to recognize the concordat between Pius VII and Napoleon. The last priest of this body died in 1847, but it lingered on for at least half a century.

Msgr. Chatel founded the "Eglis catholique francaise" in 1831. He was consecrated by Bishop Fabre-Pallaprat, who had refused to accept the 1801 concordat. This body survived until the 1890's.

Hyacinthe Loyson's schismatic sect in France, formed about 1879, was loosely associated with the Old Catholics. In 1888 the Episcopal bishop of Western New York took this French schismatic body under his wing, and helped to finance it. After Loyson's resignation in 1893 the Dutch Old Catholic bishops agreed to accept his followers into communion.

What we now know as Old Catholicism began when some German theologians refused to accept the definitions of the infallibility of the pope as well as his supreme and universal jurisdiction. Many of these had already been alienated from the Church by the publication of the Syllabus of Errors of 1864 which seemed to set the Church against most of the liberal and progressive movements of the day.

Resistance was led by the famous church historian Johann Ignaz Dollinger, who declared: "As a Christian, as a theologian, as a historian, as a citizen, I cannot accept this doctrine." The objectors called a meeting in 1871 to organize the movement. About 300 priests and laymen attended, including some Anglicans, Orthodox, and Protestants. By the end of the year 23 parishes had been established. The schismatic archbishop of Utrecht attended the next Old Catholic congress in 1872.

Dollinger respected the excommunication imposed on him by Rome and ceased his priestly functions. However, he presided at the Old Catholic congresses and guided the Church in its repudiation of the Council of Trent. He opposed the abolition of clerical celibacy and asked that his name be removed from the list of Old Catholic clergy for a few years, but it was later included. He received the last rites from an Old Catholic priest at his death in 1890.

Since no bishops had joined the rebellion, the Old Catholic, desiring episcopal consecration, turned to the Church of Utrecht. This ancient diocese had gone into schism in 1704 after refusing to endorse Rome's stand against the Jansenist heresy. Later, missionary bishop Dominique Marie Varlet, stopped for ten days in Amsterdam on his way to assume the post of bishop of Babylon. He had been in charge of French missions in what was then the Louisiana territory. He received his appointment in 1718 as coadjutor bishop of Babylon and sailed for France. On the day of his consecration in Paris he got word that the bishop of Babylon had died and that he was no longer coadjutor but bishop. He agreed to confirm 600 children in the schismatic Church. Bishop Varlet continued his journey by way of Russia to Persia. Here he was informed that he had been suspended for performing episcopal functions for the schismatics and for failing to call on the papal nuncio in Paris to give his adhesion to the bull *Unigenitus*. He returned to Holland and settled in Amsterdam.

Leaders of the Church of Utrecht finally prevailed upon Varlet to consecrate a bishop for them. He consecrated Cornelius von Steenoven in 1724 and when the latter died Varlet consecrated three other men. Through the last of these, Peter John Meindaerts, consecrated in 1739, all genuine Old Catholic bishops now trace their apostolic succession.

After its break with Rome the Church of Utrecht continued to observe all the canonical formalities. Its leaders notified the pope when they elected a new bishop and informed him of the consecration. The popes regularly replied by issuing bulls of excommunication. At the start of the schism three out of five Catholics in Holland belonged to this national Church; by 1815 only 6000 remained in the Church of Utrecht while almost one million were in communion with Rome.

It was to this remnant that the German and Swiss Old Catholics appealed. They knew that these Utrecht orders were undoubtedly valid although considered irregular by Rome. A German Old Catholic priest received episcopal consecration from Utrecht in 1873. A bishop for Switzerland was consecrated in 1876.

The various Old Catholic bodies drew up a statement of doctrine in 1899 called the Declaration of Utrecht. Among other things they agreed not to consecrate bishops without the consent of the other Old Catholic bishops. The Declaration of Utrecht also repudiated the Council of Trent: "We refused to accept the decrees of the Council of Trent in matters of discipline, and as for the dogmatic decisions of that council we accept them only so far as they are in harmony with the teaching of the Primitive Church."

Over a period of years the Old Catholics rejected the obligation of auricular confession, fasting, indulgences, the Index, stipends, the doctrine of the Immaculate Conception, veneration of relics, the Latin liturgy.

The daughter Churches of Germany, Switzerland, and Austria moved much faster than Utrecht in disciplinary changes. For example, the Old Catholic Church in Switzerland abolished clerical celibacy in 1875 and the German Church followed suit two years later, but the Dutch Church retained this regulation until 1922. Most Old Catholic bishops are now married as are practically all Old Catholic priests.

Power in the independent Old Catholic Churches rests in a synod. Synod membership includes the bishop or bishops, members of the synod council, all priests of the diocese, and lay representatives of the parishes.

The German, Dutch, and Swiss Old Catholic Churches belong to the World Council of Churches. Except for a small mission in South Africa, the Old Catholics engage in no missionary work. They have participated in ecumenical dialogues. They recognized the validity of Anglican orders in 1925 and signed an agreement at Bonn in 1931 to enter inter-communion with the Anglican Churches. In 1965 the Old Catholics also entered into full sacramental union with the Philippine Independent Church which claims 1,500,000 members.

An Old Catholic representative attended the sessions of Vatican II and a Roman Catholic observer went to the 19th International Congress of Old Catholics in 1965. This meeting held in Vienna brought together 400 Old Catholic delegates from 17 countries and included 22 bishops.

At the present time there are an estimated 30,000 Old Catholics in Germany, 35,000 in Austria, 80,000 in Poland, 22,000 in Switzerland, 12,000 in Holland and small communities in Czechoslovakia and Yugoslavia (Croatia).

The Polish National Catholics obtained their orders from the Dutch Old Catholics in 1907. The PNCC far outnumbers the rest of the Old Catholics today and it is the only Old Catholic body in the United States in fraternal relationship with the original continental Old Catholics.

For the most part the bodies claiming to be the Old Catholic Church in the U. S. are the shaky creations of religious entrepreneurs; consecrations are often bought and sold. Membership statistics are highly suspect and many congregations exist only in the imaginations of the patriarchs, exarchs, primates, metropolitans, archbishops, and bishops of the tiny sects. They are plagued by feuds and defections.

Many of these Old Catholic sects trace their origin to the remarkable and pathetic adventurer, Joseph Rene Vilatte, born in 1854.

His father, a butcher, belonged to a tiny schismatic sect called the *Petite Eglise* but Vilatte became a Roman Catholic and was educated by the Christian Brothers. After service in the French army during the Franco-Prussian War Vilatte emigrated to Canada. He left Canada for France and then Belgium and became a novice Christian Brother. This did not last long. Vilatte went back to

Canada and began studies for the priesthood for the diocese of Montreal.

For a time he left the Church but soon afterwards he was found at the house of study of the Viatorian Fathers in Bourbonnais, Illinois. In Illinois he got in touch with Pastor Chiniquy, an apostate priest from Canada. Chiniquy advised Vilatte to leave the Roman Church and labor as a Presbyterian missionary among the Belgians in Wisconsin.

It was early in 1884 that Vilatte, still a layman, started work as a free-lance Presbyterian missionary in Green Bay, with the chief object of converting the French and Belgian settlers. About a year later, apparently on the advice of Loyson, he approached J. H. Hobart Brown, Protestant Episcopal bishop of Fond du Lac, suggesting that the Presbyterian mission should be taken under his protection as an Old Catholic outpost.

Bishop Brown agreed to this, and in 1885 arranged that Vilatte be ordained deacon and priest by Bishop Herzog, the Old Catholic bishop in Switzerland. On his return to Wisconsin he worked for three years with great zeal, but after the death of Bishop Brown in 1888, the situation became difficult. Vilatte wanted to be raised to the episcopate.

At first the Episcopal bishop was prepared to consider this, but it did not take him long to realize that Vilatte was an ecclesiastical promotor, who behind his back was negotiating at the same time with the Roman Catholic bishop of Green Bay, the Russian Orthodox bishop of the Aleutian Islands, and the Old Catholic bishops in Europe.

In 1890 Vilatte severed all relations with the Episcopal Church, and on May 29, 1892, managed to get himself consecrated by Julius Alvarez. Alvarez was formerly a priest of the Latin rite, who had formed a schismatic sect known as the "Independent Catholic Church of Goa and Ceylon" after he had been raised to the episcopate in 1889 by Mar Paul Athanasius, Syrian Antiochene bishop of Kottayam. Vilatte was given the title of "Mar Timotheas, Archbishop of the Old Catholic Church of America."

Once he got back to Wisconsin, Vilatte realized that he had not gained much by his journey to Ceylon. The Roman Catholic bishop of Green Bay secured the services of French and Flemish-speaking Premonstratensian canons to counteract further conversions to Old Catholicism. At no time did Vilatte have a large following around Green Bay.

By 1894 he was in touch with the Apostolic Delegate to the United States, and with the Bishop of Green Bay, seeking reconciliation with Rome. Nothing came of these negotiations, and Vilatte turned his attention to the Poles, who were having difficulties with the American Catholic bishops. In 1898 he consecrated Stanislaus Kaminski at Buffalo. Then he returned to Europe where in the course of the next two or three years he was responsible for forming small schismatic bodies in England, France, and Italy by ordaining priests and consecrating several bishops. Early in 1899 it was announced that Vilatte was in Rome and about to make his submission to the pope, but in the end he left Europe and found a refuge in Canada for some years, hard up financially and pursued by his creditors. He was back again in France in 1906, and then the next few years he made Chicago his headquarters. In 1915 he founded there what he called the American Catholic Church but he retired from the primacy in 1920. The following year he consecrated the first bishop for the African Orthodox Church, after which he returned to his native France. In 1925 he made his formal recantation of errors, and it is said that it was the pope who asked the Cistercians of the Abbey of Pont-Colbert, near Versailles, to give him a home.

He was not allowed to celebrate Mass, and grew restless. Shortly before his death in 1929 he secretly ordained one of the novices, and even raised him to the episcopate. He was buried as a layman.

Vilatte's American Catholic Church is reported to have 5000 members in 29 churches—probably a generous estimate. Even this tiny group has split into two factions. It is amply served by an archbishop, two auxiliary bishops, and a titular bishop.

James Francis Augustine Lashley, who started the American Catholic Church, Archdiocese of New York, at the latest report in 1947, claimed 8000 adherents in 20 churches, all in New York City.

Perhaps the largest surviving sect launched by Vilatte is the African Orthodox Church. The Rev. George Alexander McGuire withdrew from the Episcopal Church in 1919 to found a separate Negro Episcopalian church. He first called his churches Independent Episcopal churches but changed the name to African Orthodox in 1921 and received consecration as bishop from Vilatte. Some of the members of the African Orthodox Church, under the leadership of Reuben Spata, a native of Uganda, are now in full communion with the Orthodox patriarch of Alexandria. They have adopted the Byzantine rite.

The African Orthodox liturgy is a combination of the Anglican, Roman, and Orthodox liturgies. McGuire now claims the title of patriarch and the African Orthodox Church reports 24 churches and 600 members. One of McGuire's bishops broke off and formed his own African

Orthodox Church of New York in Harlem.

The other prolific church founder was Arnold Harris Mathew. Born in 1852 in France, he was baptized a Roman Catholic but rebaptized at the age of two in Anglican rites at his mother's insistence. He began studies for the ministry of the Church of England but reverted to Roman Catholicism. A bright student, he completed philosophy and theology studies in only 18 months and was ordained a priest in 1877. For a few months he tasted the life of the Dominican order but returned to the diocesan priesthood. In 1889 his parishioners received a notice that their pastor could no longer serve them since he had abandoned belief in the fundamental doctrines of Christianity and was attracted to Unitarianism.

The next year Mathew changed his name to Count Arnoldo Girolomo Povoleri. In 1892 he married and subsequently fathered three children. He announced that he again accepted the doctrines of the Church but remained a suspended priest. He spent about ten years as a lay Catholic author without revealing his clerical background.

Count Povoleri now became convinced that England was ripe for the Old Catholic message. He got in touch with the continental Old Catholics in 1907 and finally persuaded the Dutch Old Catholic bishops to consecrate him. When the conservative Dutch Old Catholics discovered that their episcopal candidate was married and had a family they backed away from the consecration but finally agreed to proceed with the plan. The count was raised to the episcopacy on April 28, 1908.

Mistaken in the reception which Old Catholicism would receive in the British Isles, Bishop Mathew went ahead with the consecration of two former Roman priests. This outraged the Dutch bishops since it violated the Declaration of Utrecht. The count declared his independence of the continental Old Catholics. Before long he raised four more priests to the episcopacy so that his Church boasted seven bishops for about 100 faithful.

In 1914 Prince de Landas Berghes et de Rache of Austria, who had been consecrated by Mathew the previous year, came to the United States as an enemy alien. On his own authority he consecrated two men as his suffragans. His purpose was to unite the Old Catholic factions, but he only added to the confusion. De Landas was reconciled with the Holy See before his death in 1920.

One of his suffragans, William Henry Brothers, set up the Old Catholic Church in America and in turn consecrated about half a dozen bishops. The other suffragan, an ex-Catholic priest by the name of Carmel Henry Carfora, organized the North American Old Roman Catholic Church. He consecrated more than 20 bishops not only for his own body but for various national groups.

Carfora who gave himself the title "Supreme Primate" and claimed infallibility when he spoke ex cathedra died in Chicago in 1958. At his death his Church claimed 78,000 members in 60 parishes. Since his death this body has split into four or five factions. One is headed by Carfora's former chancellor, Primate Metropolitan Hubert A. Rogers of Brooklyn, and another by a former bishop of the Carfora Church, Richard A. Marchenna.

The remnant of the Brothers' sect, reduced to himself and two or three priests, was received into union with the Patriarchal Exarchate of the Russian Orthodox Catholic Church in America in 1962. All were reordained and Brothers is now a mitred Archpriest.

One of Brothers' collaborators, Joseph Zielonka, parted company with him in 1940 and set up the rival Polish

Old Catholic Church. He was succeeded in 1961 by a former Roman Catholic priest, Archbishop Peter A. Zurawetsky, who lives in Rahway, New Jersey. The name of this small Church was changed to Christ Catholic Church. In 1960 it claimed 22 parishes and 7,200 members.

The tiny Reformed Catholic Church (Utrecht Confession) maintains its headquarters in Los Angeles. Its estimate of membership is modest: 2217 in 20 parishes. It claims to be part of the worldwide Reformed Catholic Church with congregations in England, France, and Germany. Its archbishop, W. W. Flynn, states, "We have no arguments with Rome—she is our mother and we respect her as such." The Flynn group criticizes Utrecht for falling under Anglican domination.

The bizarre Liberal Catholic Church also derives its orders from Mathew, but its theosophical and occult orientation puts it beyond the pale of orthodox Christianity.

By 1915 most of the clergy of Archbishop Mathew's Church had become Theosophists. This occult religion was founded by an eccentric Russian noblewoman, Madame Helena Blavatsky, and propagated by Annie Besant. Madame Blavatsky claimed to receive mysterious spiritual instruction from invisible Masters. Her religion combined elements of Hinduism, pantheism, Christianity, spiritualism, Freemasonry, Buddhism, and other Eastern cults.

Archbishop Mathew consecrated a former Anglican clergyman, Frederick Samuel Willoughby, who was a convinced Theosophist. He in turn consecrated another Theosophist, James Wedgwood. Mathew lost control of the situation and the Theosophists took over the apparatus of his Church and renamed it the Liberal Catholic Church (Old Catholic). The new management promised stately ritual and valid orders but the greatest freedom of religious thought. In a few years the Liberal Catholics started missions in Australia and the United States.

The Liberal Catholics deny communion to no one who approaches their altars. They introduced the dialogue Mass in 1934, several decades before Rome gave her approval. They allow no crucifixes or images of the dead Christ in their churches.

As theosophists the Liberal Catholics believe that the Christ principle has appeared many times in history. Jesus was only one manifestation of this principle. Not only Christianity but many other world religions are divinely inspired and therefore the Liberal Catholics do not proselytize.

Reincarnation is a basic belief. Man dies and is reborn in a long cycle of death and life. Purgatory is simply the time and place between reincarnations; there is no hell.

Priests of this Church do not accept salaries or stipends and support themselves at secular jobs. Their congregations are usually small. Liberal Catholic priests often use the parlors of their homes as chapels which seat perhaps 25 worshippers.

In 1947 the Liberal Catholics in this country, who never numbered more than 4,000, suffered a schism. Now the strict Theosophists recognize a bishop who resides in Minneapolis while the smaller body, leaning more to orthodox Christianity, has its headquarters in Los Angeles.

Theosophist Liberal Catholics acknowledge the spiritual authority of an English bishop as presiding bishop of the Church. He is the Rt. Rev. Sir Hugh Sykes of London. Bishop Sykes is active in the Theosophical Society and in Co-Masonry, a form of Freemasonry which admits both men and women. In secular life the bishop works for the firm which publishes the London telephone directory.

Regionary bishops serve dioceses in Austria, Germany, Switzerland, France, French Africa, Belgium and Holland, the Scandinavian countries, Australia, New Zealand, Great Britain and Ireland, and the United States. The sect has recently established missions in Latin America.

Reunion of separated Christian Churches has been one of the major long-range goals of the Second Vatican Council and the ecumenical movement. It now appears that one of the most likely reunions will involve the Roman Catholic Church and the Old Catholic Churches of Europe.

On Nov. 7, 1966 Bernard Cardinal Alfrink of Utrecht and Andreas Rinkel, the Old Catholic archbishop of Utrecht, joined in a paraliturgical service in St. Gertrude's church. Both prelates extended a joint blessing at the common service on the feast of St. Willibrord, first bishop of Utrecht and patron saint of the Netherlands.

During the historic rite it was revealed that Rome's insistence that Old Catholics assent to the bull *Unigenitus* prior to any theological dialogue had been abandoned. This bull condemned Jansenism in 1713 and played an important part in the eventual schism.

The irrelevancy of the Jansenist controversy in the modern world, the willingness of Old Catholics to re-examine the role of the papacy and the concept of collegiality, and the renewal of Roman Catholicism, have combined to encourage the Old Catholics and the Roman Catholics to investigate possible roads to reunion.

Cardinal Bea wrote to the Old Catholics: "An encounter which is conducted in the spirit of faith and in

Christian charity is the first step on the road toward the hoped-for unity." Theological committees from both Churches are meeting to discuss the issues which must be resolved to achieve reunion.

Evidence of the friendlier climate in which the two Churches now exist is the report that 1000 Roman Catholics and 100 Old Catholics have merged their parish churches to form one parish in Rotterdam's inner city. Members of both traditions will attend Mass at the Old Catholic church building. The priests plan joint Holy Week observances and a single midnight Mass at Christmas. Old Catholic priests have served as deacon and subdeacon at Masses celebrated by a Roman Catholic priest.

While such cooperation holds promise for future ecumenical progress, dialogue between Rome and the theosophical Liberal Catholics or the many "Old Catholic" sects in the United States and England is unlikely.

FURTHER READING

Anson, Peter, *Bishops at Large* (London, Faber and Faber, 1964).

Moss, C. B., *The Old Catholic Movement* (London, S.P.C.K., 1948).

The Pentecostals
🔲🔲🔲🔲🔲🔲🔲🔲🔲

To MILLIONS OF Christians all the charisms or extraordinary powers granted by the Holy Spirit on the first Pentecost should be enjoyed by the Church today. These gifts include not only speaking in tongues but also the gifts of healing, interpretation, discernment of spirits, and prophecy.

Some students of the movement estimate that the number of Pentecostals around the world approaches 9,000,000 including more than 2,000,000 in the United States. Additional thousands belong to Roman Catholic and mainline Protestant Churches and constitute what has become known as the Neo-Pentecostal movement.

That gifts such as speaking in tongues (glossolalia) were employed by the early Christians to witness to their faith is not denied by any Christian Church. But accounts of tongue-speaking after A.D. 100 are rare and by the beginning of the fourth century, the charismatic gifts seem to have disappeared. St. Augustine declared: "Who in our day expects that those on whom hands are laid so that they may receive the Holy Spirit should forthwith speak with tongues? . . . These were signs adapted to the times. For there behooved to be that betokening of the Spirit in all tongues to show that the Gospel of God was to run through all the tongues over the earth. But that thing was done for the betokening, and it has passed away."

In the eighteenth century, John Wesley, the founder of Methodism, preached about the baptism of the Holy Spirit which was an intense personal experience confronting the Christian with the presence of God. Emphasis on this spirit-baptism or "second blessing" waned as Methodism turned into a middle-class American denomination. But the growing neglect of Wesley's "holiness" teachings disturbed some Methodists. Toward the end of the nineteenth century, some of these Methodists left the parent Church and formed separate Holiness Churches such as the Church of the Nazarene.

The re-appearance of glossolalia was reported in 1901. Charles F. Parham, a Holiness preacher, was dismayed by the aridity of his own spiritual life. He rented a white elephant mansion in Topeka, Kansas, and started a Bible school with about forty students. Together they set out on an intensive study of the scriptures and came to the conclusion that speaking in tongues was the one sign that a Christian had indeed received the baptism of the Holy Spirit. At 7 p.m. on New Year's Eve in 1900, one of the students, Miss Agnes N. Ozman, startled the assembled group when she began to pray in tongues. Within a few days many more followed suit.

Parham spent the next five years as an itinerant preacher before opening another Bible school, this time in Houston. One of his students, a Negro minister named W. J. Seymour, carried the "full gospel" message to Los Angeles. A three-year-long revival in the California city attracted people from all over the country, and these people planted Pentecostalism in most of the major cities in the U.S., as well as in many European nations. The older Holiness Churches refused to give emphasis to tongue-speaking, but dozens of independent Pentecostal Churches were soon organized.

The spectacular growth of Pentecostalism has forced scholars to pay more attention to the movement. Dr. Henry Pitney Van Duzen, former president of Union Theological Seminary, has called Pentecostalism the "third force" in world Christianity alongside Catholicism and Protestantism.

The various Pentecostal bodies furnish about four times as many foreign missionaries as would be expected. In Brazil the Asambleas de Dios claims 1 million members. In Chile 14 percent of the population now belongs to Pentecostal Churches. Elsewhere in Latin America the Pentecostals win more converts than all of the mainline Protestant Churches put together.

Sweden reports the largest percentage of Pentecostals of any nation; Swedish Pentecostals form the largest religious body outside the state Lutheran Church. Norway and Finland also have growing Pentecostal movements.

Typically the Pentecostals have won converts from the lower economic and social classes. Aggressive missionaries, the Pentecostals have been less noted for building schools, hospitals, or charitable institutions than the mainline Protestants.

Dr. Luther P. Gerlach, an anthropology professor at the University of Minnesota, recently completed a three-year study of Pentecostals. He concluded that the movement is not limited to "the discontented, the deprived, or the deviant." He added: "Our own judgment is that most of them are outstanding stable individuals. We don't see speaking in tongues as the important characteristic of the movement. It's just one of many. The significant feature of it is its function as a status symbol, a mark of identification."

Largest of the dozens of Pentecostal Churches in the U.S. is the Assemblies of God which reports 625,000 members in 8600 congregations. A number of small Pentecostal groups banded together at Hot Springs, Arkansas, in 1914 to form this Church.

True to Pentecostal principles Assemblies of God churches insist that all Pentecostal gifts found in the New Testament must be duplicated in the twentieth-century Church. The sect supports 760 missionaries and enrolls 992,000 children in its Sunday Schools. Members are expected to tithe, submit to immersion baptism, abstain from liquor and tobacco, and avoid secret societies. Affiliated branches cater to members of German, Polish, Ukrainian, and Latin American nationality.

Another large group of churches preaching Pentecostalism is made up of those bearing the name Church of God. They range from fly-by-night storefront churches with a handful of adherents to sects with a membership in the tens of thousands. Altogether probably 400,000 people belong to one of the many Churches of God. Five such churches maintain headquarters in Cleveland, Tennessee, and trace their origin to A. J. Tomlinson. Tomlinson, a Bible salesman, served as general overseer of the original Church of God from 1903 to 1923 when he was impeached and set up another Church of God. After his death his sons, Homer and Milton, headed separate Churches of God, one with headquarters in Queens Village, New York, and the other in Cleveland, Tennessee. The latter body was first called "The Church of God Over Which M. A. Tomlinson Is General Overseer" but this has been shortened to Church of God Prophecy.

Negroes participated in the birth and early spread of Pentecostalism and several of the larger churches are composed entirely of Negroes. The Church of God in Christ was founded in the 1890's as a Holiness church, but founder C. H. Jones brought his followers into the Pentecostal fold. This body had grown from 31,000 members in 1936 to 419,000.

Another Negro Church, the Apostolic Overcoming Holy Church of God, was founded in 1916 by a former Methodist minister. Members not only speak in tongues but engage in ecstatic dancing during revival services. They follow a Puritan ethic which discourages the usual vices as well as slang, the use of snuff, and idle talk. The United Holy Church of America, Inc. began as a Holiness church in North Carolina in 1886 and adopted Pentecostal positions.

Among the larger groups which include the designation "Pentecostal" in their church titles are the United Pentecostal Church (150,000 members), the Pentecostal Holiness Church, Inc. (66,000), the Pentecostal Church of God of America, Inc. (115,000), and the Pentecostal Assemblies of the World, Inc. (45,000).

Perhaps the most colorful personality in the Pentecostal movement was "Sister" Aimee Semple McPherson, foundress of the International Church of the Foursquare Gospel. In her heyday Sister Aimee would enter her 5300-seat Angelus Temple in Los Angeles wearing football togs and riding a motorcycle.

A native of Canada, she was converted at the age of 17 and married the Baptist preacher who had converted her. The pair went as missionaries to China but her husband Robert Semple died of malaria in Hong Kong and she returned to the States. She embarked upon a career of evangelism, married a grocer by the name of Harold McPherson, and came to California in 1920. Her Temple was dedicated three years later as 1000 voices sang "Open the Gates of the Temple." Sister Aimee employed every device of oratory, lighting, costuming, publicity, dramatics, and crowd psychology to gain attention and win converts. The newspapers devoted headlines to her disappearance in 1926. Two men lost their lives diving for her body in the ocean. Finally she turned up and related that she had been kidnaped and tortured but managed to escape from a hideout in the desert. At her death in 1944 her followers contributed $100,000 worth of flowers including a 600-foot floral cross. Twelve pallbearers took 20 minutes to carry the 1200-pound bronze casket a few hundred yards to her grave at Forest Lawn cemetery.

Her son, Rolf, assumed the office of president of the International Church of the Foursquare Gospel which his mother had incorporated in 1927. L.I.F.E. Bible College next to the Angelus Temple has graduated 5000 Foursquare ministers and radio station KFSG is operated by the sect in Los Angeles. The sect survived Sister Aimee's career and death and its growth from 21,000 members in 1936 to 160,000 in 1971 in this country indicates that it will continue to expand.

The best known Pentecostal preacher in the nation—Oral Roberts—was ordained by one of the smaller Churches: the Pentecostal Holiness Church. (Oral Roberts joined the Boston Avenue Methodist Church of Tulsa in 1968.) The Oral Roberts Evangelistic Association in Tulsa employs 415 people. Roberts serves as president of Oral Roberts University in Tulsa which may well become the largest and leading Pentecostal college. It includes a graduate school of theology.

In general the Pentecostals are isolated from the mainstream of Protestant church life. Their doctrines, membership, and church organization are as unfamiliar to the average Methodist and Lutheran as to Catholics. They are unlikely to join the local ministerial society or cooperate in interdenominational projects. Their preachers do not hesitate to lambast the established Churches for deserting the "old time religion." Nevertheless these groups claim a combined constituency of at least 2,000,000 and they have been registering much greater membership increases than the older Churches. Their adherents contribute far more per capita than do other Protestants even though they represent a lower income bracket. Their foreign mission programs rival those of the very largest denominations in number of workers and converts. They probably spend more time in church than most Protestants since the Sunday evening, midweek service, and revival remain features of almost all Pentecostal groups.

As members of these many sects attain a degree of financial security and social position, they exert a liberalizing influence on the sect. Some leave the sect for a Methodist or Baptist Church which carries more prestige in the community. Others remain in the sect and help transform it into a church-type organization.

As time goes on seminaries and colleges are founded, a full time minister replaces the part-time preacher, local congregations acquire property and leave their rented quarters, ministers with college and professional training move into the top positions, some of the sect's young people leave farming and factory work for white collar positions, the worship service calms down. Over a period of several generations the original protest against the established Churches becomes a curious bit of denominational history. Other groups arise to offer what the sect-turned-Church no longer countenances.

The first evidence of Pentecostalism in the traditional Protestant Churches was reported in a large Episcopal parish in Van Nuys, California, in 1960. Father Dennis Bennett, rector of St. Mark's church, had prayed for and received the gift of tongues, and had met with some of his 2,600 parishioners who also sought the Pentecostal experience. Father Bennett's espousal of tongue-speaking led to his resignation as rector. Bishop Pike, who in a few years would embrace spiritualism, forbade any public support of Pentecostalism in his northern California diocese.

Since 1960 the mutation known as neo-Pentecostalism has cropped up in Lutheran, Presbyterian, Baptist and other Churches. In some theological points these neo-Pentecostals differ from classical Pentecostals, but all agree that the charismatic gifts of Pentecost should be enjoyed and used by today's Christians.

Seldom do neo-Pentecostals leave their original Church homes to affiliate with a Pentecostal Church. They usually foster Pentecostal beliefs in their own Churches, read neo-Pentecostal periodicals such as *Trinity,* and attend a weekly prayer meeting.

The first manifestation of Pentecostalism among Roman Catholics appeared at Duquesne University in Pittsburgh in 1966. A group of faculty and students began to investigate the idea of baptism of the Holy Spirit and started to meet with a neo-Pentecostal prayer group. By February of 1967 four Catholics at Duquesne testified that they had received this baptism and the accompanying gift of tongues.

From Pittsburgh the movement spread to Notre Dame and then to Newman Centers at Michigan State and the

University of Michigan. Within four years from its beginning the Catholic Pentecostal movement has spread to dozens of areas in the U. S. and Canada. At least 30,000 Roman Catholics now participate in prayer meetings and have received or are seeking the baptism of the Holy Spirit. They form a tiny minority of the forty-seven million American Catholics and have not attracted many adherents outside of North America; however, the spread of Pentecostalism among Catholics may prove to be one of the most significant developments of the post-Vatican II Church.

Notre Dame remains an active center of Catholic Pentecostalism. The movement's best known theologian, Holy Cross Father Edward O'Connor, teaches there. He holds a doctorate in theology and has been known as a rather conservative scholar. Kevin and Dorothy Ranaghan, associated with St. Mary's College, wrote the paperback *Catholic Pentecostals* which is a basic exposition of Pentecostal spirituality and a compilation of testimonials by Catholic participants. A group of five single men operates True House in South Bend. This serves as a clearing house for the Catholic Pentecostals, distributing a directory of prayer groups around the country.

Perhaps the most active center is that at Ann Arbor, Michigan. Ralph Martin and Steve Clark started the nucleus of the group while working at the Newman Center at the University of Michigan. Now as many as 500 people attend the Thursday night prayer meeting, and another 170 from the immediate area attend the Monday meeting. A dozen or more Pentecostals devote most of their time to fostering the Catholic Pentecostal movement in Ann Arbor and neighboring Michigan cities.

Basilian Father George Kosicki is probably the best

known of the fourteen priests in the Detroit area involved in the movement. Cardinal Dearden has given the group permission to found three Houses of Prayer. In the Albany-Schenectady-Troy area, a Catholic can choose to attend one or two prayer meetings every night of the week. Other Pentecostal centers are found in Chicago, Cleveland, St. Louis, Milwaukee, Miami, Dayton, Akron, and Columbus, but the movement is spreading rapidly to other areas.

Central in the life of the Catholic Pentecostal along with the Mass is the weekly prayer meeting. Held in a home or church hall, it may well last three hours or longer. The format varies but usually includes Bible reading, singing, testimonials, fellowship, speaking in tongues, and some-times healings. Toward the end of a meeting the group extends an invitation to any who wish to ask for the baptism of the Holy Spirit. Those already so baptized pray over these individuals and participate in the laying on of hands.

Many Catholic Pentecostals testify that their involve-ment has also heightened their appreciation of the Mass and other devotions. They may now try to attend daily Mass although some admit that before hearing of Pente-costalism they skipped Mass altogether or attended only out of fear of sin. Pentecostals are regularly urged to set aside some time each day for Bible study and additional time for meditation and prayer. One midwestern Newman chaplain—not a Pentecostal—told me he formed a kindly impression of the Catholic Pentecostals when he went to a Newman conference and discovered the Pentecostals had spent five hours in a Bible study session. "Anything which can get a bunch of college students to spend that much time on the Bible can't be all bad," he remarked.

One noteworthy accomplishment of the young Catholic Pentecostal movement has been to build an ecumenical bridge between Catholics and those Protestants once considered the most hostile toward Rome. Protestant Pentecostals have been welcomed at Catholic prayer meetings and conferences; Catholics have entered into dialogue with such respected Pentecostals as David J. duPlessis, an observer at Vatican II.

Some Catholics have joined the Full Gospel Business Men's Fellowship International along with Pentecostals and neo-Pentecostals. This organization was formed in 1953 by Demos Shakarian, a California dairyman of Armenian extraction and Pentecostal persuasion. Its chapters are generally composed of business and professional men who share the baptism of the Holy Spirit and the gift of tongues.

Two books have had an unusual impact on Pentecostals and those who have investigated the movement. *The Cross and the Switchblade* tells the story of a mountain preacher who came to New York City and applied Pentecostal methods in his work with youth gangs and drug addicts. A motion picture with Pat Boone playing the role of Rev. David Wilkerson has been released. The other book which nearly every Pentecostal has read is *They Speak With Other Tongues* by John Sherrill, an Episcopalian journalist.

Almost all Pentecostals believe that glossolalia is speaking a genuine foreign language by a person who has never spoken or studied such a language. A small minority believe that the language may be a heavenly language used only to praise God.

The folklore of the movement abounds in cases in which Pentecostals spoke languages of which they were ignorant but which were easily translated by others in the group who knew the language. Authenticated cases, however, are few and far between. The kind of meticulous investigation which must be carried out before a cure at Lourdes is declared miraculous has not been undertaken. Pentecostals usually insist that such a scientific study would prove little. They note that there are now at least 2,800 languages spoken around the world and even an outstanding linguist knows only a handful. Even a roomful of linguists combining their knowledge would be familiar with only 100 or 200 languages. Besides there are the innumerable dead languages and finally the angelic or heavenly tongues. So, say the Pentecostals, a corps of linguists might well fail to recognize the tape recording of a particular "tongue," but the authenticity of the gift would remain a question mark. Not only do Pentecostals prefer to emphasize other aspects than tongue-speaking, but they point out that many other gifts were promised at the first Pentecost. One priest moderator of a prayer group estimated that about seventy-five out of 100 participants had received the gift of tongues, fifteen had the gift of interpretation, and several seemed on the verge of receiving the gift of healing.

Unlike classical Pentecostals the Catholics seldom claim that everyone must receive the baptism to be a full-fledged Christian or that everyone baptized should give evidence by speaking in tongues. Some Protestants have attended Pentecostal churches for years and never believed they had received the baptism and never spoke in tongues. This situation could obviously lead to conditions of anxiety and depression for these individuals.

The verdict on Catholic Pentecostalism by outside scholars has ranged from approval to skepticism to condemnation. Father Kilian McDonnell, O.S.B., director of the Institute for Ecumenical and Cultural Research at

St. John's College in Minnesota, has made an extensive study of Pentecostalism but is not a participant himself. He admits: "Pentecostalism conjures up images of emotionalism, fanaticism, religious mania, illiteracy, anti-intellectualism, credulity, messianic postures and panting after miracles." But the Benedictine monk attributes much of this bad image to the setting of religious revivalism into which classical Pentecostalism was born.

He maintains: "The issue in Pentecostalism is not tongues, but fullness of life in the Holy Spirit, openness to the power of the Spirit, and the exercise of all gifts of the Spirit. . . . Because Pentecostalism is not a denomination, not a doctrine, but a spirituality, an experience, a way of life, which has a scriptural basis, it can fit into a Roman Catholic, a Lutheran, a Presbyterian context."

Bishop G. Emmett Carter of London, Ontario, reveals a personal attraction for the Pentecostals because they are "old" in the sense and traditions of the Church. "They have a long standing tradition of prayer. They have returned to the fundamentals. They read and meditate upon the word of God and let the Spirit move within them."

Far harsher is the criticism of Pentecostalism of the German scholar Konrad Algermissen: "Any normal person who has been present at a Pentecostal gathering when the Holy Spirit has been poured out, or has witnessed the baptism of the Spirit, the so-called speaking in tongues or the driving out of the devil, is bound to conclude that it is not divine but demoniac, or, at least, morbid and psychopathic powers that are at work."

Some Protestant fundamentalists agree with Algermissen that speaking in tongues is the work of the devil, but most critics hesitate to attribute glossolalia to him. They simply say that ample psychological evidence exists to show that speaking in tongues occurs when an individual allows his subconscious to take over his powers of speech. For example, George B. Cutten, an authority on glossolalia, writes: "As far as I know there is no case of speaking in strange tongues which has been strictly and scientifically investigated that cannot be explained by recognized psychological laws." Dr. E. Mansell Pattison, psychiatrist on the staff of the University of Washington School of Medicine, states: "The product of our analysis is the demonstration of the very natural mechanisms which produce glossolalia. As a psychological phenomenon, glossolalia is easy to produce and readily understandable."

The U. S. bishops appointed a commission headed by Bishop Alexander M. Zaleski of Lansing to study Catholic Pentecostalism. The commission's first report was released in November 1969 and neither condemned nor encouraged the movement. In part the report declared: "It seems to be too soon to draw definitive conclusions regarding the phenomenon, and more scholarly research is needed." At the same time the commission acknowledged that the movement "has legitimate reasons for existence" and "a strong biblical base." Finally the bishops' commission said that "the movement should at this point not be inhibited but allowed to develop."

For a religious movement not yet 75 years old Pentecostalism has long since gone beyond the time when its adherents could be dismissed as "Holy Rollers." In many countries the Pentecostal Churches are the only ones to register membership gains; in a country such as Chile the Pentecostals represent 82% of all those who identify themselves as Protestants. The influence of neo-Pentecostalism on such denominations as Roman Catholicism, Methodism, Episcopalianism, Presbyterianism and Lutheranism may force established church authorities to make some difficult decisions. For millions of Christians the miracles of the early Church are repeated every day and every week in the 1970's.

FURTHER READING

Bloch-Hoell, Nils, *The Pentecostal Movement* (New York, Humanities Press, 1965).

Gee, Donald, *The Pentecostal Movement* (London, Elim, 1949).

Hoekema, Anthony, *What About Tongue Speaking?* (Grand Rapids, Mich., Eerdmans, 1966).

Nichol, John Thomas, *Pentecostalism* (New York, Harper and Row, 1966).

Ranaghan, Kevin and Dorothy, *Catholic Pentecostals* (New York, Paulist Press, 1969).

Sherrill, John L., *They Speak With Other Tongues* (New York, McGraw-Hill, 1964).

The Plymouth Brethren
🔲🔲🔲🔲🔲🔲🔲🔲🔲

A SMALL GROUP of Christians who began to meet in Plymouth, England, in 1827 gave a name to a fundamentalist and adventist movement known as the Plymouth Brethren. Their early leader was a former Church of Ireland clergyman, John Darby (1800-1882), who had rejected creeds and urged a faith based on the Bible alone. His followers have also been known as Darbyites but they reject this name as well as Plymouth Brethren. The latter name has been used for 140 years to identify the group.

The movement has been plagued by schisms. At least eight distinct groups in the United States are known as Plymouth Brethren. Darby himself was involved in the first schism. He went to the continent in 1838 and remained there for seven years doing missionary work. When he returned to England his leadership was challenged and he formed a rival sect. The basic division among Plymouth Brethren is between the Exclusive Brethren who recognize as true Christians only their fellow Brethren and the Open Brethren who admit that true Christians may be found in other denominations.

Darby visited Germany, the United States, Canada, Italy, New Zealand, and the West Indies. His collected writings fill 32 volumes.

Plymouth Brethren came to the United States in the late 19th century. The eight groups are identified by

Roman numerals from I to VIII. Plymouth II claims the largest number of members: 15,000; Plymouth I claims another 5000. The other six groups make up the remaining 13,000 Brethren although statistics for these denominations are only rough estimates. Plymouth I and II are strictly congregational in polity but III to VIII belong to Circles of Fellowship. Until 1936 VII and VIII were part of I. The movement also embraces about 15,000 people in England, Canada, Germany, and Switzerland.

The Plymouth Brethren have no ordained clergymen, seminaries, official publications or spokesmen, schools, or charitable institutions. They emphasize Bible study but oppose higher education. The Brethren meet in small groups of 25 to 40, usually in rented halls or private homes. Like Jehovah's Witnesses and Christadelphians they usually brand other Christian groups as apostate and prefer to keep to themselves. At their weekly meetings they hold a communion service, read the Bible, and pray. They follow no ritual.

The Polish National Catholics
□□□□□□□□□

FEW ETHNIC GROUPS have remained more loyal to the
Roman Catholic Church than the 6 million Polish Americans. No more than 7,000 are thought to have converted
to some form of Protestantism. Yet it was within the
Polish American community that the only serious schism
in the history of the Church in America took place.

The Church which resulted from this break survives
as the Polish National Catholic Church and reports more
than 282,000 members in 172 parishes in the United
States, 18 in Canada, and others in Poland.

The PNCC labors among Polish Americans concentrated in the nine states of Massachusetts, Connecticut,
New York, New Jersey, Pennsylvania, Ohio, Michigan,
Illinois, and Wisconsin. It is served by four bishops and
144 priests in the United States.

Externally PNCC church buildings resemble Roman
Catholic churches built half a century ago. These churches
include altars and tabernacles, sanctuary lamps, stations
of the cross, statues, crucifixes, confessionals, holy-water
fonts, etc. PNCC priests wear the historic vestments.

Most Roman Catholic scholars acknowledge that the
Polish National Catholic Church retains valid priestly
orders although no official statement has ever been issued
by Rome. These orders were obtained through the Old

Catholic Church whose bishops stand in the apostolic succession and whose priests are validly ordained.

Both Roman and Polish Churches have undertaken liturgical changes in recent years. Before 1964 the most obvious difference between the two bodies was that one used Latin in the Mass and the other Polish. Now the Roman Mass is completely in English (or some other vernacular) and the Polish National Catholics use both Polish and English. Such innovations as the celebrant facing the people, congregational singing at Mass, the recitation of portions of the Mass by the people are found in both Churches.

The Poles were not converted to Christianity until A.D. 1000. Protestant ideas spread by the Hussites and Lutherans were squelched by the Jesuits of the Counter Reformation and by 1600 the Reformation effort in Poland was dead.

During the latter part of the nineteenth century thousands of Poles entered the United States. The trickle became a flood and in the peak year of 1912-1913 more than 175,000 Poles passed through Ellis Island. These immigrants tended to settle in ethnic and language communities, mostly in the nine states mentioned.

They discovered that the Church of their fathers was not directed by fellow Poles in America but by bishops of Irish and German descent. Even though these bishops helped establish the more than 850 predominantly Polish parishes and parochial schools, a few ultranationalistic Poles objected to non-Polish direction. They seemed to want some sort of separate but equal policy such as the various Eastern rites enjoy.

A lack of Polish priests sometimes made it necessary to appoint non-Polish pastors in their parishes. A few congregations here and there rebelled and sought to win the right to choose their own pastors. They refused to listen to preaching in English and were reluctant to follow the established forms of property control set up by the Council of Baltimore. The PNCC developed in this setting from three separate independence movements originating between 1895 and 1900.

Fr. Antoni Koslowski, who had been assistant pastor of St. Jadwiga Church in Chicago, organized an independent congregation of All Saints in 1895. He obtained consecration as a bishop by the Old Catholics in Switzerland in 1897, and in the next ten years started 23 schismatic parishes from New Jersey to Manitoba. He called his creation the Polish Old Catholic Church. Koslowski died in 1907 without having consecrated any bishops.

A second stream of dissent began when Polish parishioners in St. Adalbert Parish in Buffalo objected to the bishop's control of church property. They organized a rival parish called Our Lady of the Rosary in 1895. Their pastor, Fr. Stanislaus Kaminski, paid $2,500 to Joseph Rene Vilatte, the ecclesiastical adventurer, to be consecrated a bishop. Bishop Kaminski remained a one-parish bishop until his death in 1911.

The mainstream of the present PNCC started in Scranton in a parish of miners and factory workers. The immigrants had built a church called the Sacred Heart of Jesus but, like the Poles in Buffalo, they did not want to turn over the title to the bishop. For this stand and other actions they were reprimanded by the bishop. Eventually the dispute led to a free-for-all fight in front of the church and the arrest of 20 people.

The disgruntled parishioners appealed for help to a former Scranton curate now in nearby Nanticoke, Fr.

Francis Hodur. The Polish-born Hodur declared: "Let all those who are dissatisfied and feel wronged in this affair set about organizing and building a new church, which shall remain in possession of the people themselves. After that, we shall decide what further steps are necessary."

They followed his advice, raised funds for a new building, and asked the bishop to bless it. He agreed provided they would transfer the title to him in accordance with the Baltimore decrees. They refused.

Father Hodur now became their pastor and named the new church St. Stanislaus. He went to Rome in 1898 to seek concessions for the Polish dissidents, saw two cardinals, but got no satisfaction. He canceled an audience with the Holy Father and sailed for home. Father Hodur was excommunicated on October 22, 1898, and publicly burned the notice of excommunication before the congregation.

The first Mass in the Polish language was celebrated on Christmas Eve in 1900. Other Poles began to form independent congregations that were gathered into a synod which met in 1904. By this time the movement had attracted about 16,000 adherents. Hodur was elected bishop but would have to wait three years for consecration. The European Old Catholics were unwilling to consecrate a second Polish bishop since they had already consecrated Koslowski. When the latter died, however, they agreed to consecrate Hodur. This was done in St. Gertrude church in Utrecht.

Hodur managed to incorporate most of Koslowski's parishes into his new PNCC as well as the large Buffalo church headed by Kaminski. To provide insurance benefits forfeited by their change of allegiance the Polish Nationals set up the Polish National Union in America which has been a financial success. Refused burial in Catholic cemeteries, they bought ground for cemeteries of their own.

Bishop Hodur encouraged a small group of Lithuanians to organize a parallel Lithuanian National Catholic Church in 1941.

At the PNCC's fourth synod in 1921 the Church officially authorized the new mission in Poland. Four more bishops were elected and would subsequently be consecrated by Hodur alone. This synod also approved the marriage of the clergy, but few priests at the time took advantage of the ruling because of lay opposition. Today three out of four PNCC priests are married but newly ordained priests must agree to remain single for two years. Any parish council may refuse to accept a married priest as pastor. Hodur himself never married.

From 1926 to 1936 the PNCC grew from 61,874 members to 186,000. Hodur had himself trained a few priests to supplement the former Roman priests who formed the original clergy. He bought a three-story building on a busy Scranton corner where he established his seminary called Savonarola after the 15th century Dominican who was hanged as a heretic in Florence.

The seminary enrolls between 12 and 16 students. Its three-year course is practical: Bible, church history, Polish history, moral and doctrinal theology, philosophy. Students need no college preparation nor do they need to study Latin, Greek, or Hebrew. Courses are taught in Polish, which has become something of a problem since few young men know the language well enough for classroom instruction.

Hodur headed the PNCC for almost 60 years. Blind and paralyzed for his last eight years, he used a microphone to deliver sermons from his rectory to his Scranton cathedral. He died February 16, 1953, at the age of 86.

Dominating the life of the Polish Nationals for so many decades, Bishop Hodur stamped his own peculiar theological notions into its fabric. What began as a protest against essentially disciplinary measures such as the form of property control, the language of the liturgy, the power to choose pastors, turned into avenues of doctrinal innovation.

A sympathetic historian of the movement, the Rev. Theodore Andrews of the Protestant Episcopal Church observes: "They [the creedal statements] are, of course, clearly intended as watchwords for a small but venturesome group; and their limitation is that of their being chiefly the work of one author, whose writings are not so much the carefully considered statements of a theologian as homilies of a crusading priest, eager to stir his people to action, and indignant at the pretensions of an alien hierarchy" (*The Polish National Catholic Church in America and Poland*, pp. 39-40).

The PNCC accepts the first four ecumenical councils and its own general synods as authoritative. Some questions on which Hodur spoke, such as the doctrine of original sin and eternal punishment, seem to be considered open questions today which may be defined in some future synod.

That Hodur himself denied the doctrines of original sin and hell is clear. He declared that it would show a lack of confidence in the justice and mercy of God to believe in an eternal hell. "He would not deliver His creatures into the power of evil spirits, for them to torment or destroy," he wrote. A man's conduct on earth somehow determines his status after death but eventually all men will attain the goal of union with God, Hodur believed. The soul may undergo purification or cleansing after death but will never be lost. He also maintained that faith is "helpful to man toward his salvation, though not absolutely necessary."

Bishop Hodur emphasized the value of the apostolic succession and of membership in the Holy Catholic Church which was composed of all baptized Christians. He also stated: "The leaders of the Polish National Catholic Church are of the opinion that before God and before America all beliefs, all sects, are equal. If God did not wish a certain sect to exist, He would not give it the necessary powers to exist and develop."

A student of Old Catholicism comments: "Bishop Hodur, however outstanding as an organizer, was no theologian and lacked clear theological concepts. Thus theological insecurity became one of the distinctive features of his Church. The principles and rules which Bishop Hodur drew up in 1932 and on several other occasions are not consistent with the faith of the primitive Church and bear much more resemblance to a Unitarian creed" (Victor Consemius, "Catholicism: Old and Roman," *Journal of Ecumenical Studies*, Summer 1967, p. 438).

One of the bishop's theological inventions was the elevation of the preaching, reading, and hearing of the word of God to the status of "a great sacrament of a Christian, National Church." To end up with seven sacraments he combined baptism and confirmation into one sacrament.

As for the doctrine of the Church, the PNCC declares in its current catechism: "All baptized people who are united with Christ through faith are members of the Holy Catholic Church" (p. 37). In answering the question of the need for national churches, the catechism states: "Christ called all men from all nations and races to serve

God, each to contribute its particular spiritual and cultural gifts toward the building of God's Kingdom on earth" (p. 40).

Private confession is required of children and young people up to the age of 21. After that a general confession is sufficient. The Polish Nationals still distribute communion under the species of bread only. Communicants must make either a private or a general confession and fast from midnight.

They have made some minor changes in the Roman liturgy but still celebrate the Mass, hold Benediction, have Stations of the Cross, recite the rosary. They continue the special Polish devotions to the Sacred Heart and the Lenten "Gorzkie Zale." The liturgical language is Polish although the pressure is now on from younger members to adopt more English. A few parishes use English at one or more Sunday Masses.

Hodur added a number of unique feast days to the PNCC calendar: the feasts of the Poor Shepherd, the Polish National Catholic Church, the Remembrance of the Dear Polish Fatherland, Brotherly Love, and the Christian Family. The Church holds special liturgical commemorations for Polish heroes and religious reformers such as Huss, Savonarola, and Peter Waldo.

The catechism recommends that all PNCC homes have a crucifix, holy water, and blessed candles. It also sanctions such sacramentals as the sign of the cross, the Angelus, holy oils, ashes, palms, incense, and images of our Lord and the saints (p. 34).

Both parishes and dioceses are relatively autonomous. Authority in the areas of faith, morals, and discipline resides in the clergy; in social and economic matters in the laity.

Every four years the bishops, pastors, and lay delegates meet in the General Synod. Delegates are chosen on the original basis of one for every 50 parishioners—which is becoming rather unwieldly. The four United States dioceses are the Central (Scranton), Eastern (New England), Buffalo-Pittsburgh, and Chicago.

The bishop of the Chicago diocese, Leon Grochowski, succeeded to the post of Prime Bishop. As a student at Warsaw Polytechnic College, Grochowski participated in forbidden underground activities against the Russians and had to flee to the United States. He was ordained in 1910 by Hodur and was one of the four bishops consecrated in 1924. He was an energetic organizer for the PNCC in the Chicago area and made 11 trips to his native land.

For the first time an American-born prelate heads the Polish National Catholic Church. Bishop Thaddeus F. Zielinski, a native of Wilkes-Barre, Pa., was named in 1969 to succeed the late Prime Bishop Leon Grochowski. The new Prime Bishop has sought ways to retain the loyalty of second and third generation Polish Americans whose knowledge of the language and traditions is limited. He celebrated Mass in English rather than Polish in his Buffalo cathedral in 1961 and has translated and published the first English catechism, prayerbook, ritual and hymns for his Church.

The Prime Bishop consecrates other bishops, controls the seminary and church publications, and examines candidates for the priesthood. The bishops are elected by the synod from a list of eligible priests submitted by the Prime Bishop.

The PNCC discourages formation of religious orders. It operates only one parochial school, a bilingual school in Scranton. The rest of the religious instruction is carried on through classes on Saturdays and Sundays in each parish. The Church owns its own printing plant and a 400-acre farm at Waymart, Pa., used as a summer camp and as a home for the aged.

Hodur sent a bishop to Poland in 1925 to take charge of the mission to the homeland. He also consecrated Wladislaw M. Faron as bishop in 1930 but soon learned that Bishop Faron was beginning to remarry divorced people and had himself consecrated two suffragans without authority from Scranton. Hodur deposed Faron in 1931 and the latter rejoined the Roman Catholic Church in 1949.

The founder of the PNCC visited Poland 14 times. By 1939, the PNCC in Poland claimed 56 parishes, a seminary, and about 50,000 faithful. Few priests in Poland dared to marry. A number of priests lost their lives during the war so that by the end of the war only 70 PNCC priests survived. The PNCC in Poland probably enrolls about 60,000 people today.

Isolated by a self-imposed language barrier and ultranationalistic aims, the PNCC has only recently entered into the wider fellowship of Protestant and Orthodox bodies. Holding membership in both the National Council of Churches (since 1957) and the World Council of Churches (since 1948), the PNCC has also observed intercommunion with the Protestant Episcopal Church since 1946. The statement governing this intercommunion points out: "Intercommunion does not require from either Communion the acceptance of all doctrinal opinion, sacramental devotion, or liturgical practice characteristic of the other, but implies that each believes the other to hold all the essentials of the Christian faith." The agreement was based on the Bonn agreement with the Old Catholics on the continent in 1931.

The PNCC does not allow divorce and remarriage, although the Prime Bishop may grant annulments. It has made no statement for or against contraception. This Church does not forbid membership in any society not condemned by the state, which means that the Polish Nationals may join the Masonic lodge and other secret societies.

Growth of the Polish National Catholic Church since 1926 has been greater than the overall growth of the Polish American community but the great majority of Poles have remained Roman Catholics. The fires of intense nationalism have banked in recent years and this has affected the Polish American community as well as other ethnic groups. Fewer Americans became fluent in a language other than English, limit marriage to members of their own ethnic group, and see themselves primarily as members of an ethnic minority.

Recently Bishop Grochowski told his church leaders that he had furnished information on the episcopal consecrations of Polish National Catholic bishops to Abbot Laurentius Klein, O.S.B., at the latter's request. Abbot Klein planned to forward this information to Cardinal Bea of the Secretariat for Christian Unity. Bishop Grochowski told the Supreme Council of his Church that it is "willing to unite with any Church." He added, "We came to the conclusion that if we are really united with the Lord, as we should be, the unity will come of itself."

For the first time in the history of the PNCC a Roman Catholic priest attended this Church's general synod in 1967. Msgr. Eugene Clark represented the Roman Catholic bishop of Scranton at the meeting which was attended by 120 clerical and 430 lay delegates. Other observers were the head of the PNCC in Poland and the head of the Slovak National Catholic Church.

Prime Bishop Zielinski told the synod: "Christians must face the world with a single front, a single voice, and a single faith." His own ecumenical activities included participation as consecrator of three bishops of the Philippine Independent Church in 1969 and ordination of a number of deacons and priests for the Episcopal Church.

In the nearly 75 years since the break with the Roman Catholic Church many of the specific causes of the conflict have been resolved. Father Hodur complained that no member of the American Catholic hierarchy claimed Polish ancestry; today Cardinal Krol and at least 11 other bishops in the Roman Church come from the Polish American community. The use of the language of the people in the Mass and sacraments has been adopted by the Roman Church. The Roman Catholic layman is being urged to make his distinctive contribution to the life of his parish and the entire Church. In these areas Father Hodur seemed to anticipate some of the changes of the Second Vatican Council.

FURTHER READING

Andrews, Theodore, *The Polish National Catholic Church in America and Poland* (London, S.P.C.K., 1953).

Anson, Peter F., *Bishops at Large* (London, Faber and Faber, 1964).

Fox, Paul, *The Polish National Catholic Church* (Scranton, Pa., School of Christian Living, n.d.).

The Quakers
🔳🔳🔳🔳🔳🔳🔳🔳🔳

ALL THE QUAKERS in the world add up to fewer people than the population of Grand Rapids or Omaha. Yet the 196,000 members of the Religious Society of Friends have demonstrated for three centuries how a small band of men and women can witness to the world out of all proportion to their numbers.

In New York and Geneva Quakers offer their services in the quest for peace to United Nations personnel. In the Deep South dedicated Quakers help register Negroes to vote for the first time. In Hong Kong a group of Quakers operates a day nursery for working mothers.

Young adult volunteers give two years of their lives in Quaker-sponsored projects in Guatamala, India, Tanzania, Germany, and the United States. Quaker teams present seminars on nonviolence on college campuses. Since 1943 Quakers have maintained one of the most influential lobbies in Washington; their Friends Committee on National Legislation opposes capital punishment and conscription and works for peace, foreign aid programs, and civil rights.

Two Quakers—Herbert Hoover and Richard M. Nixon—have occupied the White House. Nixon belongs to the East Whittier Friends Meeting, near Los Angeles.

Recognition of Quaker activities on behalf of peace came in 1947 when the Nobel Peace Prize was awarded jointly to the American Friends Service Committee and its British counterpart, the Friends Service Council.

William Temple, the former archbishop of Canterbury, once said: "We differ from the Quakers in every respect, but they certainly are the best Christians."

Despite their catalog of good works and the esteem in which they are held by other Christians as well as believers, the Quakers do not attract many converts. In any scale of proselytism the modern Quakers would stand at one extreme and the missionary-minded Mormons and Jehovah's Witnesses at the other. Today there are fewer than half as many Quakers in England—21,000—as there were at the end of the 17th century when the founder of the Society of Friends died.

Msgr. Ronald Knox described the competition which Quakerism faced from both Deism and the Wesleyan revival. What survived "was a religious coterie rather than a sect; a band of well-to-do reformers, distinguished by their wide influence and active benevolence, but numbering only a handful of adherents among the multitudes on whom they had compassion" (*Enthusiasm*, p. 168).

During the 18th century it looked like Quakerism would remain one of the major religious forces in America but its growth has lagged far behind other denominations. It has probably never exceeded the American membership it reported in 1800. Most Quakers show only a slight interest in winning others to their faith; some groups of Quakers have devoted more attention to purging the membership rolls of those who fail to meet some standard of conduct than to spreading "the Truth." The 122,000 American Friends comprise one of the smallest components of the American religious panorama.

The Quakers do not win acceptance because they are

numerous or because they are growing in numbers. What does distinguish the Quakers from many other Christians is their personal commitment to God and man. The Quaker worships God also by serving him through man. Although decidedly mystical, Quakerism does not understand a purely interior religion. It believes that the Christian faith must express itself in action and service.

The Quaker tries to seek direct divine illumination by jettisoning all of the Christian sacraments, rituals, hymns, formal prayers, and priesthood. He tries to live by the Inner Light and some understanding of what is meant by this term is central to an understanding of Quakerism.

The Inner Light is not conscience but it is that which enlightens conscience. Quaker theologians usually describe the Inner Light as "that of God in each man." Man discerns the Inner Light when he silently and patiently waits for God to speak to him. Such direct illumination is far superior to the written revelation of the Bible or the traditions of the Church, in the Quaker view.

Here is how the founder of Quakerism described the Inner Light:

"The Lord God hath opened to me by His invisible power how that every man was enlightened by the divine Light of Christ; and I saw it shine through all and that they that believed in it came out of condemnation and came to the Light of Life, and became the children of it; but they that hated it, did not believe in it, were condemned by it, though they made a profession of Christ. This I saw in the pure openings of the Light, without the help of any man, neither did I then know where to find it in the Scriptures, though afterwards, searching the Scriptures, I found it. For I saw in that Light and Spirit which was before Scripture was given forth, and which led the holy men of God to give them forth, that all must come to that Spirit—if they would know God or Christ or the Scriptures aright—which they that gave them forth were led and taught by."

In some basic theological positions Quakerism comes closer to Roman Catholicism than to Protestantism. The Quaker rejects the classical Lutheran view of human nature as totally depraved as a result of original sin. Most Quakers would uphold the inherent goodness of man. They believe that perfection and freedom from sin are possible in this life. The founder of the Society of Friends early preached against the Calvinist doctrine of predestination.

In his attitude toward the Bible the Quaker stands in sharpest contrast to the orthodox Protestant. Quakers consider the Bible to be a word of God but consider the Inner Light to be a manifestation of God. The same spirit of God which inspired the writers of sacred scripture can enlighten the individual seeking Christianity today. Therefore the Society of Friends does not attribute to the Bible the same final authority as do the Protestants. Some scholars classify the Society of Friends as a third form of Christianity, neither Catholic nor Protestant.

Quakers are popularly known as Protestants, however. Since many contemporary Protestants also adopt a less dogmatic position than the "sola scriptura" of the Reformers the breach between liberal Protestants and Friends is not as wide as it once was. The major Quaker bodies belong to the National and World Councils of Churches and Quaker observers attended sessions of the Second Vatican Council.

The traditional Quaker form of worship, the silent meeting, is designed to facilitate the direct inspiration of the Inner Light. At an appointed time on the First Day (Sunday) the Quakers gather at their meetinghouse. They sit quietly and wait; at times an individual will rise to give a testimony or share a spiritual thought. There is no sermon, set prayers, altar, scripture readings, or hymns.

In the earlier days of Quakerism the elders sat on raised seats facing the congregation. The men, wearing their hats, would sit on one side of the aisle and the women on the other.

Recently I attended a meeting for worship conducted by a small congregation of Quakers in Indiana. The meeting room was on the second floor of a rather shabby YMCA building. At 11 o'clock on Sunday morning the 35 or so men, women and children filed into the bare room and took their seats in a semi-circle.

A printed card handed to visitors stated: "All present are asked to join in prayer and meditation, and if moved by Divine Spirit, to give expression to prayer or to speak in the spirit of worship."

The 60 minutes of silence was interrupted only twice. After we had been sitting for about 10 minutes one of the members of the congregation told about an experience which her daughter had had while she was a Quaker worker in a prison farm in Kentucky. Her relationship to a young Negro inmate illustrated how God shows his love through human beings.

After half an hour the young children were dismissed. Most of the Quakers sat with eyes closed throughout the meeting. The only noises were those of the hissing steam radiator, a passing airplane, and the traffic in the street below. Near the end of the hour another Friend offered a reflection on Gandhi's understanding of means and ends. At noon we shook hands with the persons sitting next to us and departed.

I was told that during other meetings many more people offered prayers and testimonies and that two such offerings were below the average. This is a small Quaker group; most of the dozen or so families who belong are associated with the nearby state university.

Preceding the meeting for worship was a Sunday School for children. These schools resemble the familiar Protestant Sunday School and include Bible study, hymns, and story telling.

The Quaker withdraws to the silence of the weekly meeting only to find spiritual nourishment and inspiration and to go back into the world. There is no such thing as a Quaker hermit or a Quaker monastery where contemplatives cut themselves off from men and affairs.

A Friend will belong to a monthly meeting which meets once a week for worship and once a month for business. These monthly meetings correspond to a parish; the monthly meetings of an area get together four times a year for a quarterly meeting. Finally the monthly meetings form the 27 yearly meetings in the United States and Canada which are the counterpart of a diocese.

In all Quaker meetings the members do not seek decisions by majority rule but by the "sense of the meeting" which means unanimity. In these meetings women hold equal power and status with men.

Elders and overseers are appointed to serve each monthly meeting. The elders arrange for meetings for worship, marriages, and funerals while the overseers assume responsibilities for the pastoral care of members. The Clerk is the chief administrative officer of the meeting.

At least once a year each monthly meeting makes what amounts to a group examination of conscience. The members of the congregation answer a series of questions or queries posed by the yearly meeting which relate to the spiritual state of the meeting.

A Quaker bride and groom repeat their marriage vows during a meeting for worship after obtaining the consent of the meeting to the union. Each declares: "In the presence of the Lord and of these our friends, I take thee, . . . to be my wife (or husband,), promising with divine assistance to be unto thee a loving and faithful husband (or wife) so long as we both shall live." Then all those present sign the marriage certificate as witnesses.

Not all Quaker congregations follow the original form of the silent meetings. Many Quakers in the Middle West, West and South have abandoned the silent meeting in favor of a programmed worship service which differs little from a typical Protestant service. These are known as Friends Churches or pastoral meetings and are often served by salaried ministers. Classical Quakerism dispensed with a separate ministry; laymen and lay women were chosen to serve as clerks, elders, and overseers but drew no salary.

Even the sacraments of baptism and the Lord's Supper which were preserved by every other Protestant Church were discarded by the first Quakers. They reasoned that no rites or rituals were needed to discern the Inner Light. The born Quaker is therefore not a baptized Christian. A convert or "convinced" Quaker may have been baptized in another denomination but his entrance into the Society of Friends would involve no initiatory rite. A committee interviews the prospective convert and submits a report to the meeting.

You would not expect to find a religious conservative among the Unitarians or a liberal in the Southern Baptist Convention but you will find both Unitarians and Fundamentalists among American Quakers. Some Quakers consider Jesus Christ to be the Second Person of the Trinity while others rank him only as a great teacher who exemplified the Inner Light better than other men. These theological differences are evident not only in the two major Quaker groups but among the membership of the many yearly meetings.

To trace the history of the Society of Friends we must go back more than 300 years. During the Reformation period some Christians believed that the Protestant Reformers—Luther and Calvin—stopped short of a complete return to primitive Christianity. They formed sects often classified as Anabaptists and endured persecution by both Catholics and Protestants. These Anabaptists and their modern descendants such as the Mennonites and Baptists formed the left wing of the Reformation. In England their counterparts were sects such as the Seekers, Ranters, and the Quakers.

The Church of England threw off the spiritual jurisdiction of the Bishop of Rome but the Puritan element in Anglicanism rejected the Mass, images, and five of the seven sacraments. The Presbyterians dispensed with bishops altogether including the Anglican bishops. Congregationalists thought the Presbyterian system was restrictive of freedom and they insisted on the autonomy of the individual congregation. The Baptists denied the validity of the baptism of infants or any mode other than total immersion. Finally came the Quakers who rejected the remaining ritual, the sole authority of the Bible, and the professional ministry.

George Fox (1624-1691) founded the Society of Friends. He was apprenticed to a shoemaker while a young lad and received little formal schooling.

The young man became increasingly dissatisfied with the church to which his family belonged. By the time he was 19 he had quit attending his parish church. He could abide neither the preaching or the worship and was scandalized by the habits, especially the drinking habits, of the clergy. Now Fox left home and became a Seeker, wandering about the countryside in search of religious enlightenment, visiting Anglican priests and church reformers.

For four years Fox sought to find a new way in which man could gain direct access to God. Finally he relates "when all my hopes in men were gone, so that I had nothing outwardly to help me, nor could I tell what to do, then, O then, I heard a voice which said, 'There is One, even Christ Jesus, that can speak to my condition.' And when I heard it, my heart did leap for joy."

He developed his idea of the Inner Light within each man. In 1647 Fox began preaching his new religious ideas and won converts in northern England, especially among the Seekers. Five years later he organized the Society of Friends.

At first his followers called themselves by various names such as Children of Light and Friends of Truth. Several versions of how the name "Quaker" came to be applied to Fox's followers have been offered. According to one story Fox was once brought before a magistrate because of his unorthodox religious views. Fox warned the judge that even he must tremble and quake at the Word of the Lord and the judge asked if he were a quaker. The name Quaker stuck and is now accepted by the Friends.

For the rest of his life George Fox traveled through England and other countries preaching his brand of group mysticism. Most of his converts came from the Baptists, Seekers and Ranters; hardly any Catholics or continental Protestants joined his movement. Missionary journeys took him to Scotland, Ireland, Holland, Germany, and the West Indies. Between 1671 and 1773 he toured the American colonies organizing Quaker communities and seeking converts.

Everywhere Fox traveled he asked men to live by the Inner Light and to demonstrate their faith by deeds. The early Quakers took a particular interest in the welfare of slaves and prisoners, the care of the poor and aged, the abolition of capital punishment and war.

The Quakers refused to serve in the army or navy, swear oaths, pay tithes for the support of the established Church, doff their hats to others, or use honorific titles. They usually branded the Anglican clergy a "hireling ministry" and sometimes heckled preachers in their pulpits. They made enemies. The established Church saw Quakerism as a threat to true Christianity and the state saw the Quakers as obstreperous critics and rebels.

Fox himself was imprisoned eight times for a total of six years. Between 1650 and 1689 more than 450 Quakers died in prison for their religious beliefs and at least 20,000 spent some time in prison. Just as in 1972 some people try to smear others by calling them Communists so in the 17th century critics of Quakerism tried to accuse them of being Catholic agents. One pamphlet published in 1654 was entitled: "The Quakers Unmasked, and clearly detected to be but the Spawn of Romish Frogs, Jesuits and

Franciscan Fryers, sent from Rome to seduce the intoxicated Giddy-headed English Nation."

At the age of 45 Fox married Margaret Fell, a widow who was ten years his senior. Her home at Swarthmore became headquarters for Quaker activity. Fox died in 1691; his *Journal* was edited and published three years after his death.

The theologian of Quakerism, Robert Barclay, spent many years under Catholic influence. Originally a Presbyterian he was sent to Paris to study under his uncle who was a professor at a Jesuit college. Barclay received a thorough training in Catholic theology and scholastic philosophy and used this training to serve the apologetic needs of Quakerism after he joined the Society in 1666. His chief work was *An Apology for the True Christian Divinity*. Barclay identified Quakerism as pure and primitive Christianity stripped of unessentials.

After the death of Fox and Barclay the Quaker movement became infected with Quietism. This theory proposes that God works only when man suspends all his usual activities. As a result the Quaker movement stagnated and missionary activity ceased. The English Society has never equalled the 65,000 Friends who supported the movement at the time of Fox's death.

Two Quaker women reached Boston in 1656 but were immediately accused of being witches and were deported. Later four other Quakers were hanged in Boston and many Quakers were whipped and tortured for their beliefs. Only the Toleration Act of 1689 halted the persecution.

One of the most famous Quaker converts, William Penn, came to Philadelphia in 1682. He was the son of an English admiral to whom the king owed a large sum of money. He settled the debt by giving a charter to the son who had become a convert to Quakerism. This was a large tract of land west of New Jersey. William Penn thought of calling it Sylvania but the king suggested he call it Penn-Sylvania. It became a haven for Quakers and a center of religious freedom in the colonies.

Penn once declared: "I abhor two principles in religion and pity them that own them. . . . The first is obedience to authority without conviction; and the other is destroying them that differ from me for God's sake."

Penn signed a treaty with the Indians and sought to establish a just and peaceful commonwealth in Pennsylvania. The Quakers dominated the political life of this colony, the wealthiest and most populous in America, until 1756 when they refused to vote a tax for a war against the Shawnees and Delaware Indians. Others less concerned about fair treatment for the original inhabitants took over the reins of government.

The Quakers not only developed Pennsylvania and New Jersey but at one time controlled Rhode Island, Delaware, and North Carolina. According to the Quaker historian Elbert Russell by 1700 "Friends were the greatest single religious organization in the English colonies as a whole, both in their influence and in their promise" (*The History of Quakerism,* p. 124). Later the Quakers were overwhelmed by immigrants from other religious traditions.

Quaker concern for fair treatment of the Indians was paralleled by growing concern for the slaves. Through the efforts of such Quaker abolitionists as John Woolman the meetings adopted stricter and stricter policies regarding slave holding. By 1776 all Quakers in good standing had released their slaves. Later Quakers would be active in the underground railroad and the abolitionist movement.

Naturally their pacifism kept the Quakers out of active

participation in the American Revolution. Those Quakers who did serve the colonial cause such as flag-maker Betsy Ross and Gen. Nathanael Greene were disfellowshipped.

After the Revolution Quakerism began to harden into a "peculiar" system. The doctrine of Quietism which stifled missionary activities in England infected the American Quakers as well. The Quaker community turned into itself. The elders concentrated on winning rigid adherence to strict standards of conduct and dress. Any Friend who married outside of the Quaker community was excommunicated. Art, music, games, dances and other pastimes were forbidden. By emphasizing simplicity and plainness the Quakers sought to distinguish essentials from nonessentials and also to put the money which might be spent for frills into good works. Periodic purges reduced the ranks of the Society of Friends, the young people rebelled, and few non-Quakers were attracted by the somber and straight-laced life which Quakerism came to represent.

Quakers in both England and America adopted what was known as "plain language." This meant that a Quaker refused to use the plural "you" when addressing someone since this was the form of address to a superior and was believed to be giving special honor to a human being. They substituted the Biblical-sounding "thee" and "thou." Because the days of the week were taken from pagan forms the Quakers renamed them "First-day" for Sunday, "Second-day" for Monday, etc.

One Quaker farmer is said to have addressed his recalcitrant cow at milking time: "Thee knows that I will not swear at thee. And thee knows that I will not strike thee. But what thee does not know, cow, is that I might sell thee to a Baptist who would beat the devil out of thee."

Because of their refusal to take oaths many Quakers

suffered in courts of law or turned down possible political careers. Their main opposition to oaths was scriptural— "Swear not at all" (Matt. 5:34)—but they also objected to oaths since such swearing seemed to sanction two standards of truth, one in court and another in daily life.

No longer do any Quakers wear the distinctive plain garb which once set the Quaker apart from the rest of the community much as the Amish are identified today. In 19th century Quaker communities colors were forbidden in clothing; the men wore black and the women gray. The suits lacked lapels and extra buttons and were worn without neckties. A broad-brimmed hat completed the costume.

This withdrawal because of Quietest influence and cessation of missionary work hurt American Quakerism but the Quaker scholar Rufus M. Jones writes: "The greatest tragedy of Quaker history was the separation of the Society in America, in 1827-1828, into two branches."

The schism was precipitated by Elias Hicks, a Long Island farmer. He opposed Deism and atheism but approached a unitarian position and cared little for the historical Jesus. He led a large body of Quakers away from the more orthodox Friends in 1827. Two-thirds of the Philadelphia meeting sided with Hicks and throughout the country yearly meetings, monthly meetings and even families divided between the Hicksites and the Orthodox. A conservative group called the Wilburites separated themselves in 1845. Some of these divisions persist to this day so that the relatively few American Quakers give allegiance to three major and a number of smaller yearly meetings.

Largest of these Quaker bodies is the Friends United

Meeting which reports 70,673 members in 502 churches. This is a union of 14 yearly meetings. It has headquarters in Richmond, Indiana and was once known as the Five Years Meeting. Many meetings associated with the Friends United Meeting were influenced by the Evangelical revivals of the 19th century and some are hard to distinguish from Baptist or Congregationalist Churches. Within the Five Years Meeting is the Association of Evangelical Friends which claims to represent 20,000 Quakers of a more fundamental orientation.

The contemporary Hicksites form the Religious Society of Friends (General Conference). These Quakers incline toward a more rationalist and modernist theology than other Quakers but the Conference never did adopt the theological platform of Elias Hicks. The General Conference is made up of 31,670 Friends in seven yearly meetings in Baltimore, Canada, New England, Illinois, Indiana, New York, and Philadelphia.

In 1965 four independent yearly meetings—Ohio, Kansas, Oregon, and Rocky Mountain—formed the Evangelical Friends Alliance. These Friends favor an evangelical Protestant theology, prefer the National Association of Evangelicals to the National Council of Churches, support Billy Graham and his revivals, and seek fellowship with Holiness Churches. This new Alliance claims to represent about 30,000 Quakers and constitutes the third major grouping of Friends.

Smaller Quaker bodies include the Pacific Yearly Meeting of Friends (2,622) and the Religious Society of Friends (Conservative) whose 1,696 members continue the Wilburite tradition.

Most American Quakers will be found in Pennsylvania, North Carolina, Indiana, Kansas, Ohio, and California.

Outside of the U. S. and England the largest numbers of Friends live in Kenya (31,555), Madagascar (7,726), Bolivia (3,000), Ireland (1,875), Guatemala (1,500), and Australasia (1,500). There are only 14 Quakers in Austria and 15 in Finland.

About 4,000 men and women belong to the Wider Quaker Fellowship. They sympathize with Quaker positions but do not wish to sever their ties with other Churches.

Although the Quaker movement is fragmented most Quakers support the work of the American Friends Service Committee. This is the cooperative agency which provides continuity and supervision for the worldwide Friends efforts to achieve peace and eliminate poverty, ignorance, and disease. It was founded in 1917 and first concentrated on war relief and aid to refugees. Now the AFSC works in the fields of community relations, international service and affairs, peace education, and youth services. Its executive secretary and board of directors are all Friends but only about one-third of its 500 staff workers are Friends. All must subscribe in general to the attitudes and peace concerns which characterize the Society of Friends.

About half the staff works at the national office in Philadelphia while others manage the 11 regional offices in the United States and 17 offices in other nations. Most AFSC workers serve two-year tours although a few make a career in the Committee.

Money to support the work of the AFSC (about $5 million a year) comes from Quakers and non-Quakers, foundations, corporations, and sometimes from governments in areas where the Committee labors. English Quakers support a similar cooperative agency.

Twenty of the 26 Yearly Meetings and ten Friends organizations have appointed representatives to the Friends

Committee on National Legislation. This lobby operates on an annual budget of $115,000.

At one time the Quakers operated a number of elementary schools and academies but most of these have been abandoned. The emphasis in recent years has been on higher education and secondary schools. All but two of the Quaker colleges in the United States were founded since the Civil War. Best known of these colleges are Swarthmore, Earlham, Haverford, Guilford, Wilmington, William Penn, Friends University, and Whittier. A Quaker financier, Ezra Cornell, gave his name and substantial endowments to establish one of the nation's leading private universities but Cornell has never been affiliated with the Quaker movement.

Those Friends Churches which offer a programmed rather than the unprogrammed silent meeting also usually employ a salaried minister. Recently a Quaker school of theology to train ministers has been established at Earlham College. Pendle Hill near Philadelphia serves as a graduate school of Quaker thought.

Consistent with its philosophy of the Inner Light and the imperatives of conscience the Society of Friends does not insist that every Friend be a pacifist. During World War II about 8,000 American Quakers served in the armed forces, 1,000 served in noncombatant posts, 1,000 received deferments, and 100 were sent to prison. The Quaker who enlists in the army or navy does not suffer ostracism although in earlier days such action might have brought excommunication. The basic Quaker position of pacifism is subject to the individual's own conscience which may lead one Quaker to prison for refusing to register and another to a Marine Corps commission.

A Quaker will avoid liquor, gambling, and stock market

speculation. He will refuse to swear an oath in court but nowadays an affirmation is all that is required from those who have religious objections to oaths.

The Quaker will not join secret societies such as Freemasonry which specialize in oaths. The 1936 revision of the Book of Discipline for the General Conference oberved: "Secret societies are capable of producing much evil and are incapable of producing any good which might not be effected by open means." It added: "The Society of Friends has always borne a corporate testimony against secret organizations" (p. 61).

A Quaker is likely to show a concern for world peace, racial equality, prison reform, abolition of capital punishment, slum clearance, support of the United Nations, coexistence with Communist states, recognition of Red China, mental health programs. Yet any individual Quaker could conscientiously oppose or ignore any of these concerns. Some of the English Quakers have recently proposed controversial positions regarding premarital sexual intercourse and homosexuality which have scandalized some American Quakers as well as other Christians.

American Quakers have produced scientists and public figures far out of proportion to their numbers. John Greenleaf Whittier was known as the Quaker poet. Susan B. Anthony led the fight for votes for women and equality of the sexes.

If Quakerism has anything to tell others it may be that personal commitment is central to the Christian faith. The Quakers tend toward mysticism but they do not ignore mankind while cultivating their own spiritual lives. As William Penn wrote: "True godliness does not turn men out of the world but enables them to live better in it, and excites their endeavors to mend it."

FURTHER READING

Bacon, Margaret H., *The Quiet Rebels: The Story of the Quakers in America* (New York, Basic Books, 1969).

Brinton, Howard, *Friends for 300 Years* (New York, Harper & Brothers, 1952).

Russell, Elbert, *The History of Quakerism* (New York, Macmillan, 1942).

Sykes, John, *The Quakers* (Philadelphia and New York, Lippincott, 1958).

The Rosicrucians
🔲🔲🔲🔲🔲🔲🔲🔲🔲

EVERY DAY HUNDREDS of people respond to advertisements placed in periodicals as diverse as *The New York Times Book Review* and *Popular Mechanics* by the Rosicrucians (AMORC). The full name of this organization is the Ancient and Mystical Order Rosae Crucis; headquarters are in San Jose, Calif.

The ads promise that the Rosicrucian Order can unlock the secret wisdom of the ages, banish fears and frustration, enrich the human spirit, and open the door to self-mastery. By writing a postcard for further information the inquirer can take the first step toward a new life.

What do they receive from San Jose? In a few days a mailman will deliver a handsomely printed brochure entitled "Mastery of Life" along with an application blank, introductory letter, and return envelope.

The booklet depicts a gallery of distinguished men of history under the title "These Men were Rosicrucians." They include Benjamin Franklin, Isaac Newton, Claude Debussy, Francis Bacon, and Rene Descartes. Other Rosicrucian publications list Plato, Aristotle, Jesus, Dante, Cicero and St. Thomas Aquinas as members of this mystical fraternity.

In its literature the AMORC promises to reveal the workings of mysterious cosmic laws by which an initiate can turn his wishes and day dreams into reality. "There is no supernaturalism. Everything occurs by cosmic, natural' law."

The Rosicrucians promise that their teachings can enable a person to improve memory, develop will power, maintain health, overcome bad habits, understand the purpose of life, attain "cosmic consciousness," change one's environment, influence other people, overcome an inferiority complex, develop personality, learn the truth about reincarnation, decipher ancient symbols, etc.

Claiming to be the modern counterpart of ancient mystery schools, the AMORC traces its history to the reign of Pharoah Akhnaton in 1350 B. C. The California organization also claims as ancestors the band of colonists, calling themselves Rosicrucians, who landed in the New World in 1695. They settled in Ephrata, Pa., but by 1801 the descendants of these Rosicrucians had scattered.

Those who join the AMORC receive two monographs a month. The Order suggests that he set aside 60 to 90 minutes a week, preferably on Thursday night, to study these lessons. He also gets a membership card, the monthly *Rosicrucian Digest,* and the passwords and secret grips which will enable him to gain entry to a Rosicrucian lodge or chapter. This costs $3.50 a month after payment of a membership fee of $5. So long as a member expects to remain a Rosicrucian in good standing he will remit $42 a year to San Jose.

There is no such thing as a family membership and the candidate is warned against sharing his monographs with those who do not also pay their monthly fees. He must pledge: "I will keep confidential all reading matter, lessons, and discourses sent to me, and will carefully examine them to determine each step I am to take in being prepared for a more practical and masterful position in life."

AMORC ads bring inquiries from thousands of men and women each month but relatively few maintain membership or even pay the first initiation fee and dues. The active membership probably does not exceed 45,000 at any one time. The organization spends more than $500,000 a year on ads, printing, postage, etc.

Those who do not enroll will eventually receive a subsequent mailing from the cult. For only $1.50 a month an associate member can receive the magazine and his choice of any two of seven available series of lectures. These are Mystical Adventures, Numerology, the Doctrines of Jacob Boehme, and Astronomy. They do not qualify to enter a Rosicrucian lodge or participate in the rituals.

The full member is asked to study his first-degree lessons at home for six weeks. He then initiates himself into the Order. This initiation is simple: the candidate stares at a mirror and traces a five-inch cross on the glass while repeating "Hail, Rosy Cross." He meditates for three minutes. Finally, he places the tip of his left forefinger in the middle of his forehead and whispers, "Peace."

One famous dabbler in Rosicrucianism was Sirhan Sirhan, Senator Robert Kennedy's assassin. *Time* magazine explains: "Mail order courses in Rosicrucian mysticism had given him a new creed. They told the disturbed Christian Arab that he could unlock from the mirror image of Sirhan Sirhan the inner knowledge, happiness and power he craved" (April, 1969, p. 28).

The novice remains in the first degree for another 12 weeks and studies his lessons on mental vibrations, mystical comprehension, the life force, and other occult subjects. He spends another 12 weeks in the second degree. It usually takes from 9 to 12 months to complete the three degrees.

Like the Freemason who has reached the Master Mason or third degree, the frater or soror of the AMORC is now encouraged to further his fraternal education by advancing to the higher degrees. In the Rosicrucian Order these consist of nine Temple degrees. The diligent Rosicrucian may then be invited to join the select Illuminati.

Although most Rosicrucians receive their instruction by correspondence, a growing number belong to lodges which meet in their own temples or rented quarters. In furnishings these Rosicrucian lodges resemble a Masonic lodge but the membership includes both men and women.

A recent issue of the official publication lists 100 regular lodges in 31 states, the District of Columbia, and Puerto Rico. California leads the nation in the number of lodges with 19 and Texas is second with eight. Sixteen of these U. S. lodges own the robes and paraphernalia needed for full-scale initiation into the 12 degrees.

Listed also are 26 lodges in France, 21 in Brazil, 18 in Nigeria, 13 each in Mexico and Canada, 12 in England, 11 in Venezuela, 8 in Australia, and a few others around the world. Members of U. S. or foreign lodges pay dues to their own lodges which forward a percentage to headquarters in San Jose.

The Master of a Rosicrucian lodge sits at one end of the chamber on a triangular dias while the Matre of the lodge, a woman, sits at the other end of the room. The Vestal Virgin sits in front of the Master and guards the sacred fire which is used to ignite incense used in the rites.

She must be an unmarried girl under 18 at the time of her appointment.

In the center of the lodge room stands the Shekinah or sacred triangle, which is flanked by three candles. Members of the lodge sit along both sides and wear Masonic-type aprons and regalia; some of these are embroidered with the main symbol of the AMORC, a cross and a rose (protected by U. S. patent). Before each initiation the members swear a solemn oath to keep the secrets of the fraternity inviolate.

Rosicrucians observe two special feasts: the New Year Feast on or about March 21, at which the fraters and sorors eat a symbolic meal of corn, salt, and grape juice; and the Outdoor Fete around Sept. 23.

The Rosicrucian marriage ceremony must be held in a lodge within three days after the civil ceremony and is performed by the lodge Master or the Chaplain. Children of Rosicrucian parents may receive the Appelation rite if they are under 18 months old. Parents must agree to educate the child in non-sectarian schools. "Such ritual may take the place of, or supplant, any christening ceremony" (*Rosicrucian Manual*, p. 177).

Children are eligible to join the Junior Order of Torch Bearers. They must be between 6 and 18 years of age. The AMORC furnishes a child guidance lesson for parents once a month.

The committed Rosicrucian is urged to live by the principles of the fraternity. When he wakes up in the morning he should face east, inhale and exhale seven deep breaths, bathe, and drink a glass of water. Before meals he should wash his hands, hold them palms down over the food, and say a mental prayer. Most Rosicrucians become vegetarians.

The cult performs its own burial rites for deceased members. Ideally the funeral begins late in the evening so that it ends about midnight. The body lies in repose in the lodge chamber, garbed in a Rosicrucian apron. The mourners wear purple garments which is the proper mourning color. The body remains in the temple until cremation the next morning.

How did the Rosicrucian Order (AMORC) get started? Despite its claims to antiquity it is relatively young. In 1915 an occultist, H. Spencer Lewis, inserted an ad in a New York newspaper offering to share his Rosicrucian secrets. He claimed to have received authorization from certain French adepts to reestablish the Order in the Western hemisphere.

Lewis maintained that his organization was the public voice of the Great White Brotherhood, familiar in Theosophy and other occult systems. The adepts of the Brotherhood live in Tibet; among their former pupils were Jesus and the 12 apostles.

From New York Lewis moved to San Francisco, then to Tampa, and finally to San Jose. He composed the basic monographs still distributed to initiates and his articles still appear in the pages of the *Rosicrucian Digest*. To add prestige to his pronouncements he gave himself a Ph. D. degree. He died in 1939.

His son, Ralph, succeeded him as "Supreme Autocratic Authority" and "Imperator for North, Central and South America, the British Commonwealth and Empire, France, Switzerland, Sweden, and Africa." Ralph Lewis was born in 1904 and attended a military school but skipped college and became Supreme Secretary of the cult in 1923. The constitution of the AMORC provides that control of the organization will remain in the male succession of the Lewis family.

The AMORC has prospered. It belongs to the San Jose Chamber of Commerce and its annual payroll nears $750,000. The cult occupies an entire city block which includes a museum, temple, administration building, auditorium, planetarium, art gallery, and library.

The legend which forms the basis of the Rosicrucian Order (AMORC) and other versions was started by publication of the *Fama Fraternitatis* in Germany in 1614. This book, describing the life and adventures of one Christian Rosenkreuz, is believed to have been the work of Johann Valentin Andrea, a Lutheran theologian.

Rosenkreuz was said to have entered a monastery as a young boy and to have accompanied a monk on a voyage to the Holy Land. In Cyprus the monk died and the lad wandered about Arabia and Egypt, absorbing the mystical lore of these civilizations. Returning to Europe he founded a secret order whose members were pledged to heal the sick, pursue occult studies, attend one meeting of the fraternity a year, and choose their own successors.

Since the publication of this story groups of alchemists, occultists, astrologers, cabalists and Freemasons have laid claim to the name Rosicrucian. The only mention of the AMORC in the 649-page history of Rosicrucianism by A. E. Waite (*The Brotherhood of the Rosy Cross,* University Books, 1961), is a note in the preface. Waite dismisses the AMORC and similar cults in one sentence: "They represent individual enterprises which have no roots in the past."

H. Spencer Lewis was not the only one to use the material of the Rosicrucian legends to build a modern cult.

Max Heindel founded the Rosicrucian Fellowship in Ocean-side, Calif. When he died in 1919 his widow continued his work. Two other U. S. Rosicrucian groups are the Rosicrucian Brotherhood of Quakertown, Pa. and the Society of Rosicrucians of New York City. The Rosicrucian degree in the Masonic Scottish rite has nothing to do with the AMORC.

The basic religious beliefs of the AMORC include pantheism and reincarnation. In his book *Rosicrucian Questions and Answers* Lewis wrote: "The Rosicrucians believe and have always believed that there is but one soul in the universe, and that is the universal soul or the universal consciousness of God" (p. 206).

The cult teaches that the human personality survives death, and that after a stay in the resting place it enters a new human body in a series of reincarnations. Lewis taught that Jesus Christ was the only one to complete the cycle of reincarnations and be united with God.

FURTHER READING

Lewis, H. Spencer, *Rosicrucian Manual* (San Jose, Calif., Supreme Grand Lodge of AMORC, 1959).

————, *Rosicrucian Questions and Answers* (San Jose, Calif., Supreme Grand Lodge of AMORC, 1959).

The Salvation Army
□□□□□□□□□

MOST PEOPLE RECOGNIZE the military uniform of the Salvation Army officer and the bonnet of the Army's lassies. On bustling city streets at Christmastime these dedicated Salvationists ask help to provide a holiday meal for the homeless or the poor.

We may have encountered a fictional version of the Salvation Army in George Bernard Shaw's *Major Barbara* or in the musical, *Guys and Dolls,* adapted from Damon Runyon's short stories.

We may know something about the Salvation Army's efforts to furnish clean lodging for transients, a dignified confinement for the unmarried mother, a social and educational program for the children of working parents. But we may not know exactly what the Salvation Army stands for. Is it simply a social welfare agency with evangelical overtones? Is it an appendage to other Churches? Is the Salvation Army a sect itself?

Another question we may have asked ourselves is why the Army clothes itself in the garb of a semi-military organization with officers, citadels, marching orders, and brass bands. Why the military trappings?

As a matter of fact, the Salvation Army is a Protestant denomination with its own creed, clergy, ritual, seminaries, and hierarchy. It carries out its mission by comforting, caring for and converting, particularly members of the lower social and economic classes, just as the Episcopal Church seems to direct its appeal to the upper classes.

The *Yearbook of American Churches* tells us, "The deepest motivation of all Salvation Army service is found in its religious faith, and its fundamental doctrines are stated in its Foundation Deed of 1878 in 11 cardinal affirmations. . . . The Army is evangelical before it is anything else." Catholic writer Konrad Algermissen observes: "The Salvation Army wishes to be super-denominational. But since it possesses a separate religious doctrinal system, separate religious customs, a separate religious organization, it must be reckoned among the others as a Christian sect" (*Christian Denominations*, page 859).

True, the Army enjoys widespread community support for its welfare work and often participates in Community Chest and United Fund drives. A local unit may choose to de-emphasize its specifically religious purpose and orientation to avoid jeopardizing its financial support but the Army understands that its first and foremost aim is evangelization. An official statement of the Army explains: "The primary object of the Salvation Army is the spiritual regeneration of mankind. Whatever phase of its many activities be considered this primary object is always controlling."

To reach its constituency the Army works through a variety of agencies which offer help to the down and out, the alcoholic, the poor, the sick, the troubled. Some critics may question the adequacy of the training of a Salvation Army officer or the Army's approach, which becomes essentially a salvage operation rather than an effort to change social conditions. But no one will deny the dedication and spirit of sacrifice of Army personnel or the value of the help it has given to literally millions of men and women.

This movement began more than 100 years ago when a dynamic Methodist preacher left his pulpit to bring the gospel to the wretched people who lived in the slums of East London. He told his co-workers: "Go for souls, and for the worst."

William Booth was born in 1829 and was baptized in the Anglican Church but experienced a religious conversion at the age of 15 and became a Methodist. He worked as an apprentice pawnbroker in Nottingham from the age of 14 and later went to London where he engaged in the same occupation.

In London the young man took up lay preaching in one of the many Methodist splinter groups. He left the tiny Methodist Reform Movement to join the sect known as the Methodist New Connexion. This sect agreed to train him for ministry. A year before his ordination he married Catherine Mumford whose family was associated with the Quakers.

Booth took charge of a tent mission in London which was called The Christian Mission. When the battered tent finally collapsed he rented other quarters for his revival services including a tavern, warehouse, stable and dance hall. He discovered that his converts were not welcomed in the Methodist and Anglican Churches to which they were directed. He explained:

"From the first I was strongly opposed to forming any separate organization. . . . My first idea was simply to get the people saved and send them to the church. This proved at the outset impracticable. First, they would not go when sent. Second, they were not wanted; and third, we wanted some of them at least ourselves to help us in the business of saving others. We were thus driven to providing for the converts ourselves."

The late Fr. Gustave Weigel, S. J. observed: "Perhaps the only reason why the Salvation Army became a Church was because evangelical Churches had no place for religious orders in their organizations" (*Churches in North America*, p. 102).

Four years after walking into the tent, Rev. Booth had a wife and eight children, a magazine, a headquarters, 14 preaching stations, a soup kitchen, and a schedule of 140 worship services each week.

His co-workers began to call him "General," which was a shortened form of "General Superintendent." They called themselves "The Hallelujah Army." In 1878 General Booth was checking printer's proofs of an annual report which was entitled "The Christian Mission—A Volunteer Army." Booth crossed out "Volunteer" and substituted "Salvation" and the new name stuck. He modeled his religious organization after the British Army.

A Salvation Army poster in the same year described the membership as "recruited from amongst the multitudes who are without God and without hope in the world, devoting their leisure time to all sorts of laborious efforts for the salvation of others from unbelief, drunkenness, vice, and crime."

Not everyone applauded Booth's efforts. Some saloon keepers hired goons to harass the preacher and his converts, their former customers.

General Booth formed what might be called an army of Protestant Jesuits with a more or less Franciscan outlook. His colleagues agreed to give him absolute obedience as would any soldiers. Unlike the Society of Jesus, he demanded no lengthy training period. The General appointed subordinate officers in grades corresponding to the regular army. What would be known as members or parishioners in a traditional Church were called recruits and soldiers.

Between 1880 and 1890 the Salvation Army established outposts throughout the world. Ireland and the United States were invaded in 1880. General Booth would visit this country four times.

Army expeditions were sent to Australia and France in 1881, to Canada, India and Sweden in 1882, to New Zealand and South Africa in 1883, to Germany in 1886, to Italy, Holland, Denmark and the West Indies in 1887, to Norway in 1888, and to Argentina, Uruguay, Belgium, and Finland in 1889.

The Army's first American convert was "Ashbarrel" Jimmy who kept body and soul together by scavenging in garbage and ash barrels. The Army helped victims of the San Francisco earthquake and the troops in the Spanish-American War.

World War I brought the Army to the attention of millions of Americans. The Salvation Army officer brought comfort to the doughboys in the trenches of France while cheerful lassies staffed canteens behind the lines. The President conferred the Distinguished Service Medal on Commander Evangeline Booth, the General's daughter who headed the U. S. division. After the armistice returning veterans remembered the Army with affection and helped raise funds to build a chain of citadels in cities across the country.

Before his death in 1912 General Booth had been received by kings, emperors, and presidents; he received an honorary doctorate from Oxford. At the end he lost the sight of both eyes. His wife had died of cancer in 1890.

The last public words of the General were delivered before an audience of 10,000 in Royal Albert Hall in London:

"While women weep as they do now, I'll fight!
While little children go hungry as they do now,
I'll fight!
While men go to prison, in and out, I'll fight!
While there is a drunkard left,
While there is a poor girl left upon the streets,
While there remains one dark soul without the light
of God, I'll fight—I'll fight to the very end!"

During his lifetime the general relied mainly on his own children to fill the top Army posts around the world. For example, his son Ballington directed Salvation Army activities in the United States. When his brother Bramwell decided to shift almost everyone around, Ballington and his wife Maud objected. They had no wish to leave this country and thought their removal would jeopardize Army programs.

Finally in 1896 the Ballington Booths seceded from the Army and founded a similar but more democratic organization: the Volunteers of America. Ballington almost persuaded the majority of American Salvationists to follow his course but his sister Eva climbed up a fire escape and through a window to the hall where he was addressing Salvationists. She turned the audience away from schism.

The Volunteers of America operate 492 service units in the United States with 31,000 members and 336 officers. Like the Army, it constitutes an evangelical sect but it administers the sacraments of baptism and holy communion. Its social welfare activities parallel those of the larger Army. The only son of the Ballington Booths, Charles Brandon Booth, heads the Volunteers.

An earlier schism in 1882 by a Salvation Army leader in the United States resulted in formation of the American

Rescue Workers who report about 4,200 members. Headquarters is in Philadelphia.

Bramwell Booth seemed to view the Salvation Army as a dynasty which his children would inherit. He was removed from office in 1928 by seven commissioners who wanted to change the method by which generals were chosen. Originally an incumbent general wrote the name of his successor on a piece of paper which was sealed in an envelope and opened only at his death. Today the general is elected by the High Council.

Membership in the Salvation Army in the U. S. today stands at more than 331,000. The great majority are "soldiers," not officers. The program in this country is directed by 5,595 officers and cadets. Officers, men and women, are considered ordained ministers. The Army operates 8,913 centers and Sunday Schools which enroll some 121,000 pupils. The Army in the U. S. also employs some 15,300 civilians such as nurses and social workers.

Around the world the Salvation Army staffs 16,065 corps or outposts in 70 countries with 25,000 officers. Its institutions include 521 homes for the homeless, 205 men's work centers, 29 general hospitals, 12 convalescent hospitals, 86 maternity homes for unwed mothers, 6 leprosaria, 67 clinics, 13 probation homes, and 124 fresh air camps. The worldwide Army enlists more than 1 million soldiers.

Basic to Salvationist evangelistic techniques is the street meeting. With a brass band to attract attention, the officers station themselves on a street corner. The meeting may begin with a prayer and include Bible reading, testimonials, and hymn singing. Later on the group will march to the nearby citadel.

On Saturday night the ex-boozers may take the floor in the testimonial part of the meeting. Stubble-faced Joe Z. takes his turn. "I drank paints, liniment, extracts, anything that had alcohol in it. Denatured alcohol used to taste just like honey to me. I drank half a pint to half a gallon a day. People used to say I'd drink embalming fluid."

Joe looks over the crowd and continues his story. "I worked on high chimneys. Sometimes I'd get deliriums way up high. It would take whole fire companies to get me down when I got the death grip up there.

"But a Salvation Army man kept coming to my home. He wouldn't stay away. He told me God loves drunkards like me. And one day I saw the light. There's power in the Blood, yes, sir, there's power in the Blood or I wouldn't be here tonight."

The hall echoes with a few "Amens" and "Praise to Jesus" ejaculations. Another reformed alcoholic gets to his feet and starts to tell his story.

Rarely do recovered alcoholics ever become Salvation Army officers. Those whom the Army converts or rehabilitates may decide to remain as soldiers or may prefer to join some other Church. The Army tolerates no nominal members—every soldier must help in some way with the work of the citadel. As a soldier a convert may buy a uniform and devote his spare hours to social work, evangelism, youth programs. All Salvationists must agree to abstain from liquor, tobacco, and gambling.

Many candidates for officership come from Salvation Army families in which the parents themselves are officers. The Army expects no college training but most candidates present high school diplomas. After a six months' probationary period as a local corps cadet the aspiring officer makes application for entrance into one of the training centers in New York, Chicago, San Francisco, or Atlanta.

The two-year course covers the Bible, theology, church discipline, music, homiletics, social work, bookkeeping, English, sociology, etc. The Army pays little attention to the liberal arts of literature, art, philosophy, history, and such subjects. Eighteen months are spent in the classroom and six months in the field. The two-year curriculum seems short enough considering the range of human problems faced by Salvation Army officers and the fact that this course suffices for ordination to the ministry. It would seem that more extensive training in theology, psychiatry, marriage counseling, and psychology would be desirable.

After graduation as Lieutenants, the new officers take additional correspondence courses and read a book a month on Army history and activities. When they pass exams on these subjects they become fully commissioned officers. Their formal training falls far short of that required by the Presbyterian, Lutheran, Episcopalian, and Congregationalist denominations, but they have about as much training as many fundamentalist preachers.

From its early days the Army has accorded equal rights to women. General Booth often said, "My best men are women." The regulations of the organization state: "A woman may hold any position of authority or power in the Army, from that of a local officer to that of General." Booth's daughter Eva (or Evangeline) was elected General in 1934.

Salvation Army officers may perform marriages, preach, conduct worship, bury the dead. They qualify as clergymen before the law and may serve as chaplains in the armed forces.

Officers must marry other officers to maintain their commissions. If an officer marries a soldier, he (or she) must resign as an officer and give up active duty, but remain as a soldier and seek employment. If the non-officer marriage partner completed officers' training, the couple would be commissioned.

Moving up the hierarchy, the lieutenant may advance to captain, major, brigadier, lieutenant colonel and colonel. A lieutenant commissioner or commissioner is in charge of a territory such as the South or Midwest. The general lives in London. Since 1963 the Army has been commanded by General Frederick Coutts, a Scotsman.

Officers always wear the regulation uniform. Women officers may not wear earrings or broaches or style their hair. Each officer receives furnished quarters at his post. Base pay varies according to marital status, number of children and number of years of service. Pay now ranges from $45 a week for new married lieutenants to $85 a week for top officers.

The Army calls its doctrinal statement the "Articles of War." Prayer meetings are "knee drills" and an officer gets "marching orders" and "furloughs" instead of a new assignment and vacations. A bugler blows taps over the grave of a deceased officer when he is "Promoted to Glory." A church is a "citadel," the weekly magazine is *The War Cry*, and the weekly envelope is the "cartridge."

No longer does the Army confine its work to the skid rows and slums. It now sponsors day nurseries, hospitals, prison rehabilitation centers, a missing persons bureau, orphanages, summer camps, canteens, clinics, disaster relief programs, and an anti-suicide bureau. At 118 salvage centers men, usually alcoholics, collect old newspapers, furniture, and clothing. The clothing and furniture are repaired and sold at low cost to poor families while the newspapers, magazines, and rags are sent to paper mills for reprocessing. Proceeds are used for rehabilitation programs.

A decade ago 80% of the people helped by the Salvation Army had problems with alcohol but now 70% are involved with drugs. In a single year the Salvation Army will have contact with 800,000 young people through a variety of programs. Only a small fraction of these will ever become soldiers or officers in the Army.

In the United States, the Army operates 36 maternity homes and hospitals (often called Booth Memorial Hospitals) for unwed mothers. About 7600 expectant mothers receive care in these homes while thousands of others receive assistance from the Salvation Army. Officers who are registered nurses live at the maternity homes and other medical, professional, and technical personnel are employed as required.

More than 5000 convicts are paroled to the Army each year and another 7000 get assistance in obtaining discharges. The Army conducts evangelistic services within prison walls and sponsors the Brighter-Day league and Lifer clubs in a number of penitentiaries. Once outside the convict may get assistance from an Army employment bureau.

A French Salvation Army officer, Charles Pean, was mainly responsible for the decision to close the notorious penal colony, Devil's Island. He visited Devil's Island in 1928 and reported: "It seems impossible that in this twentieth century such an altogether scandalous and futile system could exist."

Over 400 jailers guarded 6000 prisoners whose moral and physical degradation was hard to imagine. Pean wrote three books exposing conditions in the colony. In 1945 the Salvation Army accepted the job of bringing the remaining 2000 prisoners back to France.

The Army's missing persons bureau locates more people than all the police departments in the country combined. No charge is made for this service and only rarely does the Army fail to locate its man. One rule which governs all missing persons work is that if the missing person does not want to disclose his whereabouts the Army will respect his wishes.

Salvationism has been called Methodism without sacraments. General Booth decided against administering baptism or communion. He believed that these sacraments simply divided Christians. Some Christians thought the only valid baptism was by immersion but others baptized by pouring or sprinkling. Some Churches taught the Real Presence in the Eucharist while others held it to be a simple memorial service. The General eliminated both sacraments but taught a theology similar to other evangelical sects.

The *Salvation Army Handbook of Doctrine* states: ". . . as it is the Salvation Army's firm conviction that these ceremonies are not necessary to salvation nor essential to spiritual progress, we do not observe them" (p. 160).

As substitutes for traditional sacraments the Army has its own ritual such as the signing of the Articles of War (against slumdom, bumdom, and rumdom) and the pledge of obedience and total abstinence. A ceremony surrounds the presentation of the colors, the Army flag with its blood and fire emblem. A Dedication of Children takes the place of water baptism. In this ceremony an Army officer accepts the child and recites the following formula: "In the name of the Lord and of the Corps of the Salvation

Army, I have taken this child, who has been fully given up by his (her) parents for the Salvation of the world. God save, bless, and keep this child. Amen."

A Salvation Army couple will be married in Army uniforms and participate in a cermony prescribed by Army regulations. As the bridegroom places the ring on his bride's finger he declares: "I put this ring upon your finger as a continual sign that we are married under the solemn pledges we have this day given, to live for God and fight in the ranks of the Salvation Army." The Army's *Orders and Regulations* allow some celebration after the ceremony but insist "rice, slipper throwing, or any other frivolous custom unworthy of the Army is forbidden."

In presenting the doctrine of the Fall of Man and the freedom of the will the Salvation Army leans more toward the traditional Catholic view than the Lutheran interpretation. The official handbook states that at the Fall "man's spiritual powers were marred, but not destroyed." A firm belief in the divinity of Jesus Christ and the existence of heaven and hell characterizes Salvationist preaching.

The type of practical evangelistic training which the Salvation Army supplies does not encourage theological study. Except for the lack of sacraments the Army presents a theology akin to that of any Fundamentalist or Holiness Church.

The Army does take a strong stand against the doctrine of predestination as expressed in classical Calvinism. It does not believe that some are predestined to be saved and others predestined to be lost. Salvation or damnation is a choice facing every man. Furthermore, the Army denies that because a man is once "saved" he is always saved. His salvation depends on his continuing free choice for God and against evil. Some Holiness Churches have taught "once saved always saved" but this is much too comfortable a doctrine for militant Salvationists.

Probably no American denomination enjoys the same measure of support from people of all faiths as does the Salvation Army. Rare is the man or woman who has never dropped a coin in the Army's Christmas kettle, purchased a copy of *The War Cry*, donated newspapers or old clothes, contributed to the Army through the United Fund or Community Chest, or been personally helped by the thousands of dedicated Salvationists.

FURTHER READING

Bishop, Edward, *Blood and Fire* (Chicago, Moody Press, 1964).

Chesham, Sallie, *Born to Battle*: *The Salvation Army in America* (Chicago, Rand McNally, 1965).

Neal, Harry Edward, *The Hallelujah Army* (Philadelphia, Chilton, 1961).

The Self-Realization Fellowship
□□□□□□□□□□

ONE OF SEVERAL movements to introduce Hinduism to Westerners, Self-Realization Fellowship (SRF) was founded by Paramahansa Yogananda in 1920. He had started the Yogoda Satsanga Society (SRF) three years before in his native India.

A witty and urbane guru, Yogananda came to the United States in 1920. He was born in Gorakhpur, India, and received monastic training for ten years in the hermitage of his guru, Swami Sri Yukteswar. Yogananda was made a Swami in 1914.

Through SRF Yogananda professed to present the teachings of original Yoga and original Christianity. He bought a 60-room hotel atop Mt. Washington in Los Angeles, which became headquarters for the movement. Here and in public lectures throughout the nation he instructed devotees in his mystical doctrines and the Kriya Yoga system based on scientific techniques of concentration, meditation, and exercise.

In 1932 Yogananda found a wealthy supporter in James J. Lynn who had acquired a fortune in business and insurance in Kansas City. Lynn mastered Kriya Yoga and succeeded Yogananda as president of SRF when the latter died in 1952. Lynn donated $1 million to the SRF in 1953 and bequeathed another $1 million and a stock portfolio.

The present head of the movement was born Faye Wright and raised a Mormon in Salt Lake City. She joined Self-Realization Fellowship as a renunciant in 1930. As Daya Mata (her monastic name) she became president of SRF when Lynn died in 1955.

Most SRF churches are found in California but there are meditation groups in Arizona, Michigan, New Jersey and New York as well as in Canada, Mexico, Argentina, Switzerland, India, Australia and several other countries.

Devotees come to the SRF Retreat at the colony in Encinitas, California, for meditation and spiritual instruction. The SRF Lake Shrine in Pacific Palisades has become a popular tourist attraction, as has the movement's India Center in Hollywood, which includes a small vegetarian restaurant.

Colony residents take monastic vows as monks and nuns of the Self-Realization Order, monastic branch of the Fellowship. They devote their full time to the work of the Order and to self-improvement. A new Gyanamata Ashram for nuns was completed at the Los Angeles head-quarters in 1968. The renunciants send healing vibrations by prayer to those who seek help in healing and liberation from disease, mental inharmonies, and spiritual ignorance.

Yogananda's *Autobiography of a Yogi* remains a perennial best seller as does his *Whispers from Eternity*. SRF probably counts several thousand devotees in the United States.

The Spiritualists
□□□□□□□□□□

"I HEAR THE NAME Ralph. Is there a Ralph here?"

"Here," stammers a gray-haired man across the aisle from me.

"Ralph Waters?"

"Yes."

"Your mother is standing next to me, Ralph, and says hello. And here is your brother Elmer and your Grandmother Swiggens and a whole group of your cousins. There is Alma and George and Elizabeth," reports the medium, an elderly lady in a black formal.

"And now I have a message for a Mary Elson. Are you here Mary?"

And so the recital of names and deceased relatives and messages continued for half an hour at the Saturday seance on a warm and sunny August afternoon at Camp Chesterfield, Indiana. The Indiana camp is probably the largest and best known Spiritualist camp in the world, rivaled only by the camp at Lily Dale, New York.

About 300 people had assembled in the musty, 750-seat Cathedral of the Woods for the demonstration. At the moment they were waiting expectantly for the clairvoyant to mention their names and relay a message from a dead parent or spouse or other relative.

The visiting medium, the Rev. Nellie Curry Hicock

of St. Petersburg, Florida, has been a practicing medium for 45 years.

During her clairvoyant demonstration she must have addressed 35 to 40 men and women in the audience. She called them by name and identified scores of deceased relatives and friends. Most of the spirit messages were trivial: we are fine on the other side, God bless you, your problems will be solved, etc.

At times Rev. Hicock complained that the spirits were crowding about her as she stood on the platform. There were so many spirits she had trouble sorting them out and getting their messages straight. Every now and then the medium addressed the spirits themselves and told them to kindly wait their turn and state their names and identifications clearly.

The Spiritualist camp, now in its 82nd year, attracts thousands of Spiritualists as well as the curious every summer. Some come for a day and some for a month or more to study spiritualism, participate in seances, obtain spiritual healing.

My wife and I arrived at about 4 o'clock at the little (2600 population) Indiana town of Chesterfield and drove into the grounds of the camp. No one asked for identification and there was no admission fee to the 48-acre camp grounds.

We parked near a row of cottages occupied by the mediums, some of whom stay at Chesterfield all year round. All told, the camp now has 24 resident mediums, six visiting mediums, and six spiritual healers. Each cottage has a sign which identifies the medium and her specialty: "Materializations at 8 p.m.," "Clairvoyance and Trumpet," "Private trances and direct voice." To visit a medium you had to make an appointment and pay a stipend averaging $3.

Before the 6:30 seance we strolled through the park-like grounds. We browsed at the Universal Bookstore which handles not only spiritualist literature but books on theosophy, New Thought, metaphysics, astrology, Unity and other occult fields. Later at the camp's gift shop we examined crystal balls, statues of St. Francis of Assisi, photographs of the late President Kennedy, and other souvenirs.

A leaflet gave practical instructions for crystal gazing:

"Keep the crystal clean and bright; only handle it when in use. Warm by holding near a fire and place on a piece of black or dark purple cloth. . . . The room should have a north aspect and be quiet and free from disturbances. The time most suitable is two hours after a light meal. Draw the window curtains so as to exclude nearly all light and leave the room in comparative darkness. Let what light there is fall over your shoulder on the crystal which may be held in the hand or placed on a small table. It should be about the same distance from your eyes as a book would be when reading. Concentrate your attention on the centre. Look into, not at it, and do not stare or inconvenience yourself. Some see at once, others take about ten minutes the first time of trying. If you do not succeed or cannot see clearly after looking for half an hour, put away the crystal and try again at the same hour the next day."

We stopped at the Merry-go-Round, a clean and bright snack bar. Here as elsewhere around the camp we noticed that at least two-thirds of the people were women, middle-aged or elderly. There were some family groups including small children, about 15 Negroes, and one group of Spiritualists who were speaking Spanish.

We paused at the Garden of Prayer which resembles a grotto. Two prie-dieux were placed before a life-size statue of Jesus. Plaster angels hovered on either side of the statue.

Inside the grotto several Spiritualists were engaged in a lively discussion of phenomena they had witnessed at the camp and back home. One gentleman explained that his favorite medium had actually raised to life a child declared dead 24 hours before. Another man told about his Master, a spirit who guides him in his development and introduced him to the mysteries of the unseen world. He insisted that he had seen his Master in person which the other Spiritualists considered quite unusual.

Near the Garden we came upon the Congress of Religion. In a large semicircle were busts of the founders of the world religions. The bust of Jesus stood in the center of the display against a background of the figures of Moses, Buddha, Zoroaster, Mohammed, and other religious leaders. Nearby, the Hett Memorial Museum housed relics of the founders of Spiritualism, spirit paintings, etc.

We decided to dine at the camp's cafeteria and by the time we finished it was almost 6:30. We walked past the outdoor fountain, noticed the lavender benches under the trees (lavender is a particularly good spiritual color), saw the chapel and the amphitheater known as The Grove, observed statues of an angel and an Indian, saw the three hotels where Spiritualist guests can stay for as little as $2.50 a night.

At the Cathedral we paid an attendant a dollar and received a hymnal and slip of paper on which was printed:

"Please address your billet to one or more loved ones in spirit, giving first and last names. Ask one or more questions and sign your full name."

The interior resembled an ordinary Protestant church. On the platform were a pulpit, chairs for the mediums, a table, and two candelabra. On one wall was a painting, at least 12 feet tall, of the Virgin and Child.

Before the service started the ushers collected the completed billets. A balding gentleman in his 60's stepped up to the pulpit and announced a hymn session. An enormously fat man played the piano on one side of the stage and a thin woman played the organ at the other side.

For about 20 minutes the congregation joined in singing such familiar hymns as "What a Friend We Have in Jesus," "Beyond the Sunset," and "Nearer, My God, to Thee." The song leader invited people to suggest their favorite hymns, which was a tactical mistake. People began to shout out names and numbers of hymns and those rejected seemed to take the rejection in a personal way. One lady named a song but the leader said it was not well known. She snorted, "You're never going to learn any new ones this way." The lady closed her hymn book and quit singing.

Finally two mediums entered from the rear of the stage and took their places. The younger medium in a chartreuse formal delivered an invocation and the audience stood to recite the Lord's Prayer. Nellie Curry Hicock stood next to the table and started to call out names and spirits.

Was her demonstration of clairvoyance a genuine spiritualistic phenomenon? I do not know. I do know that she was introduced as someone who was known to almost everyone in the audience, the regular visitors to the camp. I knew too that everyone who filled out a billet had signed his or her full name, indicated several spirits, and asked one or two questions. These had been collected and were probably available to the mediums. On the other hand the medium might have enjoyed telepathic sensitivities that enabled her to read the minds of some of the people in the Cathedral.

She was relieved by the Rev. Penninah Umbach, who took off her glasses, carefully pasted adhesive tape over her eyes, and covered them with a green blindfold. The Rev. Umbach sat at a table and fondled what were said to be the billets written by the audience. She too claimed to be able to converse with spirits who surrounded her and begged to be allowed to say hello. The messages seldom went beyond a greeting or a "God bless you."

In front of me sat a sad-faced man, a widower with two teen-age children. They held hands and were trying to get in touch with the recently deceased wife and mother. Neither the clairvoyant nor the billet reader had any messages for them.

At the finale of the seance a male medium took over the platform and announced an experiment in spirit writing. He handed a pack of supposedly plain 4 x 5 cards to the Rev. Umbach to be "magnetized" and passed other cards to members of the congregation to examine. These were collected and dumped into a wicker basket. A handful of pencils was thrown into the basket and the basket was covered by another basket and then a large cloth. The medium said that sensitive souls could probably hear the scratching of the pencils as the spirits wrote their messages. He passed among the people and held the covered basket to their ears. Many nodded in agreement. Meanwhile the congregation sang several verses of "In the Garden."

The medium took his basket back to the stage, uncovered it and looked to see if any of the spirits had chosen to deliver messages. Sure enough, there must have been 20 or more messages among the many blank cards. As he called the names of recipients an usher delivered the cards. The middle-aged lady back of us wept, "I got a letter from my daddy." I examined some of the cards; they were handwritten and each had a simple colored pencil sketch of either a trumpet, lilies, or Bible.

This concluded the seance. Many of the participants now hurried to the cottages for private appointments with the resident mediums. The spirits still had a couple of hours of work ahead of them.

From early June to late August the Camp Chesterfield mediums offer all types of spiritualistic phenomena. A devotee would have to spend weeks to witness all of them including table tipping, trumpet voices, spirit photography, the production of ectoplasm, spiritual healing, rappings, crystal ball gazing, ouija board, levitation, direct voice.

For five days in late August the camp offered a short course in Spiritualism for believers. During these days they could study such subjects as the human aura, occult anatomy, numerology, ESP, biblical spiritualism, and graphology.

To most of the serious visitors to Camp Chesterfield Spiritualism not only demonstrates that the living can communicate with the dead but that Spiritualism itself is a religion, a science, and a philosophy of life. Some Spiritualists reveal a hostility toward organized Christianity and to all dogmas and creeds.

Spiritualists may read the Bible and revere Jesus but only because he was the greatest of all mediums. His healings are understood as spiritual healings, the Transfiguration is a "materialization," the angels of the Bible are spirit messengers, etc.

The National Spiritualist Association of Churches defines Spiritualism as "the Science, Philosophy and Religion of continuous life, based upon the demonstrated fact of communication, by means of mediumship, with those who live in the Spirit World." A medium is "one whose organism is sensitive to vibrations from the spirit world and through whose instrumentality, intelligences in that world are able to convey messages and produce the phenomena of Spiritualism."

Technically spiritualism is a philosophy opposed to materialism and the correct name for the religion we are discussing is "Spiritism." Yet members of the cult never use this term and we will use the more common term.

Evocation of the spirits of the dead for purposes of divination goes back to ancient history. The Hebrews dabbled in necromancy and God condemned them for it:

"Neither let there be found among you any one . . . that consulteth soothsayers, or observeth dreams and omens. Neither let there be any wizard, nor charmer, nor any one that consulteth pythonic spirits, or fortune tellers; or that seeketh the truth from the dead. For the Lord abhorreth all these things: and for these abominations he will destroy them at thy coming" (Deuteronomy 18:10-12).

To this and other Old Testament condemnations modern Spiritualists counter with quotations such as from 1 John 4:1, "Believe not every spirit: but try the spirits if they be of God."

Despite the antiquity of necromancy, the modern religion of Spiritualism dates back to 1848. Its advent had been prepared by the spirit communications of the Swedish mystic Emanuel Swedenborg. Swedenborg claimed to be able to converse with spirits, and Stockholm became a center of early seances. The forerunner of hypnotism—mesmerism—also aroused people's interest in mysterious powers and forces.

Even before the founding of Spiritualism, Andrew Jackson Davis, the Poughkeepsie Seer, had produced trance writings and was giving trance lectures in New York City in 1844. He eventually produced 26 volumes of spiritualistic speculation which has remained the Bible of the movement. He called his chief work *Nature's Divine Revelations*.

In 1847 John Fox, his wife and two small daughters moved from Rochester to the village of Hydesville, New York. Neighbors said their new house was haunted and soon after the Foxes moved in they were startled to hear strange noises and rappings. One day when the rappings began, young Katie snapped her fingers and said, "Here, Mr. Splitfoot, do as I do!" The invisible rapper responded with the same number of raps. A simple code of raps was worked out and the spirit provided answers to various questions posed by the family. The date the spirit first answered Katie—March 31, 1848—is accepted as the birth of modern Spiritualism.

The spirit rapper revealed that he had been murdered in the Fox cottage many years before. The family dug in the cellar and found a skeleton.

Now an older Fox daughter, Leah, took over the management of the sisters, Margaret and Katie, and all three became professional mediums. They toured the country giving demonstrations. In a few years Spiritualism had won at least 100,000 adherents and you could find 100 mediums in New York City and another 60 in Philadelphia. Distinguished Americans such as Horace Greeley,

Henry James, W. Lloyd Garrison, James Fenimore Cooper, William Cullen Bryant, Daniel Webster, Harriet Beecher Stowe, and Hamlin Garland either embraced Spiritualism or took a keen interest in its claims.

The cult spread to Europe in 1852, taking first root in Scotland. A Scot, Daniel Dunglas Home, became the most famous of all mediums and the only leading medium of his era who was never compromised in any fraud or trickery. After giving a number of seances in the United States, Home returned to Europe and married a rich Russian noblewoman. Among his phenomena are levitation, elongation of his body by as much as 11 inches, and spirit accordion playing. Home joined the Roman Catholic Church in 1856 and gave up his mediumship.

William Stainton-Moses, an Anglican minister, started to hold seances in 1872. He specialized in levitation, apparitions, and automatic writing. Victorian England turned to seances as an amusing pastime.

In France and elsewhere on the continent most Spiritualists adopted the doctrines of Allan Kardec. He taught that some spirits return again and again to earth in a series of reincarnations. Few American Spiritualists accept reincarnation. In October, 1930 the National Spiritualist Association passed a resolution which declared that "acceptance of the doctrine of Reincarnation as a principle of Spiritualism subverts the chief premise of our teaching, which is that of continuity of life, recognition of departed friends and reunion."

Life did not treat the Fox sisters kindly. Margaret was sent to school by Horace Greeley, then entered a common-law marriage with an Englishman who went back to his native country and left her pregnant. She started to drink. She startled the Spiritualist world by joining the Catholic

Church. On October 21, 1888 Margaret and Katie both appeared at an anti-Spiritualist meeting in a New York auditorium. Maggie told the crowd: "I am here tonight as one of the founders of Spiritualism to denounce it as absolute falsehood . . . the most wicked blasphemy known to the world." She then showed how she and her sister had produced the raps by cracking their big toes. The sisters said they started by trying to fool their parents and then were exploited by their older sister Leah.

But a year later Margaret renounced Catholicism and retracted her confession. She turned again to mediumship to make a living. Within a few years both Fox sisters were dead, victims of alcoholism. The vices and confessions of the Fox sisters embarrass devout Spiritualists but they are still honored as the high priestesses of the religion.

By the end of the 19th century interest in Spiritualism had waned; the exposé by Maggie and Katie and the many cases of fraud repelled most inquirers. The revival of interest came during and after World War I when bereaved relatives turned to seances to make contact with fallen soldiers. In England in particular the movement gained a roster of distinguished converts which gave Spiritualism a prestige there that it has never enjoyed in the land of its birth.

Three British Spiritualists of great integrity and reputation were Sir William Crookes, Sir Oliver Lodge, and Sir Arthur Conan Doyle. Crookes (1832-1919) served as president of the British Association for the Advancement of Science and was the discoverer of the element thallium. Lodge, another former president of the BAAS, to be the spirit messages of his son who had been killed in battle in France. Sir Arthur Conan Doyle, the creator published a book entitled *Raymond*, which purported of Sherlock Holmes, promoted the cause of Spiritualism by pen and lecture platform. In more recent years Lord Dowding, former head of the Royal Air Force, was a convinced Spiritualist as was Mackenzie King, prime minister of Canada.

The Sunday Times of London has estimated there are 1000 Spiritualist churches in England with 250,000 members. English Spiritualism displays a distinctly anti-clerical and anti-Christian character which is rare in U. S. Spiritualism.

James A. Pike, the controversial Episcopalian bishop, participated in six seances in 1967 in which he reported that he had made contact with his deceased son. One of the mediums at these seances was the Rev. Arthur A. Ford of Philadelphia, an ordained Disciples of Christ minister. Through his spirit control—"Fletcher"—the medium relayed messages from the bishop's son who had committed suicide in 1966. Fletcher told the bishop: "This boy says that before he came over he was confused and mentally disturbed. He wants you to understand that neither you, nor any other member of the family, has any right to feel that you have failed him in any way." The bishop considered the evidence of the seances to be convincing proof of life after death.

Perhaps the largest body of Spiritualists in the world is that in Brazil where the cult poses a serious threat to Christianity. *Time* magazine estimated that in 1959 there were 10,000,000 Brazilian Spiritualists out of a total population of 61,000,000. The Brazilian Spiritual Federation, only one of many Spiritualist organizations, claims 3600 centers. The Brazilian government issued a special stamp in 1957 commemorating the "First Centenary of Organized Spiritism"; the stamp featured a portrait of Allan

Kardec. There are at least another 1,000,000 Spiritualists in other countries of Latin America, such as Haiti.

How many Spiritualists are in the United States is hard to determine. The International General Assembly of Spiritualists reported 209 churches with 164,000 members in 1956, but more current figures are not available. The National Spiritualist Association of Churches, probably the most influential body, lists 4962 members. The National Spiritual Alliance of the United States of America reports 3180 members; it broke from the National Spiritualist Association in 1913 over the question of reincarnation. There are at least a dozen smaller Spiritualist groups including the Spiritual Science Church, Aquarian Brotherhood of Christ, Independent Spiritualist Association, Spiritualist Episcopal Church, and the Universal Spiritualist Association.

Some students of the movement suggest that for every enrolled member in a Spiritualist church there are from 10 to 15 people who dabble in Spiritualism. Most Spiritualist congregations are small and meet in rented halls or rooms. Spiritualist Churches, publications, and organizations seem to be plagued by financial problems. Growth areas for the cult seem to be in Florida and Southern California, indicating possibly that the mediums enjoy the sunshine.

Spiritualist pastors and mediums may attend a two-year course at the Morris Pratt Institute in Whitewater, Wisconsin. This seminary is sponsored by the National Spiritualist Association and seeks to raise educational and ethical standards. A Spiritualist pastor will ordinarily perform as a medium but not all mediums seek ordination to the ministry. Mediums who engage in fraud and trickery find refuge in ordination since few public officials care to tamper with freedom of religion by prosecuting an ordained clergyman.

Spiritualism teaches that death is easy and painless. After death the spirit finds himself inhabiting a body similar to the one he had during life except that his spiritual body exhibits no deformities or disease.

A common Spiritualist description of the spirit world includes seven spheres. The unrepentant wicked go to the two lowest spheres but most people start at the third or Summerland sphere. The spirits in Summerland live much as do human beings except that they experience no sorrow or evil or disease. They live in houses, wear clothes, keep pets, marry their soul mates. As these spirits undergo purification they may advance to higher spheres such as the fourth sphere for philosophers, the fifth for contemplatives, the sixth or love sphere, and the seventh known as the Christ sphere. Spiritualists are universalists, that is, they believe that every soul will eventually be saved. All true Spiritualists emphatically discard the belief in a heaven and hell.

The messages received in the seance room usually originate from the spirits in Summerland who have died recently. As the spirit's own loved ones pass to the next sphere the spirit loses interest in communicating with the living. Most of the spirit messages come through a guide or control and most of these seem to be North American Indians. They are known to mediums and Spiritualists by such names as Silver Birch, Red Cloud, and White Feather. The messages come from the spirit to the control to the medium to the receiver. Psychologists suggest that these controls are really secondary personalities of the mediums who take over while the medium is in a trance.

Naturally most people entertain a healthy skepticism

about the authenticity of spiritualistic phenomena. The circumstances of the typical seance lend themselves to trickery. Seances are usually held in a dark or semi-darkened room. The medium may insist that everyone hold hands, which frustrates tactile investigation, or sing, which muffles mechanical sounds. When scientists investigate these phenomena in the light with accurate instruments nothing happens.

Houdini, the master magician, contended that he could duplicate any feat of any medium. He advertised a standing offer of $10,000 to any medium who could fool him. Houdini knew what sleight-of-hand, wires, mirrors, and hidden apparatus could accomplish, especially when the audience consisted of credulous people in a dark room. On the other hand Conan Doyle intimated that Houdini himself was one of the greatest of all mediums and performed many of his tricks through preternatural methods.

Most of us have very little idea how a professional stage magician performs his tricks and illusions. A lady vanishes in a locked trunk, a message is found in an egg, a man floats in mid-air. We are mystified and yet we know that the conjurer is simply fooling us. How much easier it is for a dishonest medium to perform the relatively simple tricks of the seance room for bereaved and emotionally disturbed people.

The Catholic Church has never pronounced on the authenticity of any spiritualistic phenomena, nor does she maintain that all mediums and Spiritualists seek to evoke demons; common sense tells us that most people who frequent seances simply seek to communicate with dead loved ones.

The Roman Catholic Church does forbid the faithful in general from participating in seances and dabbling in

Spiritualistic phenomena. The Holy Office condemned Spiritualism in 1898 and again in 1917. Fr. Herbert Thurston, S. J. explains:

"The attitude of Catholic authority in the matter is based upon the matured conviction that for the ill-instructed, the idly curious, and the emotional, who are for the most part the very people upon whom the occult exercises the strongest attraction, any contact with the intelligences which purport to communicate from the other world can only be disquieting, and morally, if not physically dangerous" (*Spiritualism*, p. 18).

Serious scientific investigation is another matter and to this the Church raises no objection. For example, the Society for Psychical Research, founded in 1882, attempts to subject phenomena to laboratory tests. Dr. J. B. Rhine pioneered in the areas of parapsychology at Duke University. He explored such phenomena as telepathy and clairvoyance.

As a religious movement almost 130 years old, Spiritualism has little to show for itself. Its devotees believe that Spiritualism conclusively proves human immortality, but even if the phenomena were assumed to be genuine they would not prove this much. The survival of some spirits who communicate in a seance does not mean that all human beings survive death. Again, the survival of any particular spirit would not prove immortality but only that this spirit had so far escaped extinction. The question of imposture plagues Spiritualism. A spirit may claim to be a person's mother or father but what proof can there be that the spirit is not an imposter, not to say an evil spirit?

Even Spiritualists must ask themselves occasionally how the spirits can be trustworthy guides since the volumes of published spirit communications are patently contradictory. When all has been said, nothing of any great consequence has ever been communicated to the living by the spirits. Their messages are commonplace, trivial, and contradictory.

Spiritualism as a movement lacks any cohesion. Most of its capable intellectual defenders have themselves gone to the spirit world. No doubt the most famous American clairvoyant today is Jeane Dixon, not a Spiritualist at all, but a Roman Catholic.

A convinced Spiritualist, Hunter Mackintosh, discussed the future of Spiritualism in the November, 1965 issue of *Two Worlds,* the leading English journal. He imagined himself a future historian and observed:

"There will be few contemporary records of this movement for our historian to examine because Spiritualism made so little impact on society, on culture and on religion that its very existence was mostly ignored in the chronicles of the times. . . . Undoubtedly he will be surprised to find that a movement which promised so much actually achieved so little. . . . Spiritualism was unequal to the task of persuading the world to accept the notion that we continue to exist after death. Our historian will clearly perceive that this lamentable failure was due to a lack of spiritual perception and intellectual vigour which ultimately destroyed Spiritualism more effectively than any persecution or suppression by its enemies could have done" (p. 387).

Mackintosh noted that the Spiritualist movement is more than a century old and contrasted its slow growth with that of Buddhism, Christianity, Islam, and Communism 100 years after their births. He condemns Spiritualism's distrust of scientific research and its anti-intellectualism.

FURTHER READING

Braden, Charles, *These Also Believe,* Chapter 9, "Spiritualism" (New York, Macmillan, 1953).

Liljencrants, Johan, *Spiritism and Religion* (New York, Devin-Adair, 1918).

Pike, James A. with Diane Kennedy, *The Other Side* (Garden City, N. Y., Doubleday, 1968).

The Spiritualist Manual, 7th ed. (Washington, D.C., National Spiritualist Association of the United States of America, 1944).

Thurston, Herbert, *The Church and Spiritualism* (Milwaukee, Bruce, 1933).

The Swedenborgians
🔲🔲🔲🔲🔲🔲🔲🔲

MOVIE AND THEATER goers who watched the Irish nurse Anne Sullivan break through to the dark world of the little girl in *The Miracle Worker* might be surprised to learn that when the girl grew up she joined one of the oldest and oddest Christian sects: Swedenborgianism. The late Helen Keller who broke out of the prison of blindness and deafness was a Swedenborgian.

Although far older than Mormonism or Christian Science and tiny in comparison to their memberships, Swedenborgianism has exerted an influence on these and many other religious movements which would be hard to overestimate. Spiritualism, Mormonism, New Thought have all felt the impact of Swedenborgian theology.

Swedenborgians follow the curious doctrines of scientist-turned-theologian Emanuel Swedenborg (1688-1772). The two U. S. branches of this faith enroll fewer than 7000 adherents and Swedenborgianism is otherwise confined to England, Australia, and a few foreign missions.

Swedenborg, born in Stockholm, was raised a Lutheran. In fact his father was chaplain to the king and later Lutheran bishop of Skara. Emanuel was a brilliant student who received a doctorate from Upsala at 21, toured Europe, and threw himself into many fields of science. Before turning to religion at the age of 55 he had authored 60 scientific books and papers.

This latter-day da Vinci was a professional philosopher, physicist, geologist, metallurgist, mathematician, botanist, musician, zoologist, astronomer, mining engineer, chemist, physiologist, bookbinder, clockmaker, lens grinder, editor, and mineralogist. Charles XII appointed him assayer of mines in 1716.

Henry James called Swedenborg the "sanest and most far-reaching intellect this age has known." Thomas Carlyle said of him: "A man of great and indisputable cultivation, strong, mathematical intellect, and the most pious, seraphic turn of mind; a man beautiful, lovable, and tragical to see. . . . One of the loftiest minds in the realm of mind." Balzac, Coleridge, Emerson, and the Howells all discussed the ideas of Swedenborg. The Swedish seer also influenced Kant and Goethe whose *Faust* represents the Swedenborgian world view.

After this remarkably fruitful career in the sciences and government services, Swedenborg issued a claim that he was able to converse with inhabitants of the spirit world. In 29 books on religion, including his *True Christian Religion,* he described in minute detail the flora and fauna of heaven, hell, and the intermediate spirit world. His writings were all in Latin and the complete set fills two or three library shelves.

Swedenborg reported lengthy conversations with Luther, Melanchthon, and Calvin. He persuaded Luther that he had been wrong about his ideas of faith without works. One of Swedenborg's "discoveries" was that marriage continues after death with some possible reshuffling of mates, while the unmarried like himself may find their soul mates in the next world.

The Swedish theologian declared that the Old Testament, four Gospels, and Book of Revelation were authoritative but that St. Paul and Luther were in error. He devised an allegorical interpretation of the Bible. In his system cites in the Bible always typify systems of belief, stones stand for truth, houses are intelligence, snakes are carnality, etc.

He denied the Trinity. Jesus Christ was God Himself and the Trinity represented three aspects of Christ. He claimed that Jesus appeared to him in 1745 and introduced him to the spiritual meaning of Scripture.

At death men go to the realm where they will feel most at home. It may be heaven, hell, or the spirit world which is a sort of purgatory. The other world is much like this one and men go about doing what they like to do, living in houses, etc. He was also sure that other planets were inhabited by races of men far superior to those on earth.

The Last Judgment was not to come. It had come in 1757 and had been witnessed by Swedenborg himself. He especially hated the Protestant doctrine of justification by faith alone which, he said, was the great dragon of revelation. However, despite his quarrels with orthodox Lutheranism he never left the Church; he quit attending services because the spirits constantly interrupted the sermons to correct the preachers' mistakes.

He went to England in 1771 and remained there until his death a year later. For many years he had moved from Stockholm, to Amsterdam, to London, and back. In 1908 his body was returned to Sweden where it is buried in the cathedral in Upsala.

His writings antedated modern spiritualism by almost a century but certainly gave direction to the spiritualism spawned by the Fox sisters in 1848. Prof. Emeritus Charles Braden of Northwestern points out that Swedenborg's books were well known at this time and prepared many people to accept spiritualism.

His ideas on eternal marriage found permanent roots in the marriage doctrines of the Mormons. The latter marry not for time but for time and eternity. Swedenborg was revered as a "divinely illuminated seer and revelator" by his followers; Joseph Smith took the title "prophet, seer, and revelator" of his new Church.

Warren Felt Evans, a Swedenborgian clergyman healed by Phineas P. Quimby, wrote two books on mental healing before Mrs. Eddy was able to get her own *Science and Health* to press. She certainly knew Evans' theories which were colored in part by his Swedenborgianism.

Swedenborg himself never founded a Church. About a dozen years after his death a group of Englishmen including two Anglican preachers, Thomas Hartly and John Clawes, organized the Church of the New Jerusalem. The movement won converts in the Lancaster area. It spread to America in 1792 and societies were established around Baltimore. A church was set up in 1817. In 1890 a large number of Swedenborgians in Pennsylvania left the original group and established a second branch. In general the New Church has been confined to the Atlantic seaboard.

The original group, known as the General Convention of the New Jerusalem in the United States of America, claims only 4070 members in 56 churches. It operates a tiny theological seminary at Cambridge, Massachusetts. Well endowed by some wealthy members it can offer seminary training for an annual tuition of only $25 and provides free room and board to ministerial candidates, single or married. The student body rarely numbers more than four. There are 32 ordained Swedenborgian ministers.

This older branch also controls the Swedenborg Foundation of New York City which publishes and distributes Swedenborg's writings. A modest advertising campaign to acquaint Americans with the teachings of the cult is also financed by the Foundation.

The smaller General Church of the New Jerusalem maintains headquarters at Bryn Athyn, Pennsylvania. It supports 12 churches, a seminary, and academies for boys and girls. Its current membership is given at 1805. The General Church claims to adhere more closely to Swedenborg's theology and accords him more divine honor than the older branch. It has a mission in South Africa.

The English Swedenborgians number about 7000. The two American groups are barely holding their own. In fact the General Convention reported more members in 1911—8500—than it does today. Despite efforts at proselytizing, the cult seems unable to interest many in Swedenborg's dreams and allegories.

Miss Keller, who called Swedenborg "one of the noblest champions true Christianity has ever known," was converted to Swedenborgianism early in her life. She declared that he had found "the word of God . . . freed from the blots and stains of barbarous creeds." Her friends, the Macys, thought Swedenborg was a bit crazy, and, when Helen referred to the seer Anne Sullivan Macy rebuked her saying, "You know perfectly well you're talking moonshine."

A number of other Americans have been Swedenborgians, including the father of Henry and William James who was a Swedenborgian clergyman, the financial expert Barron, poet Vachel Lindsay, landscape painter George Inness, and popular newspaper poet Edgar Guest.

The liturgy of the New Church is based on the Anglican Book of Common Prayer. The Church celebrates the

Lord's Supper four times a year. It baptizes infants as well as adults and confirms adult believers. The best known Swedenborgian church is probably the Wayfarers' Chapel at Portuguese Bend, California. Designed by the son of Frank Lloyd Wright, the chapel is built of glass supported by redwood girders. It is the picturesque scene of many weddings, some from the movie colony.

The Church of the New Jerusalem seems doomed to extinction. It has difficulty holding its own adherents much less winning converts to Swedenborg's bizarre notions. Americans are likely to dismiss the Swedish seer as a brilliant scientist who "flipped." Still Swedenborgianism has had its influence on American religious life and directly on several flourishing cults. It cannot be ignored in any consideration of contemporary religious sects.

FURTHER READING

Swedenborg, Emanuel, *The True Christian Religion* (London and New York, J. M. Dent and E. P. Dutton, 1933).

Trowbridge, George, *Swedenborg: Life and Teaching* (New York, Swedenborg Foundation, 1944).

The Theosophists

SCORES OF CONTEMPORARY occult movements owe a debt to the imaginative creation of Madame Helena P. Blavatsky known as Theosophy. The revival of interest in the occult which began in the late 1960's has given new life to Theosophy. Theosophy's mystical teachings are once again attracting attention.

Madame Blavatsky, a Russian noblewoman, was born in 1831 and even as a child was known as clairvoyant and psychic. She married a Russian general at the age of 17 but left him after two months and spent the next quarter century wandering throughout the world. She visited Paris, London, Greece, Egypt, India, South America, and the United States.

She became a spiritualist medium and claimed to have received special revelations from mysterious Masters or Mahatmas. These Masters were said to be men who were eligible to reach the state of nirvana but chose to remain in human bodies in order to assist mankind in its spiritual evolution. They lived in remote regions of Tibet, China, India, Syria, and the Far East.

Joined by a former Civil War colonel and lawyer, Henry S. Olcott, Madame Blavatsky founded the Theosophical Society of New York in 1875. Her occult sytem borrowed heavily from Buddhism and Hinduism as well as spiritualism and gnostic Christianity. The Society also resembled Freemasonry in its rituals.

She wrote several of the basic texts of the Theosophical movement including *The Secret Doctrine* and *Isis Unveiled*. Fr. C. C. Martindale, S. J., a student of occultism, wrote: "Her information was encyclopaedic, but altogther confused, always inaccurate, often entirely misleading, and wholly at the mercy of her riotous imagination and unscrupulous methods. The Society for Psychic Research investigated Madame Blavatsky while she was living in India and declared that she was 'one of the most accomplished, ingenious and interesting imposters in history.' "

Relations cooled between the Madame and the Colonel and she withdrew from an active role in the Theosophical Society to direct a secret Esoteric Society in London. Under the leadership of William Q. Judge the American branch withdrew from the world movement in 1895. One of the earliest American Theosophists was Abner Doubleday, also noted as the inventor of baseball.

Madame Blavatsky died in 1891 and Col. Olcott in 1907. Mrs. Annie Besant (1847-1933) assumed control of the Theosophical Society. Mrs. Besant had married an Anglican clergyman, divorced him, lost her faith in Christianity, embraced atheism, and finally adopted Theosophy. She claimed the right of succession when the Madame died and produced a green ring given her by the founder as proof of her claim.

Mrs. Besant moved to India where she became active in Indian politics and the independence movement and was elected president of the Indian National Congress in 1917. She founded a college of Theosophy which became the University of Benares. Wealthy patrons supported her activities and she won the allegiance of most English, Indian, and Dutch Theosophists.

A former spiritualist medium, Mrs. Katherine Tingley, took charge of the American branch when Judge died. She declared she was the "Purple Mother" of Theosophical mythology and founded the Point Loma Theosophical Community in San Diego, Calif. She acquired 490 acres and built a number of buildings the largest of which was called The Homestead. This was a residence with 90 rooms and a green glass dome. Initiates from 25 countries turned over their money to Mrs. Tingley and lived in the community.

Annie Besant feuded with Mrs. Tingley for years. She carried the fight to California where she set up a temple and vegetarian restaurant in Hollywood. The two Theosophical rivals excommunicated each other and bid for the loyalty of Madame Blavatsky's students.

Annie played a trump card when she adopted an Indian lad by the name of Krishnamurti and announced that he was the reincarnation of Christ. He was the messiah the world was awaiting. Krishnamurti traveled throughout Europe with Mrs. Besant and arrived in New York City in 1926 with the publicity usually reserved for heads of state. He lectured in major U. S. cities and was hosted by members of the Order of the Star, Mrs. Besant's American followers.

Plans for a huge Theosophical colony in Ojai, Cal. were revealed by Mrs. Besant but never materialized. Interest in Theosophy sagged and within a few years both Mrs. Tingley and Mrs. Besant had died. The Homestead went bankrupt and the faithful remnant moved to Pasadena.

Theosophy today is fragmented with a total world

membership of perhaps 35,000 in 1300 lodges. Adyar in India, where the Society owns a 266-acre estate, is world headquarters. The independent American movement has its headquarters in Wheaton, Ill. and reports approximately 5000 adherents. Smaller groups of Theosophists belong to separate organizations in California.

As in Madame Blavatsky's day the Theosophical Society lists three basic objectives: "To form a nucleus of the Universal Brotherhood of Humanity, without distinction of race, creed, sex, case, or color; to encourage the study of comparative religion, philosophy, and science; and to investigate the unexplained laws of Nature and the powers latent in man."

Theosophists teach that besides the material world there are six invisible worlds of subtle matter. These worlds interpenetrate the visible world as water interpenetrates a sponge. Man himself possesses three bodies: the physical body of activity, the astral body of emotion, and the mental body of thought.

Man is perfectible and passes through a series of reincarnations to rid himself of his impurities. The law of Karma explains the misfortunes and sufferings of this life as a consequence of sins in a previous life. Man is ultimately responsible for whatever befalls him, even though he has no remembrance of previous existences.

Theosophical ideas have been incorporated by such groups as the Rosicrucians (AMORC), I AM, Unity School of Christianity, Liberal Catholics, sections of the New Thought movement, and the countless cults which inhabit Southern California.

Given the new interest in Eastern religions and mysticism, as well as the revival of astrology, numerology, and the like, the prospects for Theosophy in the immediate future are brighter than they have been for several decades. The Theosophical Society of America has expanded its book publishing program and lecture series. Not many who read Theosophical literature will be moved to join a Theosophical lodge but the rebirth of occultism in recent years has given the movement new hope.

FURTHER READING

Blavatsky, Helena P., *Isis Unveiled and The Secret Doctrine,* various editions.

Symonds, John, *The Lady With the Magic Eyes: Madame Blavatsky—Medium and Magician* (New York, Thomas Yoseloff, 1960).

Williams, Gertrude Marvin, *Priestess of the Occult* (New York, 1946).

The Unity School of Christianity
□□□□□□□□□□

ALTHOUGH IT CLAIMS more than 260 Centers in the United States alone and offers spiritual guidance to millions of people, it is not even mentioned in the standard *Yearbook of American Churches* which enumerates some 265 churches and sects.

It calls itself a "nonsectarian religious educational institution" and disclaims any identification as a separate denomination but it trains and ordains ministers, operates churches and Sunday Schools, provides rituals for baptism, worship, communion, weddings and funerals.

Its founders insisted that its teachings comprised a school of practical Christianity yet they attempted to mix Christian truths with a firm belief in reincarnation. Most of their followers have adopted a similar belief in a cycle of birth, death, and rebirth which orthodox Christians would reject.

This is the amazing Unity School of Christianity and some of its paradoxes.

From its magnificent 1200-acre headquarters in Lee's Summit, Mo., Unity sends out millions of magazines and tracts each year and yet many of its supporters know little or nothing about Unity's religious basis. At every hour of the day and night a corps of 150 men and women in the Silent Unity department receives requests for prayers and counsel. In a typical year 600,000 such petitions pour into Lee's Summit from Protestants, Catholics, and others.

In many ways Unity resembles Christian Science and yet we shall observe some basic differences between the two systems. More precisely we would classify the Unity School of Christianity as the largest and most successful of the dozens of New Thought groups which find their ultimate inspiration in the work of the 19th century New England faith healer, Phineas P. Quimby.

Unity and the other New Thought groups often display a familiar Christian vocabulary but attach quite different meanings to the terms. For example, they distinguish between Jesus (an historical person) and Christ or the Christ (the divine principle in every man). When they speak of God, the Trinity, or salvation they understand these words in a special metaphysical sense utterly foreign to the thinking of Catholics or most Protestants.

All New Thought groups including Unity emphasize health, prosperity, and happiness as everyone's birthright. God created man to be rich, healthy, beautiful, serene. Through prayer and affirmations an individual can overcome poverty, anxiety, ill health, alcoholism, personality defects.

A typical affirmation is the "Airplane Blessing" which may be recited by passengers and crew: "This is God's airplane. His intelligence is in every part of it. As He keeps the stars in their courses and the sun and moon in their paths, so He guides and directs this plane. He knows every highway and byway of the air even as He knows the highways and byways of the earth. I rest secure in His protecting presence, and all is well."

The main lesson to be learned is to get your mind off a particular trouble and think about God. This is essentially the message of all of the New Thought Churches whether

Unity, Divine Science, Church of Truth, Religious Science or others.

Some of the New Thought groups meet in rented hotel rooms or private homes while others have built substantial church buildings and enroll sizeable congregations. None of the other New Thought groups has anything to match Unity's headquarters at Lee's Summit.

At Unity Village some 500 full time workers write, print, and distribute the attractive publications which carry Unity's gospel of optimism around the world. All workers receive salaries competitive with those in the business world. The Village, which resembles a college campus, includes the administration building, 165-foot tower, Silent Unity center, an artificial lake, golf course, picnic areas, tennis courts, motel, swimming pool and one of the largest printing plants in the Midwest. To Unity Village come men and women preparing for ordination as ministers.

This entire plant as well as the extensive publishing operation is maintained by free will offerings. Although more than 1,000,000 copies of Unity's six major periodicals go to subscribers each month the cost of printing usually exceeds the subscription price. But the 6,000 letters received daily at headquarters often contain offerings in gratitude for healings or other help from Silent Unity. Some followers remember Unity in their will. Thousands of Prosperity Banks are distributed to Unity devotees. They are invited to meditate on the Prosperity Prayer and drop a contribution into the cardboard bank which is mailed to Lee's Summit after seven weeks.

The founder of this spiritual empire was a mild mannered, frail real estate broker who got the original idea for Unity from his wife. Charles Fillmore was born in a log cabin in Minnesota in 1854 and received a sketchy grade school education. As a youngster, he began to work as a printer's devil and then became a bank and grocery clerk, bookkeeper, mule-team driver, assayer, and finally a real estate broker. He made money in real estate but the bust of the Kansas City real estate boom in the mid-1880's drove him into near bankruptcy.

He married a former schoolteacher, a graduate of Oberlin College who belonged to the Methodist Church. His wife, Myrtle, had once contracted malaria and later suffered from tuberculosis. Charles was handicapped by a withered leg, curvature of the spine and deafness in one ear.

Despairing of medical help the Fillmores delved into an assortment of occult and faith healing systems. One of these systems had been worked out by Emma Curtis Hopkins, a former associate of Mary Baker Eddy and ex-editor of the *Christian Science Journal*. She and Mrs. Eddy had a falling out and Mrs. Hopkins began to teach her own version of Christian Science in Chicago. One of her students came to Kansas City to deliver a lecture and in his audience were Mr. and Mrs. Fillmore.

This lecture and further metaphysical study in the Kansas City College of Christian Science brought Myrtle Fillmore to the discovery of what she believed to be the secret of divine healing. Her recovery from TB took a full two years but she convinced her somewhat skeptical husband of the value of her healing methods. She capsulized her belief in the phrase: "I am a child of God and therefore I do not inherit sickness."

The basic Unity textbook by H. Emilie Cady states flatly: "There is no evil," and, "Pain, sickness, poverty, old age and death cannot master me for they are not real"

(*Lessons in Truth*, pp. 44-5). This echoes Mary Baker Eddy's assertion that "Sin, disease and death have no foundation in Truth."

Despite its debt to Christian Science, Unity differs from Mrs. Eddy's Church in several important respects. Unlike members of the Christian Science Mother Church those who wish to apply certain Unity principles to their lives need not sever connections with their own Churches. Unity also allows its adherents to submit to medical treatment without compromising their standing in the movement since Unity believes that not all men have reached the high spiritual plane which allows them to forego medicine and drugs in favor of spiritual healing. Unity healers never charge for their services while Christian Science practitioners bill their clients just as do M.D.'s. The use of spiritual power for evil ends known as Malicious Animal Magnetism in Christian Science has no place in Unity. Finally the authoritarianism of Christian Science has been rejected by the Fillmores and their children who direct the Unity movement.

While Christian Science denies the theory that germs or microbes cause disease, Unity admits the existence of microbes and advances a curious theory as to their origin. Fillmore explained that "thoughts of health will produce microbes to build up healthy organisms" while "thoughts of disease will produce microbes of disorder and destruction" (*Talks on Truth*, p. 18). Elaborating on his theory the founder of Unity explained: "Every thought that flits through the mind of every man, woman, and child in the universe produces a living organism, a microbe of a character like its producing thought" (p. 21). The medical doctor simply tries to kill the bad microbes but the student of Unity will get at the source and stop thinking bad thoughts which generate bad microbes and begin thinking good thoughts which will produce good microbes. It is rather futile to attack the microbes themselves. "To apply the remedy to the poor little microbe is like trying to stop the manufacture of counterfeit money by destroying all that is found in circulation" (p. 21).

Charles Fillmore began publishing a magazine called *Modern Thought* in 1884 and later changed the name to *Christian Science Thought*. This infuriated Mrs. Eddy who considered *Christian Science* her personal property. She threatened legal action against the Fillmores if they persisted in calling their magazine by this name. The Fillmores then chose the name "Unity" to designate their teachings.

The Fillmores promoted the ideas of Swami Vivekananda, an Indian yogi, who arrived in the United States in 1893. Over a period of years they obviously incorporated many aspects of Hinduism into their own religious system.

Threads of Theosophy, Rosicrucianism, Buddhism, Christianity, and other religious systems were also woven into Unity's eclectic fabric. In an early issue of his magazine Fillmore wrote: "We have taken more than 40 courses (in metaphysical subjects), some of them costing as much as $100."

At first Charles tried to carry on his business along with his religious work but from 1889 the Fillmores devoted all their energies to the promotion of Unity. They opened an office in Kansas City. Charles and Myrtle taught classes in spiritual healing, wrote articles for their publications, eventually set up a radio station (since abandoned).

In accordance with their dietary beliefs the Fillmores established a vegetarian restaurant in Kansas City. They believed that a meatless diet was more humane, healthy, and conducive to spiritual thinking. On one occasion some-one unthinkingly brought along some hot dogs to a Unity picnic; Charles laughingly nailed the hot dog to a nearby tree.

The Fillmores adopted the symbol of a winged globe to identify all Unity publications. Explained Charles: "It is an ancient Egyptian symbol and I remember that when I first saw it I felt that I had had something to do with it in a previous incarnation." They avoided using the Christian cross. The historian of the movement observed: "Charles Fillmore did not want his teaching to be connected with symbols associated with suffering. He did not believe that true religion is sorrowful. Although he taught that conduct should be governed by the highest ethical standards, he did not teach that there is any virtue in penitence and suffering" (*The Story of Unity*, p. 174).

Myrtle Fillmore originated the Society of Silent Help in 1890; it promised healing in absentia. In the early days a group of followers would meet at 10 o'clock every evening to pray for those in need. Letters came from almost every state of the union. In 1903 Silent Unity was receiving 10,000 requests for help each year; now it receives more requests than this every week. The Silent Unity workers today receive an assigned case load and work in shifts around the clock. Their job is to pray, recite affirmations, answer telephone calls, write letters of comfort and inspiration to their clients.

Not every Unity devotee today believes in reincarnation but Charles Fillmore not only accepted this doctrine but told others that he could remember incidents in his previous lives including his incarnation as St. Paul. His "Statement of Faith" which is not absolutely binding on Unity ministers but which naturally exercises a great influence on the movement includes Article 22:

> "We believe that the dissolution of spirit, soul and body, caused by death, is annulled by rebirth of the same spirit and soul in another body here on earth. We believe the repeated incarnations of man to be a merciful provision of our loving Father to the end that all may have opportunity to attain immortality through regeneration, as did Jesus."

Indulgence in sex except for the specific purpose of procreation had always been frowned upon by the Fillmores. This rules out intercourse by married couples during pregnancy or after the menopause. The Fillmores taught that men and women can refine their physical bodies by avoiding sex expression, meat, dancing, tobacco, liquor, and negative thoughts.

In his book *The Twelve Powers of Man*, Fillmore wrote: "Through the sins of the sex life (casting away of the precious substance) the body is robbed of its essential fluids and disintegrates. The result is called death, which is the last great enemy to be overcome by man. Immortality in the body is possible to man only when he has overcome the weaknesses of sensation and conserves his life substance" (p. 23). He adds: "Sex sensation has made a broken cistern of man's consciousness; for generations the life stream has been turned into this receptacle and lust has robbed the bodies of the whole race making them mere shells, void of life. The failing eye, the deaf ear, the festering or withering flesh, all bear testimony to this perversion of God's life" (p. 165).

Myrtle Fillmore died in 1931 and Charles later married

his secretary. In his declining years he divided his time between a home in the San Fernando Valley and Kansas City. Freeman writes: "Early in his study of spiritual principles, Charles Fillmore came to the conclusion that ill health is unnecessary, that old age is unnecessary, that death is unnecessary" (p. 198). Nevertheless death claimed Charles Fillmore in 1948 at the age of 94. His son Lowell (born 1882) is president of Unity School; the executive administration of all Unity activities is directed by a grandson, Charles R. Fillmore.

A statement on the purpose of Unity is reprinted monthly in the pages of *Unity* magazine:

"Unity School of Christianity is a religious educational institution teaching the use of the Jesus Christ doctrine in everyday life, and is not a church. However in disseminating the teachings of Unity, based upon the Bible and especially upon the teaching of Jesus Christ, teachers have formed independent organizations for study and worship, and these organizations have evolved into groups called centers, societies, assemblies, and churches. These groups are a part of the Unity fellowship and work in close co-operation with the Unity School of Christianity, but Unity is not a denomination nor a sect. Those who study the Unity teachings and who attend a Unity church are free to keep their affiliation with any church they desire. Unity teachings explain the action of mind, the link between God and man. They explain how mind affects the body, how it brings man into an understanding of God. Accept what, in Unity, appears to you to be Truth, and withhold judgment on the remainder until you understand it."

Unity Centers have been established in 39 states, the

District of Columbia, and Puerto Rico. Of the 265 Centers recognized by the Unity School of Christianity in this country the largest numbers are found in California, Florida, Illinois, Michigan, New York, and Ohio. There are eight Centers in Chicago, and six in New York City and four each in Detroit and St. Louis. The impressive Unity Temple in Kansas City seats 1500 worshippers and the new Detroit edifice accommodates 1600. As many attend the Sunday services at Carnegie Hall in New York City. Unity's executive director, J. Sig Paulson admits: "We'd be hard put to distinguish our centers from the little white church around the corner."

Unity also carries on its work in Centers in Canada, the West Indies, England, Australia, Japan, Germany, Switzerland, the Netherlands, France, Italy, Nigeria, Ghana, New Zealand, and South Africa.

A follower of Unity can receive the same spiritual ministrations from a Unity minister in a Unity Center that he could in any Protestant Church. Unity's ritual, based largely on the Book of Common Prayer, includes ceremonies for baptism, communion, weddings, and funerals. The Centers schedule Sunday worship services as well as healing and testimonial meetings. Children can enroll in Unity Sunday Schools. (The ritual allows a Unity clergyman to baptize an infant with rose petals instead of water if he wishes.)

Unity ministers must meet the standards set by the Unity School of Christianity. Centers belong to the Association of Unity Centers, an incorporated body separate from the Unity School. While lay members may pick and choose among Unity's doctrines an ordained minister must agree to conform to the details of Unity's philosophy.

It is possible for a high school graduate to complete Unity's theological course and receive ordination by the age of 20. Admission to the ministerial program is open to any man or woman 18 years or older. The Unity School for Ministerial and Religious Studies at Lee's Summit offers three semesters a year which enables the student to complete the program in two years.

Obviously preparation for the Unity ministry is less thorough than the three-year seminary course following college graduation expected by most Protestant denominations. For example, Unity attempts to cover both the Old and New Testaments in only 64 class hours.

For every member of a Unity Center congregation the movement probably reaches 20 people who have no formal connection with Unity. Prof. Marcus Bach estimates that one third of all U. S. church goers have read Unity literature. Millions have heard Unity programs on radio and TV. "Unity Viewpoint" is now carried by 50 radio stations.

More than 1,000,000 copies of Cady's *Lessons in Truth* have been distributed since its first publication in 1894. Unity publishes 70 books in English and others in various foreign languages.

Besides English the modern Unity printing plant publishes magazines, tracts, and booklets in English and Spanish. Overseas Unity publications are printed in such languages as Afrikaans, Dutch, Finnish, French, German, Greek, Italian, Japanese, Russian, and Swedish. For most people, however, their contact with Unity will be through one of the six magazines. Best known of these is *Daily*

Word, a pocket-sized magazine featuring prayers, affirmations, testimonials, poems, and inspirational features; it goes to 450,000 subscribers each month.

Like Christian Science publications those of the Unity School feature letters and testimonials from devotees attesting to the cures and help received by following the methods of the cult. In a recent issue of *Unity* magazine such letters reported cures of bronchitis and deafness, success in obtaining a new job at 73, the withdrawal of a law suit in an automobile accident, the sparing of a house in a nearby brush fire, an increase in an insurance business, conquest of the smoking habit, the appearance of good weather for a vacation trip, and the passing of a college examination.

The oldest children's magazine in the nation—*Wee Wisdom*—was founded by Unity in 1893 and has a current press run of 87,000. Other popular Unity periodicals are *Unity, Weekly Unity, Progress* and *New.* A group of Unity adherents known as the Silent Seventy gives away enormous quantities of Unity material in prisons, hospitals, waiting rooms, etc.

Those who begin to study the principles of Unity are assured that they need not question or abandon any of their present religious convictions. But they soon discover that the idea of God and Jesus Christ elaborated by Unity bears little resemblance to that taught by the Churches. That God is a person is basic to Christian theology but Cady explains: "God is not a being or person having life, intelligence, love, power. God is that invisible, intangible, but very real, something we call life" (p. 18). A Unity publication tells us: "God is not loving. . . . God does not love anybody or anything. God is the love in everybody and everything. God is love. . . . God exercises none of His attributes except through the inner consciousness of the universe and man" (*Jesus Christ Heals,* pp. 31-2).

Fillmore wrote: "Drop from your minds the belief that God is in any way separated from you, that He occupies form or space outside of you, or that He can be manifested to your consciousness in any way except through your own soul" (*Jesus Christ Heals,* pp. 27-8).

Here is Unity's understanding of the Trinity: "The Father is Principle, the Son is that Principle revealed in a creative plan. The Holy Spirit is the executive power of both Father and Son carrying out the creative plan" (*Statement of Faith*). Again: "Unity believes in Jesus as the one man who brought into full expression His divine nature, the Christ. . . . The difference between Him and us is not one of inherent spiritual capacity but a difference in demonstration of it."

Like every other man Jesus underwent a series of incarnations according to Fillmore. In the Old Testament Jesus appeared as Moses, Elisha, David, and others. Fillmore explained: "These were his days at school, and he arrived at a state of consciousness, while manifesting as Jesus of Nazareth, where he remembered his past lives" (*Unity,* Vol. 14, p. 149).

Unity's teachings about the nature of God, the Trinity, Jesus Christ, the Church, the sacraments, sin, salvation, and reincarnation challenge those of traditional Christianity. Yet the Unity School of Christianity influences millions of Christians in the Churches and its network of active Centers and attractive publications indicate that this influence will grow rather than diminish in the years ahead.

FURTHER READING

Bach, Marcus, *The Unity Way of Life* (Englewood Cliffs, N. J., Prentice-Hall, 1962).

Braden, Charles S., *Spirits in Rebellion* (Dallas, Southern Methodist University Press, 1963).

Cady, H. Emilie, *Lessons in Truth* (Lee's Summit, Mo., Unity School of Christianity, 1954).

Freeman, James Dillet, *The Story of Unity* (Lee's Summit, Mo., Unity School of Christianity, 1954).

General Bibliography

Algermissen, Konrad, *Christian Sects* (New York, Hawthorn, 1962).

Braden, Charles S., *These Also Believe,* rev. ed. (New York, Macmillan, 1960).

Clark, Elmer T., *The Small Sects in America* (Nashville, Abingdon, 1949).

Davies, Horton, *Christian Deviations* (Philadelphia, Westminster, 1965).

Ferguson, Charles W., *The Confusion of Tongues* (New York, Doubleday, Doran, 1928).

Ferm, Vergilius, ed., *Religion in the Twentieth Century* (New York, Philosophical Library, 1948).

Gerstner, John, *The Theology of the Major Sects* (Grand Rapids, Mich., Baker, 1960).

Hoekema, Anthony, *The Four Major Cults* (Grand Rapids, Mich., Eerdmans, 1963).

Judah, J. Stillson, *The History and Philosophy of the Metaphysical Movements in America* (Philadelphia, Westminster, 1967).

Martin, Walter R., *Kingdom of the Cults* (Grand Rapids, Mich., Zondervan, 1965).

Mathison, Richard, *Faith, Cults and Sects in America* (Indianapolis, Bobbs-Merrill, 1960).

Mayer, F. E., *Religious Bodies of America,* 4th ed. (St. Louis, Concordia, 1961).

Mead, Frank S., *Handbook of Denominations in the United States,* 4th ed., (New York and Nashville, Abingdon, 1965).

Needleman, Jacob, *The New Religions* (Garden City, N. Y., Doubleday, 1970).

Neve, J. L., *Churches and Sects of Christendom* (Blair, Nebraska, Lutheran Publishing House, 1952).

Piepkorn, Arthur C., *The Religious Bodies of the United States and Canada* (St. Louis, Concordia, 1972).

Van Baalen, J. K., *The Chaos of Cults* (Grand Rapids, Mich., Eerdmans, 1960).

Whalen, William J., *Separated Brethren,* rev. and enlarged ed., (Huntington, Ind., Our Sunday Visitor, 1972).

Yearbook of American Churches (New York, National Council of Churches of Christ in the U.S.A., published annually).

INDEX